VOLTAIRE

Haydn Mason

VOLTAIRE

A Biography

The Johns Hopkins University Press
Baltimore, Maryland

B
Voltaire

First published in the United States of America, 1981, by The Johns Hopkins
University Press, Baltimore, Maryland 21218

First published in Great Britain, 1981, by Granada Publishing in Paul Elek Ltd.

Library of Congress Catalog Card Number 80-8868
ISBN 0-8018-2611-X

For David and Gwyneth

Contents

Plates

Preface

It has been suggested that before he wrote his comedy with the whimsical title *Amphitryon 38*, the dramatist Giraudoux had enumerated, more or less, thirty-seven previous versions of the Amphitryon myth. One might approach the writing of a biography of Voltaire in a similar vein, seeing it as an *Arouet 38*. Histories of Voltaire's life have never ceased to pour forth ever since the first contemporary accounts by such as Longchamp and Wagnière.[1] At the moment of writing, a team of scholars is working under the direction of Professor René Pomeau to produce a comprehensive ten-volume account that will do for our age what Gustave Desnoiresterres[2] single-handedly managed for the nineteenth century. Where in all this activity is there a place for the present volume?

André Delattre had a point when he wrote some twenty years ago:

All biographies of Voltaire are bad, except the one by Desnoiresterres, which is an encyclopaedia and discovers in that its purpose and unity. They are bad, because they tell his life, accepting the servitude of following him into an infinite number of twists and turns; and that always in the end gives the impression of a grand bazaar inventory.[3]

The conclusion, in his view, is inescapable: only an encyclopedic account of Voltaire's life can hope to succeed if the biographer wishes to be comprehensive. Otherwise, to follow Voltaire step by step is to become lost in an impossible labyrinth. 'There is too much to say on Voltaire'; one must, adds Delattre, escape from 'the rut of compiling a true-to-life inventory'.[4]

We shall never know how Delattre would have solved the problem, as he died prematurely, leaving only a mass of highly perceptive notes which we owe it to M. Pomeau to have classified posthumously and published. Perhaps a Delattre biography would have looked at various aspects of Voltaire's personality in turn. At any rate, even in fragmentary form the results are impressive. Few biographers have captured the vitality and complex ambiguities of Voltaire's character with such force.

The present study attempts a different approach. It shares Delattre's scepticism about realistic reportage – unless the results are spread over ten volumes. Instead, it concentrates on certain periods in the *philosophe*'s life, when we may hope to find the essence of the man revealed under the pressure of circumstances. The continuous thread will of course not be lost to sight, and the addition of a Chronology will help to support the linking narrative. But inevitably certain priorities have had to be established. Some phases of Voltaire's life cannot be ignored: the stay in England or in Berlin, the high noon of partnership with Mme du Châtelet at Cirey; Geneva at the time of writing *Candide*; the final entry into Paris, death and apotheosis. Others commend themselves not quite so insistently. The twenty years of Ferney are so superabundant in activity that any choice will be arbitrary. Perhaps a view of the great man after the La Barre execution and when embarked on writing *L'Ingénu*, and again of his very last years at Ferney (a time that tends to be somewhat neglected in most biographies) may not be entirely without value.

The narrative will also allow space to pause at times and reflect upon certain abiding aspects of Voltaire's character: his attitudes to health and to money; his capacities for friendship and hatred; his susceptibilities as an author; his prodigious energy and zeal; the personal charisma and conversational brilliance.

The completion of Theodore Besterman's definitive edition of the Correspondence (to which reference will be made throughout this biography)[5] provides us at last not only with a comprehensive view of Voltaire's 'least contested masterpiece'.[6] It gives us also a priceless new tool for examining the writer's life and attitudes under innumerable lights. The vast range of his interests, the mass of correspondents (over 1800),[7] the vitality which suffuses these letters in profusion – all these factors make Voltaire's correspondence an indispensable key to our understanding of him. There are however dangers. Voltaire's letters are very often public statements, their author well aware that he is on display.[8] Each one has to be assessed in the light of its addressee and of the circumstances prevailing at that moment. Much is ignored or played down; and many letters (perhaps most notably those to Mme du

Châtelet) are lost. Only in the minority of them can he feel free from censorship or prying eyes. Furthermore, letters to an old and close friend like d'Argental are different in tone from those to, say, Mme du Deffand – also a friend of long standing, but one whose satiric tongue and pen are not to be trusted. It is impossible in the course of a biography which makes great use of the letters to evaluate each one specifically or even mention to whom in most cases it is addressed; one can say only that such considerations are constantly present in the author's mind as he moves through the years of Voltaire's life.

Quotations, especially from the letters, have almost invariably been translated into English. Where the savour of the original French is deemed essential, it has been quoted and a translation appended. One complication occurs in writing the biography of a man so versatile: a considerable number of Voltaire's letters were actually written in English! Where these are cited, a brief indication is made to that effect.

As Giraudoux saw Amphitryon afresh in the thirty-eighth incarnation, so too may we hope that some new perceptions of Voltaire will emerge from these pages. No attempt has been made to analyse his literary works, on which something has been said elsewhere.[9] What is attempted here above all is to disclose the particular personality which could produce those writings and undertake so many personal crusades in the cause of civilised living. We shall be content if by the end Voltaire's personality stands out in a rather clearer light in consequence of the approach we have taken.

It is a pleasure to record my debt to the Leverhulme Foundation, whose generous award enabled me to prepare this book for some months in the Paris libraries, as too of the enlightened arrangements of the University of East Anglia, whose provision of study leave permitted me to work on it free from other distractions. My warm thanks, once again, are extended to the Library of that University, willing as always to assist the researcher in every way, including their invaluable Inter-Library Loan service. To my wife Gretchen goes my gratitude for typing the first draft speedily and making many useful suggestions; and to Susan Davis for typing it accurately under pressure of time; to Andrew Brown for his assistance, courteous and generous as ever; and to Adrienne Redshaw my appreciation for reading the whole manuscript and, on many occasions, leaving a permanent impression upon it through her persuasive comments.

VOLTAIRE

1 Youth, and England

Voltaire (*né* François-Marie Arouet) was born, in all probability, in Paris on 21 November 1694.[1] Was he a vigorous baby in his mother's womb, as one might be tempted to expect of someone who was to display such abundance of energy all his life? The question is only slightly more otiose than attempts to psychoanalyse Voltaire, and the evidence is almost as meagre. Information on his early childhood is almost non-existent. We may speculate on the early death of his mother – who according to a cousin had a difficult time at his birth[2] and whom Voltaire represents as being of fragile health ([*c.* February 1729], D344)* – when he was just seven years old and on the gap which it left in his life, but there is little of direct significance to go on. He scarcely ever refers to her,[3] and in his writings there appears to be none of that mother-absence which plays a part in, for instance, Prévost's works. It is however possible to discern, as we shall see later, an emotional deprivation in his make-up which may be related to the loss of his mother when very young, but at best the link must remain speculative.

Rather more can be said about Voltaire's relationship to his father. The latter, a *grand bourgeois* of some importance in the legal world as a high-placed official in the Chambre des Comptes (Audit Office), found his younger son a constant trial. Until the time of his death in 1722, he remained persuaded that the latter was a ne'er-do-well. By the terms of his will Voltaire was not to be allowed to touch the capital of his share in the inheritance until he was thirty-five (over seven years away), and

* All references to Voltaire's correspondence are to *The Complete Works of Voltaire*, ed. T. Besterman, Vols 85–135 (see Select Bibliography), Besterman's definitive 'D' numbered citation system being used ('app.' denoting appendices). Dubious dating is indicated by square brackets.

1

even then only if his life had taken on 'an ordered conduct and such as I should have wished to inspire in him'; the matter was to be judged at the appropriate time by no less than the *premier président* of the Chambre des Comptes (D. app. 11). At twenty-seven, Voltaire was disturbingly well on in years still to be a scapegrace, and Arouet *père*'s exasperation can readily be imagined.

To begin with, his son, having completed his studies as a brilliant pupil at the Jesuit collège Louis-le-Grand, had followed his father's bent by beginning a legal career, but then rejected it. Starting as a law student in 1711 on leaving school, he went into a law practice three years later, but the legal world with its routine and discipline was not for him. The only lasting effect of this abortive career was that he met in the office Nicolas Thieriot, who was to remain a lifelong friend, albeit an often unreliable one. By 1716 he was already in trouble with authority, being exiled for several months from Paris; worse was to come in 1717 when he was locked up in the Bastille for several months, apparently without pen or paper. On both occasions the reasons appear to have been scurrilous political writings. Ever since 1706 he had moved in the libertine world of the Société du Temple, a group of worldly men, under the guidance of his godfather the abbé de Châteauneuf, a close friend of Voltaire's mother (cf. D4456). By 1707, it seems, he was already precocious enough to be borrowing five hundred francs from a professional money-lender.[4]

In 1718 the revolt against his father was completed by a profoundly symbolic act of liberation: young Arouet deliberately chose to adopt a new name, the one by which the world at large was soon to recognise him. The origin of the name still remains mysterious, despite resolute scholarly efforts to uncover it.[5] More significant is the fact of the change. Beginning with a letter of 12 June 1718 signed 'Arouet de Voltaire' (D62) the young writer moved, appropriately enough in a letter to the Regent duc d'Orléans, to a full public affirmation of his new name 'Voltaire', from which all family connections had been removed (D70). He was later to claim on occasion that he was an illegitimate child.[6] Whether or not this was true, by the time of Arouet *père*'s death in 1722, François-Marie had manifestly become the black sheep of the family.

Voltaire had an older brother and sister. The latter, who became Mme Mignot, was to die in 1726 during the early months of his stay in England; the news of her death coincided with some of the blackest moments of his life. It was to express his grief at this loss that he quoted Shakespeare for the very first time, from the 'To be or not to be'

I love
Becky

monologue in *Hamlet* ([26 October 1726], D303). Later he was to take an increased responsibility for his sister's daughters when their father died in 1737 and to busy himself in looking after their interests. As he wrote to Thieriot at that time, 'I really have no family but them' (D1408). His close relations with his sister and subsequently his nieces (not just Mme Denis, who became his mistress, but also Mme de Fontaine, who later became Mme de Florian[7]) clearly demonstrate that Voltaire never revolted against the family as a whole nor against the notion of a family.

But with his brother Armand the situation was quite different. Arouet *père* had had Jansenist leanings; with Armand these were intensified into an austere and fanatical faith representing all that Voltaire detested. On the latter's departure for England Armand tried to exploit the opportunity to block his brother's access to the family inheritance. Voltaire presumably had this grievance amongst others in mind when complaining in English to Thieriot in 1728 of the

ill usage I have received from him since I am in England. I have tried all sorts of means to soften if I could the pedantic rudeness and the selfish insolence with which he has crushed me these two years. I own to you in the bitterness of my heart, that his unsufferable usage has been one of my greatest grievances.

(D336)

One can scarcely mistake the voice of deep personal pain, the more striking because it could hardly have been prompted by any recent occurrences, as Voltaire had been out of France for two years. Here, if anywhere in Voltaire's family relationships, one senses an unusual sensitivity, the brooding resentment of the younger brother who has in every way been deprived of his family portion.

As René Pomeau rightly notes, the anti-Christian revolt of Voltaire the deist is an anti-Jansenist rebellion in its first phase, against belief in a rigorously cruel God and a life of ascetic habits. He argues with force the case for believing that the young writer is seeking to escape from the suffocating environment in which he was brought up and of which Armand remains an odious representative.[8] Voltaire will always reject with contumely a way of life handed down by an unattractive father and maintained by a profoundly antipathetic brother. Here may be some of the roots of Voltaire's restless dynamism. But to describe the family situation is not to explain in itself the complexity of Voltaire's character; it is the latter which must be our concern.

There are reasons for sympathising with Arouet *père*'s distrustful views of his prodigal son. To see Voltaire, however, as a simple profligate at the time of his father's death in 1722 is to misread his

life-history at that point. True, he had twice experienced arrest for
scurrilous writings, with consequent exile or imprisonment. Nor had
his first visit abroad, to Holland in 1713, been such as to encourage
confidence in his sense of responsibility. He had gone to The Hague in
September as secretary to the new French ambassador, the marquis de
Châteauneuf, again profiting from family connections with the
Châteauneuf family on his mother's side. But before Christmas he was
sent home for irregular conduct. It was in Holland that Voltaire
experienced (so far as we know) his first great passion; Olympe
Dunoyer was a compatriot whom he met in French émigré circles in the
Dutch capital. With that reckless indiscretion which was to serve him
ill on so many occasions over the next sixty-five years, he laid serious
plans to elope with her. The plot miscarried and deep scandal ensued;
Voltaire was bundled back to France in haste and disgrace.

However, he was revealing his talents in more impressive ways as
both thinker and writer. There is no reason to doubt the anonymous
denunciator of Voltaire who, when the latter had been conducted to the
Bastille once again in 1726, expressed the wish that he might have been
imprisoned there long before, as he had been preaching deism openly
for more than a decade, declaring himself an enemy of Christ and
maintaining that the Old Testament was full of myths. Already Voltaire's free-thinking had passed well beyond the light badinage of the
Société du Temple and become a militant crusade.[9] Even as early as
1716, in the *Epître à Mme de G. . . .*,[10] Voltaire had begun the Biblical
criticism that would come to full maturity only at Ferney.

In the literary world too the young man had established his creden-
tials. With boundless ambition, not to say supreme arrogance, he laid
early claim to pre-eminence in two of the most exalted domains of
letters: tragedy and the epic. For his very first play Voltaire chose the
Oedipus theme, competing directly with Sophocles and Corneille
(whom he explicitly criticises in the prefatory *Lettres sur Oedipe*). *Oedipe*,
first performed in 1718, was an immediate success and at once placed
him in the front rank of tragic dramatists. The novice had acceded to
the status of master overnight. It was the beginning of sixty years'
dominance at the Comédie Française.[11] The daring assault on the
equally lofty citadel of epic poetry was also well under way. Voltaire
had decided to take as his hero Henri IV, the one French king who had
shown enlightened religious tolerance. The poem (first published as *La
Ligue*, but later to become *La Henriade*) was probably begun as early as
1716;[12] by 1719 he was reading passages from it to the British ambassador in Paris, Lord Stair. Probably encouraged by Stair, Voltaire

addressed a dedicated copy of *Oedipe* to George I that same year, the
English monarch replying with a fine gold watch and a gold medal
bearing his effigy.[13] It would have been unlikely to impress Voltaire's
hard-headed father even if he had been aware of it; but it testifies, as do
Voltaire's other literary conquests, to the brilliance of his promise well
before 1720. Here was a dazzling young author, sure (too sure, as it
would turn out) of his destiny. It comes as no great surprise to find him
writing, about the year 1721, to his fellow-poet Louis Racine about the
possibility of entering the French Academy (D101). That particular
success was to prove unusually long-delayed for a writer of such promise, since Voltaire would need to wait another quarter of a century for it,
but it fits with his great self-confidence to find him already contemplating such a spectacular achievement.

La Ligue duly appeared in 1723 and had enormous success, to the
point of bringing epic poetry back into fashion.[14] Even a critic like
Mathieu Marais, who generally regarded Voltaire with considerable
detachment, was full of praise; it was, he said, 'a marvellous work, an
intellectual masterpiece, as beautiful as Virgil . . . One does not know
where Arouet, so young, has been able to learn so much . . .' There are
qualities, he added, 'which reveal the genius of an accomplished man'.
In short, it was a poem 'which brings glory to our nation' (D135,
Commentary). Despite severe criticisms from some, particularly in the
conservative camp in literary, political or religious matters,[15] Marais
represented the prevailing opinion.

Already, too, Voltaire's remarkable capacity to learn from new
places was becoming apparent. His second visit to Holland yielded
more substantial results than the first. Travelling to The Hague in 1722
with the widowed Mme de Rupelmonde, he reports to his friend the
marquise de Bernières in a letter full of acute observation which one
might well call a fledgling *Lettre philosophique* (D128). Holland is a
'paradis terrestre' from The Hague to Amsterdam. The capital thrives,
as 'warehouse of the universe'; the port full of ships, not a parasite or a
poor man to be seen. The focus of interest and aspiration is not the
Court but 'work and modesty'. The opera may be detestable; on the
other hand Voltaire sees religious tolerance actively being practised:
'Calvinist ministers, Arminians, Socinians, rabbis, Anabaptists, who
all speak wondrously and who in truth are all correct'. In many ways
this letter prefigures his observations of England: bourgeois prosperity
achieved by hard work not rank; sectarian diversity revealed without
fear or constraint; and the whole controlled by the spirit of modesty
('not one insolent man'). Dutch culture may, like to a lesser extent that

of England, fail to match the glories of French classicism; but the basic
social attitudes are right. No time is lost by fawning courtiers or by idle
crowds gathering to see a prince pass by. Not that Voltaire's hostility to
aristocratic values is accompanied by austerity. As ever in his life, he is
appreciative of social splendour and finds it in Holland too – but there it
relates to useful political activity ('the concourse of ambassadors').
Already one finds an awareness that an inter-dependent relationship
exists between commercial success, social equality, intellectual liberty
and political freedom.[16]

These Dutchmen all preaching their diverse faiths, but not insisting
that each one alone has the monopoly of truth, anticipate the famous
remarks that open the fifth *Lettre philosophique* a decade later about
England: 'This is the country of sects. An Englishman, as a free man,
goes to Heaven by the road he chooses'.[17] The spirit of modesty which
informs this society is paralleled by that of the London Quaker who
explains to Voltaire why they allow anyone in their meetings to get up
and say anything: . . . 'in doubt, we listen patiently to everything'.[18]

Thus far the resemblance is close. What is however missing in the
1722 letter is a philosophical *rationale* to explain all this. Later, in the
Lettres philosophiques, the twin masters – Locke and Newton – are
revealed as great thinkers not just because of their innate genius but
also because both practised intellectual humility. It is a marvellous
paradox that Locke 'dares' to doubt (Letter XIII); while Newton,
brilliant enquirer into verifiable phenomena, stops short of attempting
to explain first causes – 'The cause of this cause is in God's bosom'.[19]
None of that intellectual justification enters into the earlier account of
Holland.

But this philosophic initiation is not far off, and it comes from an
Englishman, Bolingbroke, whom Voltaire first met at La Source, near
Orléans, shortly after his own return from the Netherlands. His admiration for the Tory exile was great, and though in later years he was to
become more detached about Bolingbroke, this admiration flourished
over the next couple of years.[20] They saw each other frequently during
this period, Voltaire profiting from the wide erudition which he had
remarked in Bolingbroke at their first encounter. The Englishman
wrote to him in 1724 a letter full of invaluable philosophical advice. He
introduces Voltaire to Locke's *Essay on Human Understanding* and puts to
him that precise point about intellectual modesty which would become
a keynote in the *Lettres philosophiques* but to which, as the 1722 letter to
the marquise de Bernières already shows, Voltaire is already well
attuned: 'It is a great science to know where ignorance begins, and it is

a science which those great men [Descartes and Malebranche] did not possess' (D190). Because of such arrogance, Descartes's physics and Malebranche's metaphysics are reduced to poetic fiction. Huyghens and Newton have come along to show that almost all the Cartesian laws of movement are false and that Descartes's famous vortices ('tourbillons') are quite unfounded. Similarly, Malebranche tried to go beyond the limits of human understanding and in so doing produced merely 'the most beautiful nonsense in the world'. The letter has a magisterial quality about it and it came at the right moment in Voltaire's evolution. Even the advice which Bolingbroke also gives on the joys of gardening, linking cultivation of the soil to intellectual culture, may have been the seed that eventually bore fruit in the famous last line of *Candide*.

Here then we are witnessing, in the early 1720s, Voltaire's swift maturation of talent through writing, travel, reading. It is a dazzling progress; chequered, it is true, but intensely vigorous and rewarding. The reversal of fortune occasioned by the chevalier de Rohan is as yet unforeseen – though eminently foreseeable, given Voltaire's endless capacity for impetuous indiscretions. Are there no clouds in this sky? There are: Voltaire's health is fragile; and it is already becoming one of the leitmotivs of his life.

From as early as 1723 we find complaints from Voltaire in his correspondence of being unwell.[21] The milk diet on which he has been living is giving him much trouble, he tells Thieriot ([*c.* 10 June 1723], D153); and the mournful expressions of self-pity are already as strong as they will ever be: 'My health and my affairs are ruined to a degree that is unbelievable' (to Thieriot, D155); 'I am as sick as a dog' (to marquise de Bernières, D156); 'The pen falls from my hands, I am so sick that I cannot write more' (to marquise de Bernières, D157). One may take back this concern about health a little earlier in his letters to the previous year and his stay in Holland, whence he writes to Thieriot: 'I go riding here every day. I play tennis, I drink Tokay wine, I am so well that I am amazed by it' (2 October [1722], D125). The very expression of surprise at finding himself in good health is itself as significant as the more characteristic complaints of illness. Why should he, in the full vigour of early manhood, feel anything but contentment at ordinary rude health?

No simple explanation of Voltaire's hypochondria is likely to be forthcoming, nor indeed are we in a position to judge whether there were abiding physiological causes to explain it in whole or in part. That he himself suffered greatly from his health can however scarcely be doubted. What is the nature of these 'continual sufferings', this

'network of pain' (to marquise de Bernières, D220)? One of the clearest
indications comes in a letter to Thieriot in early 1729. Voltaire begins
by counselling his friend on the latter's health, but almost immediately
he turns to talking about his own. This is the period when he is in hiding
after his clandestine return from England, and his life is solitary and
depressing. With three police arrests already to his account during his
lifetime and a particularly unhappy beginning to his stay in England,
he has every right to claim: 'I have suffered many misfortunes.' Yet he
goes on to add that from sad experience, 'illness is the worst of them all'.
He proceeds to distinguish between specific maladies and what he
undergoes:

> To suffer fever or smallpox now and then is nothing, but to be overcome by
> languor for years together, to see all one's tastes annihilated, to have still
> enough life to wish to enjoy them and too little strength to do so, to become
> useless and intolerable to oneself, to die by degrees, that is what I have suffered
> and what has been more cruel to me than all the other trials.

> (D344)

'To die by degrees': it seems a constant state rather than a particular
affliction. Speculations arise. Do we see here one possible sign of
maternal deprivation? Is this the appeal of the man who never had
enough love bestowed on him as a child? In support of this thesis, it is
noteworthy that many of the most dramatic complaints are made to
women: in 1723–4 the marquise de Bernières, in the 1740s Mme
Denis, in Berlin Countess Bentinck; we know that Mme Denis was his
mistress, and most probably the other two were as well. However,
Thieriot is also a recipient of heart-rending testimonies of sickness, so
the theory cannot be conceived along narrowly heterosexual lines. But
the need to appear ill is often overwhelming. When in Berlin the
Academician Formey, in reply to Voltaire's assertion that he had 'four
mortal illnesses', replied that his eye looked healthy, the *philosophe*
riposted in tones of great indignation: 'Don't you know that sufferers
from scurvy die with their eyes inflamed?'[22] He represented as calumny
a report by the sculptor Pigalle that he was in good health (D16536,
16540). A British visitor to Voltaire's château at Ferney in 1774 wrote:

> His common salutation is, qui veut voir une Ombre. Vous êtes bien bon,
> Monsieur, vous venez voir un mourant, un cadavre. It is very difficult to
> converse with him on this subject. If you are sorry – And pray Sir why should
> you be sorry? Or if you insist that he is wonderfully well and robust for his age,
> he complains of the colic which is universally understood as a signal to leave
> the house.[23]

The 'languor' can scarcely betoken sexual deficiencies, given the long succession of mistresses through Voltaire's life until at least the 1750s. Such explanations as are possible are likely to be more complex and to take close account of Voltaire's temperament. In part, it may relate to a fragile constitution, which he believed he inherited from 'parents in poor health who died young'.[24] In part, it came to be an ever more useful excuse for avoiding tedious social obligations and confining himself to his study or bed, as he admits.[25] But the hypochondria is also an indication of depression and anxiety. Significantly, the earliest complaints in the correspondence link Voltaire's illness to other matters: 'The milk that I wanted to go on taking, alongside the worries of business and the melancholy with which I am teased in Paris, has done me much harm' (D153); 'My health and my affairs are in ruins . . . ' (D155). His abnormal sensitivity, which caused him, he claimed, to suffer physically on the anniversaries respectively of Henri IV's assassination and the Saint Bartholomew Day massacre (letter to comte d'Argental, 30 August 1769, D15855), ensured that he lived his life at the limit of his nervous reactions. Exaltation could give way quickly to gloom.

The impression that these valetudinarian protests are linked to some deep inadequacy and appeal for love and attention is only heightened if one notes that, paradoxically, when he had suffered a stroke in 1767 and again ten years later, he tended to play it down (cf. e.g., D13790, 20615). Was this because, in later years, fame and recognition had assuaged some of the sense of void? Or that he felt no need to dramatise unduly an obviously serious attack with which everyone could easily sympathise?

Needless to say, Voltaire's enemies gleefully seized upon this character trait. A satirical work of 1761, for instance, solemnly proclaimed that he had been in much better health of late, cured of dysentery, epilepsy, consumption, hoarseness, spitting blood, the stone, and gout.[26] Le malade imaginaire is a perennial figure of fun. Voltaire lends himself easily to the superior amusement of his biographers because the wails of pain are so often comically absurd, and because, notwithstanding, the frail body stood up to eighty-four years of intense activity. His hypochondria is the more open to mockery because on this subject the great ironist appears singularly devoid of self-irony. But it behoves us to set these reactions in the context of his whole personality. For whatever reason, a sense of physical insufficiency early became part of his subjective existence. To overlook it is to suppress a fundamental aspect of his psyche. Indeed, by doing so one risks obscuring a stoical side. Writing to Frederick of Prussia, he says:

I prefer a thousand times more to be languid and prone to fever, as I am, than to think sad thoughts. It seems to me that virtue, study and gaiety are three sisters whom one must not separate: these three goddesses are your attendants; I take them for my mistresses.

(D1359)

Here is a truer, less caricatural aspect. Illness is something he must live with (albeit not without perennial protest); but a highly nervous temperament need not for that abandon the aspiration towards joyfulness through hard work. Nor did he, ever. We must accept that the susceptibility which made him the ardent defender of the Protestant merchant Calas is the same as that which lies at the root of his everlasting complaints about his afflictions.

Let us return to the thread of our narrative. By the autumn of 1725 Voltaire had attained the heights of success. He moved easily at Court, attended Louis XV's marriage in September, and had three of his plays (*Oedipe, Marianne,* and *L'Indiscret*) performed as part of the celebrations (D252). In November he obtained a pension of 1500 francs from the Queen. His future seemed in every way assured. Yet this was the precise moment at which a quarrel was to change his comfortable existence fundamentally; for the quarrel was with a scion of one of the proudest families in France, the chevalier de Rohan. Voltaire might mingle with the aristocracy, even, since 1718, affect his new name Arouet de Voltaire. He remained none the less of bourgeois origins. His father's connections, aided by his own endeavours, had given him an excellent start in society, but faced with a true aristocrat, Voltaire was to discover unambiguously his real social standing.

The squabble apparently began, in late January 1726, with a sneer from the chevalier at Voltaire's new name when they ran into one another at the Opéra: 'M. de Voltaire, M. Arouet, what are you called?' (D261). Voltaire, doubtless somewhat sensitive on the matter, made a sharp retort, sufficiently rude for the chevalier to decide that the insolence of this *parvenu* merited a lesson. The poet was summoned from the hôtel de Sully, where he had been dining with the duc, to find awaiting him servants despatched by the chevalier de Rohan who administered him a beating. In physical terms, Voltaire may well have suffered little. Duvernet (who claims that Thieriot provided a large number of the facts for his book and who therefore can probably be relied upon for the details of this particular episode) states that of the two servants sent by the chevalier, one held Voltaire by his coat, while the other applied five or six blows on his shoulders with 'a small stick'.[27] Even so, it remains, for the history of eighteenth-century French literature, the most important punishment meted out to a writer before the

Revolution. The psychological provocation was immense. It was increased by the fact that the chevalier had chosen to witness the beating from a carriage nearby and to make the insult quite intolerable by calling out instructions (D263). Voltaire's rage knew no bounds. He rushed back to the duc de Sully, who agreed with him that the act was 'violent and uncivil' (D261), but offered him no other help. He went to the Opéra to seek the sympathy of the influential marquise de Prie (mistress of the prime minister, the duc de Bourbon) and from there to Versailles; the reactions of all his high-placed friends proved to be the same as the duc de Sully's. Thrown back on his own resources, Voltaire began seeking desperate measures of revenge upon Rohan. Perhaps to escape detection, perhaps because his inner agitation dictated it, he took to changing his residence frequently. He began fencing lessons with the idea of a duel in mind; he sought help, it seems, from members of the King's Guards (who were available, as Prévost's *Manon Lescaut* shows, for hiring out on private expeditions of this kind). Whether all these rumours were correct, he was clearly heading for disaster, and the decision to arrest him and take him to the Bastille in April was as much for his own good as in the name of public order. When arrested, he was found to be carrying pistols.

Meanwhile, the world of Paris and Versailles looked on with interest and amusement at this undignified brawl between the exalted nobleman and the renowned young poet. Opinion generally considered Voltaire foolish to have objected so sharply to Rohan's taunt, but it also felt that the latter had gone too far in undertaking the dishonourable expedient of having Voltaire chastised by his servants instead of performing it himself. On the whole, therefore, the public blamed both parties, but Rohan the more severely. However, any sympathy that Voltaire might have won was forfeited by his ridiculous projects for revenge. Instead of complaining formally to the judicial authorities, he impulsively took the law into his own hands.[28] Had he succeeded in provoking a duel, he could have received the death sentence; having the chevalier beaten up might well have been tantamount to the same thing. His immoderate rage made him an object of ridicule. The marquise de Prie summed it up in a letter to the duc de Richelieu which is not lacking in sympathy (both writer and recipient were Voltaire's friends): 'I feel very sorry for poor Voltaire; in substance he is right; but by the way he has gone about it, he has committed a thoughtless act which is inexcusable . . . ' (D270). Not for the last time Voltaire, with much right initially on his side, had destroyed his own cause – at least, in the short term – by the disproportionate violence of his reaction.

Thus was lost in the space of a few months Voltaire's enviable position of affluence and security, to be replaced by one of isolation, without prestige and power. A change of climate seemed indicated. Voltaire chose to go to England. It satisfied the condition of his release, that he live at least fifty leagues from Paris. Early in May, he left Calais, probably by the *Betty*, sailing from Calais to Gravesend on the 10th.[29]

Why England? Several reasons may relate, not least the admiration that Voltaire had discovered for this country as a result of his friendship with Bolingbroke. But one precise motive must not be overlooked, the more so as it antedates the Rohan incident. When the writer completed a new version of his epic poem *La Henriade* in 1725, he at first considered publishing it in Holland, with consequent easy entry into France. But he quickly realised that no support would be forthcoming in France, and so by October 1725 he had decided to look to England.[30] On the 6th he wrote to George I, asking for his help in assuring publication of the work, and adding: 'I eagerly seek after the honour of coming to London to pay you [my] deep respects . . . ' (D250). When, therefore, Voltaire insists to the Chief of Police Hérault just before his departure for England that he is going there of his own free will and does not want a police escort or any suggestion that he has been banished from France (D291), we should read this as no bravado but the literal truth. Later that same month the British Ambassador in Paris, Horatio Walpole, is writing to George Bubb Dodington of 'Mr Voltaire . . . being gone for England in order to print by subscription an excellent poem, called *Henry IV*, which on account of some bold strokes in it against persecution and the priests, cannot be printed here' (D295). By the time Voltaire arrived in England, his plans in this respect were well known, as both the *Daily Courant* and the *British Journal* speak of them in mid-May.[31] Voltaire had a distinct purpose in going to England, even though the circumstances and the manner of his arrival and early stay were far from what he would have wished.

The epic poem (although known unofficially as *La Henriade* from 1724, it would acquire its definitive title only with the 1728 edition) did not represent only a bid by its author for literary honours; its meaning is closely bound up with French politics under the Regency. The duc d'Orléans who had, on Louis XIV's death in 1715, assumed control of the kingdom as Regent, was uncle and guardian to the five-year-old Louis XV, a sickly child whose imminent death had to be considered a strong possibility. In that event, the Regent hoped to succeed to the throne; but the threat came from Philip V of Spain, Louis XIV's grandson and therefore in direct line of descent. So the duc d'Orléans

turned for support to England, and from 1716 an alliance was established which, despite its fragility, survived until the early 1730s.[32]
Voltaire's *La Ligue* had already fitted into Orléanist pro-British policies, and the presents given by George I to the French poet in 1719 are
best understood if one sees them as the British King's recognition of
Voltaire's propaganda value rather than awareness of his literary
talents.[33] It is surely no accident that in the poem Henri IV is sent by
Voltaire on a purely fictitious errand to England while still a prince to
seek help from Elizabeth I, or that England (as it will be a good decade
later in the *Lettres philosophiques*) is represented as a land of peace,
prosperity and tolerance.[34] The philosophical spirit of freedom in England had already impressed the poet. This admiration for England had
accorded well with support for the Regent during the latter's struggle to
retain power in the contingency of Louis XV's death. Now that the
Regent was dead, Louis XV not only still alive but fully a king, and
Voltaire in London rather than Paris, the political stance had survived
into a very different world, but with effectiveness undiminished to serve
Voltaire's personal cause, as we shall see.

However, the departure for England was not propitiously timed, and
Voltaire left with a residue of bitter hatred against Rohan, so much so
that he returned to France briefly in July in order to seek him out,
though without success (D299). A letter of exchange arranged for
him with the English banker d'Acosta fell through when the banker
went bankrupt; Voltaire returned from France on his summer visit
with new bills of exchange drawn upon another banker, Medina,
who also contrived to become insolvent before he had presented
them. The result was wretched misery, desolation and, as one might
expect in such circumstances with Voltaire, illness: as he put it in
English to Thieriot: 'I was without a penny, sick to death of a violent
agüe, a stranger, alone, helpless, in the midst of a city, wherein I was
known to no body.' As for his hopes of publishing his epic poem on
'Poor Henry' at his own expense, 'the loss of my money is a sad stop to
my design . . . ' (D303).

But even before the second bankruptcy Voltaire had disappeared
from view after his arrival in England. Where did he go? We do not
know, except that it was not, it appears, to London. Only after his July
excursion across the Channel does he surface, in a letter to Thieriot in
August (D299). From it we gather that he expects to settle permanently
in England. About London he has mixed feelings. He knows that
artistic merit wins true recognition there, that writers are not scorned,
that 'the people think freely and nobly without being held back by any

servile fear': some of the major keynotes of the future *Lettres philosophiques* are already being struck. But he is held back from the 'tintamarre
de Witheall [din of Whitehall]' by three factors: his exiguous resources,
his poor health and his love of retreat.

The letter sounds quite wraith-like. Voltaire doubts he will ever see
Thieriot again and asks those who still preserve his memory in France
to talk of him occasionally. The self-dramatising ghost sounds as if he
has absented himself from true felicity; though he recognises England's
great merits, it is as a reluctant exile. But from August he is installed
in Wandsworth at Everard Fawkener's house, and the home of this
English merchant will become his geographical and spiritual centre.[35]
Fawkener's generous action in taking Voltaire to his country house was
the turning-point of the latter's life in England; after that time purpose
and meaning were restored to it. As André-Michel Rousseau has acutely
observed, Voltaire will later commemorate this action when narrating,
in *Candide*, the magnanimity of Jacques in rescuing the naïve hero from
a similar estrangement and distress.[36]

So passes the moment of profound self-doubt, when Voltaire can
write in almost Pascalian terms: 'I feel how little I am worth, my
weaknesses fill me with pity and my faults with disgust' (D302). With
renewed hope come activity, social intercourse, letters, what we tend
to think of as the more characteristic Voltaire. But we should accord
due importance also to the silent figure of those early months, persuaded that fortune has abandoned him and that he is 'destined to be
unhappy in any case' (D299), a man who expects his life to end in
profound obscurity. Periods of such deep depression were mercifully
uncommon in Voltaire's life, though we shall encounter them again.
Beyond that, however, the summer of 1726 will serve to introduce an
element in Voltaire's personality for which his future years were to
provide ample opportunity: the alternation between love of the 'tintamarre', whether of Whitehall, Paris or Versailles, and 'my inclination
for the deepest retreat' (D299).

Voltaire has still however to overcome the jaundiced attitude about
aristocrats he had acquired in the wake of the Rohan incident. In his
October 1726 letter to Thieriot he says that Lord and Lady Bolingbroke have been as kind as ever, indeed even more so, 'in proportion to
my unhappiness'. But he could not accept their generous offers,
'because they are lords', whereas 'I have accepted all from Mr. Faulk-
near, because he is a single gentleman'. The same inhibitions affect his
plans for publishing *La Henriade*. He is tempted to obtain subscriptions
through Court patronage. But 'I am weary of courts my Thieriot. All

that is King, or belongs to a King, frights my republican philosophy
. . . ' The extent to which Voltaire has suffered from the events at the
beginning of that year can be gauged from this surprising affirmation.
Voltaire had already in 1725 revealed his ambivalent feelings about the
French Court, while yet remaining a courtier;[37] he will do so again to
much greater extent in the 1740s. But he did not normally question the
need for a monarch at the head of government; the remark to Thieriot
in October 1726 sounds much more the product of Rousseau's pen.

However, all this will now begin to change very quickly, as Voltaire
returns to city life. He moves into London, using Bolingbroke's address
but probably not living there, meeting Pope, Gay, Arbuthnot.[38] In the
New Year the 'republican' of three months earlier is received by George
I. Socially, his life has begun to resume the successful course it had had
in France until a year before; but not yet financially. Not even being
presented to the King (nor yet the fine gift of 2000 crowns from him)[39]
can replace the deficit incurred through the two bankruptcies, the loss
of income from 'rentes' and pensions, not to mention medical expenses
occasioned by his illnesses (D308). By March 1727 he is seeking
permission from the French Government to return to Paris and by May
it seems fairly certain that he has obtained it.[40] He no longer expects to
spend his life in exile from his friends in Paris.

But the moment for returning to France has not yet arrived, and
there is one great project to complete before he does: the publication by
subscription of *La Henriade*. In the meantime, he extends his literary
acquaintanceships, most notably by meeting Jonathan Swift. The link
with Swift was to prove much closer than that with Pope, though
originating later. Voltaire and Pope had learned of each other through
Bolingbroke, Pope had read works by Voltaire before they met; there is
a strong probability that they had even corresponded before 1726.[41]
Voltaire's first literary connections in London were established
through Pope and his circle in the autumn of 1726. But the link did not
go deep. Pope had little to learn from those works of Voltaire which had
yet appeared; the deist Voltaire had nothing to learn from Pope the
Roman Catholic in philosophical matters. Swift, however, had much
more to commend him to Voltaire. The latter had mixed opinions
about *Gulliver's Travels*, finding that (as he put it in English) 'The
reader's imagination is pleased and charmingly entertained by the new
prospects of the lands which Gulliver discovers to him, but that continued series of new fangled follies, of fairy tales, of wild inventions,
palls at last upon our taste' (D310). Nevertheless, he must have
responded deeply to a mental landscape which anticipates that of

Micromégas, Zadig and *Candide* in many respects. Voltaire helped Swift with letters of introduction to French friends (unfortunately, Swift had to abandon the projected trip). Later he sought Swift's help in promoting, from the latter's base in Dublin, Irish subscriptions to *La Henriade*, and Swift appears to have made a warmly positive reply.

Voltaire's penetration into the English literary world was considerable, thanks initially to Bolingbroke and Pope. Through Pope he met Gay, who showed him the manuscript of his *Beggar's Opera* and introduced him to Colley Cibber.[42] Cibber handed Voltaire on to Chetwood, the prompter at the Theatre Royal, Drury Lane, who assisted him in his desire to attend the playhouse frequently and thereby made an important contribution to Voltaire's contacts with Shakespeare. We know that Voltaire saw *Hamlet, Julius Caesar* and *Richard III*; the list is probably a good deal more extensive, given his passion for theatre.[43] In addition, Voltaire met James Thomson, famous author of *The Seasons*, and Edward Young, who was to acquire equal renown for his *Night Thoughts*. It was Young who, after listening to Voltaire's strictures upon Milton's allegorical figures in *Paradise Lost*, is supposed to have rejoined wittily about Voltaire, while looking him straight in the eye:

> So much confusion, so wicked and so thin
> He seems at once a Chaos, Death and Sin.[44]

Quite apart from the ingenious way the sentiments are expressed, it is interesting to note that already, in Voltaire's early thirties, his thinness is striking. René Pomeau is probably right to suspect that the famous Largillière portrait of 1718, which gives Voltaire an elegantly filled face, may well be touched up.[45]

By contrast, Voltaire met few scientists, nor is this surprising at a time when he was only just beginning to become seriously interested in science. He did not, for instance, seek out Newton, as he might well have done during his first year in England. On the other hand, he already knew Pemberton's vulgarisation of Newton's philosophy in 1727 (D315), well before its publication in May the following year. Perhaps the interest had come from attending Newton's prestigious funeral at Westminster Abbey on 8 April, a month earlier; probably he had received from Pemberton, then or at some other time, a copy of his forthcoming gospel of Newtonianism.[46] Voltaire was to learn about Newton from meeting the latter's niece, Mrs Conduit, and her husband. Remarkably, we owe the story every schoolboy knows about Newton and the apple not to any compatriot but to this French visitor, who first recounted it in his *Essay on epick poetry* (1727) and then repeated it for a wider audience in the *Lettres philosophiques*.[47] It is an early indication of Voltaire's flair for spotting the sort of detail that will mobilise general interest and (in the Ferney period particularly) act as propaganda for crusading action.

If, however, his links with scientists in general were limited, Voltaire managed to make contact with no fewer than eleven doctors in England, the most famous being Sir Hans Sloane, President of the Royal College of Physicians and of the Royal Society.[48] One is inevitably tempted to see some correlation between this large number and Voltaire's constant concern about his health, especially when one remembers that he suffered greatly from illness in England. By contrast, he frequented little the ecclesiastical world, apart from the Quakers. A signal exception to this was his meeting the Norwich-born Samuel Clarke, then Rector of St James, Piccadilly. Voltaire pays tribute in later years to the brilliance of Clarke's mind; it may well have been, as W. H. Barber suggests, the first time since he had been taught by the Jesuit Fathers at Louis-le-Grand for him to encounter a distinguished intellect trained in philosophical debate. Possibly, too, Clarke initiated Voltaire into Newtonian thought.[49]

As we have seen, Voltaire eventually attained the English Court. He came to know and admire Princess Caroline, who became queen on George II's accession in 1727; she wins his applause in the *Lettres philosophiques* for her support of the arts and of such enlightened scientific advances as inoculation against smallpox. He established a cordial friendship with Lord Hervey (whom he was to see again in Paris and with whom he was to maintain a correspondence over the years); he acquired the support of Lords Chesterfield and Peterborough. The Duchess of Marlborough, according to Goldsmith, 'found infinite pleasure in the agreeable vivacity of his conversation' but thought his levity unprincipled. When, having offered her his help with the writing of her Memoirs, he began also offering criticisms, she grew angry, tore the papers from his hands, crying: 'I thought the man had sense, but I find him at bottom either a fool or a philosopher.'[50] An interesting reflection, which makes Voltaire sound like a veritable Pangloss! Notwithstanding the Duchess' hot-headedness, the anecdote bears witness once more to Voltaire's lack of discretion with people of high station.

But if Voltaire had connections with some of the most eminent in English society, his links with those at his own embassy in London were virtually non-existent. Almost the only Frenchmen he encountered in England were Huguenot refugees like Desmaizeaux, whom he met at

the Rainbow coffee-house in Charing Cross (D334). He was a suspect
figure to French authority following on his many past escapades, of
which the Rohan quarrel was only the most recent. The French ambassador to Saint James's, the comte de Broglie, wrote to the comte de
Morville, minister for Foreign Affairs in the French Government,
reporting that Voltaire had approached him with a request to find
subscribers for *La Henriade*. Broglie is wary, not having seen the new
edition, and worried that Voltaire, like other French authors, may
abuse the liberty they enjoy in England and write what they like on
religion, the Pope and the Government (D309).

The result was that the French Embassy did not subscribe to Voltaire's new edition. Not only was it they who abstained; so did all the
official representatives of Catholic powers in England, whereas
Denmark, Brunswick, Sweden and Holland were all included on the
subscription list through their diplomatic corps. It is this striking fact,
as René Pomeau says, which gives *La Henriade* a clear political
significance in 1728, as a manifestation of Protestant, liberal Europe
under English leadership, arrayed against Catholic, absolutist
Europe.[51] The impression is strengthened when one sees the astonish-
ingly strong list of official British representatives amongst the subscribers – all six ambassadors to Paris between 1715 and 1741, three
ambassadors to Turkey, representatives in Lisbon, Madrid, Hanover
and elsewhere.[52] One has the impression of a three-line whip to show
the British flag by supporting Voltaire. The appearance also on the
subscription list of so many merchants, the two Fawkener brothers
pre-eminent among them,[53] strengthens further the impression of a
liberal world where the hierarchies of French society hold little sway.

The organising of a subscription list for *La Henriade* was therefore a
success, and it testifies to Voltaire's strategic brilliance in planning
such a campaign. From George I and Princess Caroline, who headed
the list at the poet's request, thereby setting the example, through the
ranks of nobility and government, the merchant class, the cloth, men of
letters and of science, Voltaire indefatigably orchestrated his attack.
When George I died in June 1727 and was succeeded by his son who felt
only indifference for Voltaire, the writer felt he needed to extend his
publicity. Consequently, as appetising precursors of *La Henriade*, he
brought out two essays in English, on the Civil Wars of France (to
prepare English readers for the subject of his poem) and on epic poetry
(to explain the evolution of the *genre* and his own concept of it).[54] The
success of these two works when they appeared in January 1728 urged
Voltaire on to yet further efforts. Letters of about that time to Richard

Boyle, Earl of Burlington (D324) and to Edward Harley, Earl of Oxford (D325: the latter being suitably reminded that an ancestor of his makes an appearance in the epic) are probably typical of many such, now lost, that were sent out to potential subscribers. Curiosity was whetted. As one journal put it: 'we also hope every day to see Mr. de Voltaire's *Henriade*. He has greatly raised the expectation of the curious . . . '[55] In the end, 343 people subscribed for a total of 475 copies. Voltaire's success was impressive, albeit of ephemeral duration. On the one side, he had overcome George II's apathy, being admitted to the King's private supper parties. On the other, he recouped a large profit, probably in the region of 30,000 francs (if one includes George I's generous present of 2000 crowns).[56] If he had arrived in England 'without a penny . . . a stranger, alone, helpless', he would leave it comfortably well off[57] and in the public eye.

Yet the departure was made in circumstances as mysterious as the arrival. The classic reference is a letter from the Earl of Peterborough of 14/25 November 1728, which speaks of Voltaire having 'gone to Constantinople in order to believe in the gospels, which he says it is impossible to do living among the teachers of Christianity' (D342). But Peterborough, although he had earlier been Voltaire's chief patron, having subscribed for twenty copies of *La Henriade*,[58] seems not to have been informed by the poet of his departure;[59] and a rather garbled account dating from 1797, which tells of a great row between writer and protector ending in Voltaire's abrupt flight from England,[60] may have some elements of truth in it, even though it can hardly be entirely authentic as it stands.[61]

Firm evidence, however, is lacking, and we are prevented from reaching any assured conclusion on the motives for Voltaire's return to France. One can equally well argue that he had been preparing his return for some time, that he had received favourable signs from the French authorities, that he had achieved what in fact he came for, and that the time was now ripe. On this hypothesis, the clandestine return to France could be explained simply by the need to be sure of official approval before he dared to appear in public. A letter to Richard Towne (in English) in the summer of 1728 gives a hint of his going: 'I want a warmer climate for my health, which grows worse and worse in England' (23 July/3 August 1728, D340). If Voltaire was concerned about his physical state in the height of summer – and surely someone so susceptible must have genuinely feared the English climate, as many another Frenchman since – one would expect him to have fled before the onset of winter. Another letter of this time, to Thieriot, is equally significant. After numerous letters in English to his friend over the last two years, Voltaire this time writes in French, commenting that Thieriot will be surprised (4/15 August 1728, D341). Does this represent a psychological shift? The prospect of France must have seemed imminent.

Yet, knowing Voltaire's propensity for quarrels and his impatience with aristocratic figures, the possibility of a forced departure cannot be ruled out. Peterborough's letter seems to suggest a possible disillusionment with English religion. Perhaps, in the end, Voltaire found the 'teachers of Christianity' in England just as disappointing as those in France? The *Lettres philosophiques*, full of praise though they are for the English philosophic spirit of tolerance, are tepid at best towards all Christian spokesmen except the Quakers (and the latter too come in for their share of criticism).

Whatever the reason, Voltaire took ship for France some time in early autumn and lay low until the following April. In March he tells Thieriot that he hopes to arrive at Saint-Germain before the 15th ([10 March 1729], D345). Where was he in between? Lucien Foulet long ago shrewdly guessed 'une petite ville de Normandie'.[62] After him, Theodore Besterman perceptively drew attention to the fact that the holograph version of a letter from this period is to be found in Dieppe (D350, Commentary, n. 7). The Dieppe hypothesis now seems conclusively demonstrated in the light of recent new evidence coming from an apothecary of that town, who speaks of Voltaire spending a winter there and becoming his disciple.[63] It looks as if, when Voltaire has Candide set out from Dieppe for England (only to be repelled by the execution of Admiral Byng), a strong personal memory lurked behind the detail.

Voltaire, in England, retrieved success from disaster. But André-Michel Rousseau has done well to remind us, by comparing Voltaire's visit with that of other French contemporaries, that it was no exceptional triumph, neither in its intrinsic prestige nor in the wealth and number of connections Voltaire made.[64] Furthermore, Voltaire left some disquieting impressions behind him. The story of his supper with Alexander Pope and his mother at Twickenham, where Voltaire held forth about how 'those d—d Jesuits, when I was a boy, b(u)g-g(a)red me to such a degree that I shall never get over it as long as I live',[65] highly diverting though it is, betokens Voltaire's capacity for crude insensitivity on occasion, particularly in a foreign language; it could have done little to improve relations with the English poet. Other more sinister rumours also prevailed.[66] M. Rousseau even resurrects, with some cogency, the old allegation that Voltaire was a spy for the Whig Government, citing the recent disquieting discovery of a payment by the British Treasury to Voltaire in 1727 for no obvious reason. He goes on to point out that to think of Voltaire as a professional spy in the modern sense would be misleading; but he concludes that Voltaire was probably not wholly guiltless in matters of State intelligence while in England.[67]

That said, the more serious accusations against Voltaire rest on uncorroborated evidence. By his very nature, wherever he moved he left sharp reactions, not all of them by any means favourable, behind him. In this respect the English visit runs true to form. Whether deliberately creating publicity or not, he could not fail to arouse it.

For us, however, the importance of England for Voltaire lies in the extent to which it matured the *philosophe*. From the beginning of his stay, he was impressed with the fact that in England 'the people think freely and nobly' (D299), that it is 'a nation of philosophers' distinguished by their wisdom and honesty (D303). Later on he is struck by the individualism which tolerates all kinds of eccentricity (like walking six miles a day for one's health!) but alongside which obedience to the law is considered essential and placed above all arbitrary whims (to des Alleurs, [11 April 1728], D330). Here are the germs of the *Lettres philosophiques* which, when published in 1734 in France (having appeared first in English as *Letters Concerning the English Nation* in 1733), adumbrate the programme for a whole civilisation. The French should learn from their cross-Channel neighbours to use the experimental approach for matters of verifiable enquiry, keep questions of faith out of science and politics, encourage trade, cultivate literature and the arts. There is a place for the nobility in such a society, but it must justify its existence by active social pursuits. Hierarchy for its own sake is rejected; instead, the creed preached is based on work and scientific values whereby man improves the lot of humanity. We shall shortly discover what virulent reactions were aroused in France by the *Lettres* and why. For the moment, this brief summary of the *Lettres philosophiques* may serve to conclude an experience in which Voltaire, having fled from arbitrary privilege, found a land where 'Reason is free' (D330) and which he proceeded to import, embroidered in polemical guise, as a new concept into French public opinion.[68]

2 Luxury, and Cirey

Though Voltaire returned from England comfortably off, he had had sufficient experience of poverty. Nor was it the first time. Until 1722 his financial situation had been good, but with his father's death he found himself deprived of regular support. Not only was he forbidden to touch the capital of his inheritance; Arouet *père* had left his affairs in such a disorderly state that the ensuing complications prevented his son for some years from even using the interest accruing on it. By 1724, things had taken such a bad turn that he realised he might even have to take up gainful employment (D212). Here was a threat to his whole intended career as a man of letters. The situation seems to have got worse the following year ('I have never felt my poverty more acutely': D241) before the pension of 1,500 francs from the Queen in November 1725 changed Voltaire's mental outlook ('I begin to have reasonable expectations': D255). But England put paid to such hopes.

Returning to France clandestinely and with uncertain prospects, Voltaire must have felt a keen desire to establish a firm financial base once and for all if possible. Such an opportunity was soon to present itself, and the story merits recounting because it throws such a clear light on the Voltairean personality.[1] In 1728 the city of Paris instituted a monthly lottery for the repayment of municipal bonds (*rentes*), whereby those who owned *rentes* had the right to buy tickets *pro rata*. As these bonds had lost some of their original value, the government decided to add 500,000 francs monthly (rising to 600,000 in 1730) to the repayments. Hence a profit of that sum was available at each draw to some lucky ticket-holders.

Voltaire, with the aid of his mathematician friend La Condamine, spotted that if all the tickets in a given lottery were cornered by one

person or syndicate, the profits would automatically follow; so they got
to work to ensure that this might be arranged. Voltaire was back at
Saint-Germain in March 1729 and permitted by the minister
Maurepas to return to Paris itself in April (D354). From the documents
extant relating to the lottery, it is clear that the syndicate had already
been organised by the May draw, as the same names (some of them
known acquaintances of Voltaire, some almost certainly fictitious)
begin to recur. The operation continued at least until February 1730
(from which point the documents have ceased to exist) and probably
until the lottery ceased in June. The gross rewards available would
therefore seem to have been in the region of seven and a half million
francs! Voltaire had achieved the dream of every lottery gambler –
absolutely certain success. When the government saw what was hap-
pening, it tried through a royal edict of the Conseil d'Etat (21 January
1730) to change the rules; but in vain. Voltaire and his companions
were acting in perfect legality, and the loophole they had discovered
could not be blocked up under existing arrangements.[2] The profits were
such that even if his own part of the winnings was fairly small, he had at
last an impregnable financial base.

   Thus Voltaire achieved a brilliant success in characteristic Voltairean
manner by cocking a snook at authority. The effect was delightfully
enhanced by a detail that allowed the writer free play for his satiric
verve. Participants in the lottery were expected to inscribe *devises*
(mottoes) on their tickets as a proof of identity. These *devises* provided
some extra entertainment for the public when read aloud on the day of
the draw. Until Voltaire appeared on the scene, they tended to run on
conventional lines, such as 'a win would make me happy'. Suddenly, a
more piquant turn of phrase appears: 'All men are equal' or (surely an
allusion to Voltaire's supposed Anglomania) 'me, for the English, oh!
what a fable!' Already, long before the Ferney years, one sees in embryo
the ironic epigrams that will become a hallmark of Voltaire's style.
Boldness, imagination, decisive intervention in the world of public
affairs – all these qualities of the future *philosophe* are here brilliantly
displayed.

   The lottery was not the only avenue Voltaire took to wealth. He also
began speculating with success in such markets as the corn trade. But
these were less spectacular and also required large sums of initial
capital; the lottery gains provided him with the necessary springboard
for that. Thereafter, despite many financial vicissitudes, Voltaire never
knew real poverty again. By the 1750s he had vast sums of money at his
disposal, using them henceforth mainly to purchase annuities. By the

time of Les Délices he could afford to employ two secretaries, a valet,
two lackeys, a French cook and a scullion, and own six horses and four
carriages.[3] During the decade 1759–68, before the high peak of expensive development at Ferney, he spent well over a million francs on his
properties there and elsewhere.[4] He had become the *seigneur* of a small
principality, as one sees strikingly in the coincidental detail that the
sum of 20,000 francs which he allotted monthly to Mme Denis was
exactly the same amount as King Stanislas gave his *intendant* at the
Court of Lorraine in Lunéville.[5] As Voltaire put it in his *Mémoires* in
1759: 'after living with kings, I became King in my own household'.[6]

Voltaire built up his fortune as a tool for his activities as a *philosophe*.
But what of his attitude to wealth and ease, in and for itself? It provides
another important clue to our understanding of him and is perhaps best
seen in relation to his most explicit statements on affluence, the two
poems entitled *Le Mondain* (1736) and *Défense du Mondain* (1737), which
relate closely to his life at Cirey. But first we must discover what
brought him to Cirey.

Voltaire's relations with the authorities, never easy where publication of his works was concerned, soon became difficult again after his
return to Paris. Without official permission appeared three works in
swift succession: the *Histoire de Charles XII* (1731), the dedicatory epistle
to *Zaïre* (1733), and the *Temple du goût* (1733). Part of the edition of
Charles XII was seized; Voltaire turned to Rouen for help in illicit
printing from the bookseller Claude François Jore and got copies
distributed in Paris by smuggling them in from Versailles in the
carriage of the duc de Richelieu, whose help was invaluable because his
eminent rank placed him above suspicion.[7] The author had himself
hesitated about returning from Rouen to Paris, first ascertaining from
Thieriot the official attitude to his work (D414). One need hardly be
surprised that the Garde des Sceaux, Chauvelin, whose official permission had gone unsought for all these works, should have become 'piqué'
by the spring of 1733 and wished to put Voltaire in prison for a few days
by way of revenge (D586). So Chauvelin gave clear warning that if the
much-heralded *Lettres philosophiques*, with their considerably more controversial contents, were to appear without his approval, Voltaire
would risk severe punishment (D638).

So Voltaire felt a growing apprehension from 1732 on as he worked
upon the *Lettres*. He was determined to publish them and present the
French with a practical model of society that could teach them useful
lessons. But equally he wished to avoid the miseries of renewed imprisonment or exile. His correspondence resounds with doubts and fears.

Will the letter on Locke cause trouble? But he has not dwelt on Locke at great length, he has watered it down a good deal (D545) and is really saying nothing contrary to religious teachings (D637). What then about the Reflections on Pascal, which he adds as a twenty-fifth letter to the original edition? It is a bold venture, he admits, to take on the sublime thinker, but Pascal's misanthropic view of human nature is wrong and must be attacked (D626); besides, Voltaire has ignored sensitive matters such as Pascal's discussions on miracles and prophecies (D637). Perhaps the sallies against the Quakers will lead his audience to think he is mocking Christianity as a whole? Voltaire takes care to read two of these letters to the eminent Cardinal Fleury in 1732 so as to gain his approval (D542). He wants to believe that all will be well when the *Lettres* appear, but as the months advance towards that event, resolution and uncertainty are mixed in roughly equal proportions. The plan is to publish first an English-language version in London, where a more reasonable nation will react more favourably than the French. Voltaire, with true businessman's flair, wishes to try out his product first in a controlled and generally benevolent market.[8] So Thieriot is entrusted with the task, though he must make sure to say in the preface that these letters were written to him by Voltaire for the most part from England in 1728. (In this way, presumably, Voltaire was hoping to count on the lenifying effect of time and distance.) Thieriot must add that as the manuscript had become known and translated he had found himself obliged to print the original (D635, 24 July 1733). Even this is not enough, however. A few days later, in a fit of apprehension, Voltaire orders Thieriot to suspend publication of the *Lettres*: the Garde des Sceaux has told Voltaire (as the latter reports it in English) that 'he will undo me if the letters come out into the world' (D638, 27 July 1733).

But the English edition appeared. Voltaire's orders must have arrived too late; but it is likely that Thieriot would have blithely disregarded Voltaire's wishes anyway, as he was to do on other occasions. Voltaire is pleased to discover that the work has met with success in England; but his anxiety regarding French reactions is undiminished. Jore has already printed 2,500 copies; they must all be carried away with total secrecy, leaving no incriminating correspondence behind, and stored at the homes of Voltaire's Rouen friends Cideville and Formont (D260). The French publication must be delayed until Voltaire is in a happier situation with the authorities, the more so because the Garde des Sceaux suspects (wrongly, in the event) that the English edition was itself printed in Rouen (D640).

Once again, Voltaire's wishes were overtaken by events. In April 1734 the *Lettres philosophiques* were leaked to the public in Paris, despite Voltaire's efforts to prevent it. For a time he was not only frightened, but also bewildered and angry. It seemed as if Jore had let him down. The true culprit became known only several weeks later: Voltaire had imprudently lent the Parisian printer François Josse a copy in order to have it bound, and Josse had seized the opportunity to pirate the edition (D752). If the reaction of the abbé Le Blanc was a general one, then the objections to Voltaire's *Lettres philosophiques* extended more widely than even he had anticipated. For the abbé took offence at everything except the Quaker letters (towards which he was merely condescending). The general scorn which Voltaire had shown for his own nation, government, ministers, and religion was 'appallingly in-decent' (D718, 15 April 1734).

The storm caught Voltaire in the provinces at Montjeu in Burgundy, whither he had gone with Mme du Châtelet to celebrate the marriage of the duc de Richelieu. He was fortunate to be out of the way; he was equally fortunate to have in the comte d'Argental an influential friend in Paris who could give him warning of imminent arrest (D738). Immediate flight was the only possible answer. At first he considers going into exile, in London or Basle (D728); later, he gives out that he is departing for Lorraine, and leaves precipitately on 6 May. Thereafter his whereabouts are a mystery, until he turns up at Richelieu's military quarters in Philippsburg at the beginning of July, before settling at Mme du Châtelet's château at Cirey in Champagne later that month. As will happen many times again, Voltaire goes completely to ground, while playing for time in order to appease the authorities. He gradually succeeded in this respect, by dint of repeated denials that he had anything to do with the unwonted appearance of the Letters, indeed had strenuously opposed it.[9] Although the work was condemned to be torn apart and solemnly burnt in Paris on 10 June 1734, he was officially told nine months later by Hérault, the Chief of Police, that he could return to Paris (D848), and in March 1735 he did so (D854). Meantime, he lay low at Cirey.

Mme du Châtelet was 'stricken with grief' at Voltaire's hasty leave-taking in Montjeu (D730). They had met and become lovers in 1733, the affair was still fresh and new. Mme du Châtelet[10] had been born in 1706, the daughter of the baron de Breteuil, an important figure at Louis XIV's court, and grown up in luxurious comfort in the family *hôtel* in Paris. From early years she had been an ardent student. She translated Virgil's *Aeneid*, discussed physics and astronomy with Fontenelle, read *Robinson Crusoe* in English; but she was a society woman too, enjoying theatre, opera, ballet. In 1725 she married the marquis du Châtelet, scion of a noble line going back to Charlemagne and himself a professional soldier: a decade older than his wife Emilie, he was a kind, generous and tolerant husband to her but quite foreign to her intellectual interests. Three children were born of the marriage – the only son would die by the guillotine in 1793. Voltaire had met her when a young man, but she was then still only a child. The decisive encounter came when she had long since tired of her husband's limitations and sought consolation elsewhere; while Voltaire for his part, weary of exiles and harassments, was ready for a more settled life. The *Lettres philosophiques* alarum was to set the seal on their relationship. For the rest of the 1730s, Cirey was to be the centre of Voltaire's existence. It would remain his base until Mme du Châtelet's death in 1749, and when he returned to the château one last time a few weeks afterwards to collect his effects, their volume amounted to two cartloads, including twenty-five large cases (D4028): evidence enough that for fifteen years it was his only real home, amidst all his wanderings.

What was Cirey like? The most informative account comes from the voluminous letters of the gossipy Mme de Graffigny, written during her stay at the château from early December 1738 to mid-February 1739. Voltaire's room, small and low, is hung with crimson velvet; little tapestry but much panelling, admirable pictures, mirrors, lacquered corner-cupboards, porcelains, a clock supported by marabou storks – 'an infinity of things in that fashion, expensive, choice, and above all so clean you could kiss the floor'; a jewellery box containing ten or twelve rings with cut stones and another two with diamonds. From Voltaire's room one goes into the little gallery (for this one is only thirty or forty feet long), of varnished wood. Between the windows stand two small, beautiful statues of Venus and Hercules. Although it is winter, a furnace set in the wall makes the air springlike. Neither the dark room (for Voltaire's optical experiments) nor the one for his scientific instruments is yet ready; the latter find a temporary home in the gallery. Only one sofa, no comfortable armchairs, only stuffed ones; as Mme de Graffigny sagely remarks: 'Bodily comfort is not, it seems, his pleasure.' Mme du Châtelet's apartment is much finer still. These luxuries did not extend, however, to poor Mme de Graffigny's lodgings. She had to put up with a temple of the winds; only one window to admit the light, but draughts came in through the many cracks around it (D1677)!

It is easy, therefore, to see echoes of Voltaire's comfortable existence in the poems on luxury, *Le Mondain* and *Défense du Mondain*. *Le Mondain* is an apology for worldly affluence, as the ninth line makes quite explicit: 'J'aime le luxe, et même la mollesse.'[11] Affluence is the 'Mère des Arts et des heureux travaux [Mother of the arts and of successful enterprises]'; both culture and the economy benefit. By contrast with the crude primitivism of the Garden of Eden (to which Voltaire devotes a satiric passage shot through with condescension), the good life is lived in Paris, London, or Rome. The true *honnête homme* surrounds himself with products of art (Correggio, Poussin), sculpture (Bouchardon), silverware (Germain) and Gobelin tapestries; his house is resplendent with mirrors and carpets, his garden with fountains, his carriage with gilt and glass. His bath is perfumed, he enjoys rendezvous with delicious actresses, attends the Opéra, goes on afterwards to exquisite suppers with champagne. After this brilliant scene, the conclusion is trenchant. To the proponents of austerity like Fénelon and his kind Voltaire says: Keep your Golden Age, where people were virtuous only because they were poor and had no other choice. For me, he concludes with every appearance of self-contentment, 'Le Paradis terrestre est où je suis'.

The link with Cirey is heightened when we read a letter such as Voltaire wrote to Thieriot on 3 November 1735, where he celebrates the marvellous suppers with Emilie, replete with excellent food and champagne, at which they read his works or Newton or Locke (D935). But the analogies only heighten the differences. In *Le Mondain* the man of fashion does not read Voltaire or indeed anything else. Furthermore, whatever the delights of Cirey, they did not rise to the *grand luxe* depicted in the poem and could not compete with the Opéra and the company of actresses. If Voltaire had been a *mondain* at Cirey, it would have had to be on a very restricted scale.

In fact, he was not a *mondain* at all. Mme de Graffigny provides equally valuable information on the habits of work practised by Voltaire and his mistress. On a typical day, there is a morning break for coffee and lunch lasting an hour or so, a pause for *goûter* at four o'clock and supper at nine, which lasts till midnight (D1686). Later in her stay there appears to be no reunion before the dinner hour itself (D1769). Mme du Châtelet works almost invariably throughout the night, sleeping a mere two hours a day; she quits her desk only for coffee and supper. Even when Voltaire leaves his papers to come and visit Mme de Graffigny he never sits down and says that one should not waste a minute, for 'the most costly expense possible is that of time'. He keeps his secretary by him at supper for half the meal and wants to get back to his work as soon as possible (D1807). These details are not wholly consistent, and one suspects that, as Mme de Graffigny's sojourn progressed, the work pattern became more intense and excluded her more. What is sufficiently clear is that existence at Cirey in the depths of the country was for the most part, despite its elegance, austere and rigorous. The same impression of hard work at eccentric hours is conveyed by another visitor in 1736 (D1205). Although Mme de Graffigny's stay ended with an orgiastic climax of theatre in which they performed forty-four acts from various plays (mainly, it would appear, Voltaire's) in forty-eight hours, this very immoderation by its contrast only enhances the intense devotion to study the rest of the time.

It could hardly be otherwise, when one takes into account Voltaire's remarkable output during these years. William Barber sums it up trenchantly:

In the seven years 1734–40 alone, he was engaged upon the composition or revision of one serious and one burlesque epic, five tragedies, four comedies, two operas, two major poems of moral and philosophical reflexion, two *contes philosophiques*; two works on metaphysics, a handbook on Newtonian science, a prize essay based on original research into a contemporary scientific problem; a major contribution to French historical literature, a literary biography, an essay on contemporary economic theories, and the editing of Frederick of Prussia's attack on the politics of Machiavelli.[12]

Professor Barber goes on to add that this takes no account of Voltaire's occasional verse, journalism, minor pieces, or the wide reading which bore fruit only in later periods of his life. *Le Mondain*, by contrast, speaks of work only in so far as luxury creates employment for others. Voltaire's views on the symbolic place of champagne in life are unequivocal. As he counselled Thieriot in 1735, drink it by all means with pleasant companions – but make sure you work hard so that you can afford to drink your own (D875).

When *Le Mondain* appeared, another untimely publication,[13] in November 1736, Voltaire had been back to Paris only for visits since his precipitate flight after the publication of the *Lettres philosophiques* in 1734. Cirey had proved to be the happiest of sanctuaries, especially when he knew that he was free to return to Paris again. The year 1735 is full of expressions of contentment. Voltaire is 'calm, happy and busy' (D885, 26 June 1735); he is working principally on the *Siècle de Louis XIV*. He has also, in return for bed and board, been putting his money into restoring the château, building and planning. Earlier, when Mme du Châtelet had joined him at Cirey in October 1734, she too had become involved, though it is characteristic of her strong will that she should quickly assume command of the enterprise: 'she is putting in windows where I had put doors', writes Voltaire with some ruefulness, though clearly full of admiration for her abilities (D800, [c. 1 November 1734]). He on his side busies himself with importing locks and turpentine and trying to prevent fires from smoking (D897, 4 August [1735]). Cirey offers him a delightful retreat. In a letter to Thieriot he claims that they are both happy, Thieriot with fine concerts, new plays and all the social and literary whirl in Paris, and he with peace, friendship and study with a woman unique of her kind (D899). At Cirey he can follow his bent in ranging from the sublime to badinage; if only Newton could have written vaudeville songs – Voltaire would have respected him the more! (D903, 24 August 1735). In brief, he dares affirm: 'Never have I been happier' (D987, 13 [January 1736]). It is the high tide of his relationship with Emilie.

She too has been surprised by happiness. Voltaire's first return to Paris from Cirey lasts from March to May 1735. She follows him back to Cirey a few weeks later, not without some trepidation yet knowing that only in the country can she keep his energies under control and hold on to him. As she tells her friend and former lover the duc de Richelieu, she finds it impossible to reconcile in her own mind so much reason in Voltaire concerning most things, allied to so much blindness as to what can destroy him irremediably (D874, [c. 30 May 1735]). Yet to her astonishment, the life at Cirey brings naught but vigour, love, happiness, as she reports to Richelieu several months later (D943). She confesses that she has never felt true passion except for the one who is now 'the charm and the torment' of her life, 'my principle of good and evil' (D955, [c. 1 December 1735]).[14]

Voltaire's second visit to Paris from Cirey between April and July 1736 was destined only to confirm his views of the capital. The journey was undertaken principally to effect a final settlement of the troubles with Jore arising from the Lettres philosophiques. In setting out for Jore what he considered to be the true account of the matter, Voltaire foolishly admitted on paper what he had taken great care to avoid confessing anywhere else, that he was the author of the work (D1045, 25 March 1736). Jore seized the opportunity to blackmail him and then published a factum denouncing him. Voltaire was able to bring pressure via Maurepas and Hérault to have Jore desist and hand over the offending letter; but it was a pyrrhic victory, as Hérault insisted that in compensation for the money he would not now have to pay Jore,

Voltaire should give 500 francs to the poor (D1107)! The latter pro-
tested to Chauvelin the shame and dishonour of it all (D1109), but the
authorities were unrelenting. It was a bitter stay in Paris. Voltaire tells
his friend the writer Cideville that he is 'overwhelmed with business affairs, illnesses and afflictions' and feels himself in exile there (D1072, 6
May [1736]); he repeats these complaints to Cideville towards the end
of his visit (D1108). His reputation had suffered from the mean squabble; the abbé Le Blanc rightly surmised that it ruined any present
expectations of his being elected to the Académie Française (D1089). A
'triste voyage' indeed, as one observer of the events commented
(D1114). The imprudence and headstrong tactlessness which Mme du
Châtelet knew so well were never more evidently displayed.
Significantly, she was not by his side in Paris to curb his errors of
judgment.

   Le Mondain ends, as we have seen, with the line 'Le Paradis terrestre
est où je suis.' That, however, is not how it appeared in the first printed
edition, where the statement is balder: 'Le Paradis Terrestre est à
Paris.'[15] It is possible, as has been suggested,[16] that Voltaire subsequently made the change out of gallantry to Mme du Châtelet. The
thesis does not, however, rule out other more subjective interpret-
ations. To assign the good life simply to Paris did not fully render the
poet's complex attitude to *mondanité*. We have already noticed the
differences between the locale of *Le Mondain* and Cirey, in contrast to
the more superficial resemblances. The paradox needs to be taken further; after the poem is written, Voltaire begins to build up the parallels.

   When he sends the poem to Cideville in September 1736, Voltaire
takes the same simple view as in the first edition: it is Parisian life which
is described in *Le Mondain* (D1154). But later one finds a change in
attitude taking place. A letter to Thieriot of late October waxes eloquent on the appointments at Cirey, Voltaire adding for good measure
that their life is very like *Le Mondain* (D1179). Inviting La Faye to the
château about the same date, he quotes lines from the poem to reinforce
the delightful impression (D1178). Cirey itself becomes a 'paradis
terrestre' (D1366, [c. 20 August 1737]; D1410, 23 December [1737]), or
'Notre petit paradis de Cirey' (D1375, [c. 12 October 1737]).

   In short, Voltaire transforms Cirey into myth. Life is made to imitate
art. A certain ambivalence underlies the whole attitude to Cirey, which
moves from being an *anti-Mondain* to a rather privileged form of *mondanité*. The ambivalence is less marked concerning Paris in Voltaire's
correspondence; yet one has only to read *Le Mondain* (which, as we have
seen, was conceived unambiguously with Paris as subject) to gain a

sense of Voltaire's fascination with the sophisticated world of the capital. By 1744 his letters explicitly return to the original affirmation of *Le Mondain*: 'Paris will always be the earthly paradise. Music, suppers, balls, the theatre, love affairs, science and society . . .' (D2931). The oscillation between attraction and repulsion for Paris will become a major theme in the years of *Candide* and Ferney, when Voltaire's return from exile seems blocked for ever. But already one sees the shifting complexities. Cirey is fine, if one is working hard in peaceful seclusion. But even in the year of high contentment 1735, and in one of the most joyous celebrations of Cirey to Thieriot, the satisfaction is balanced by a longing for news from outside. He is happy in his retreat, he says, but he is starved for information and calls on his friend to 'inundate me with news' (D928, 13 October 1735).

So it seems appropriate that, if we are to believe Mme du Châtelet, *Le Mondain* was composed neither in Cirey nor in Paris but in the post-chaise carrying him back to Cirey from his disastrous visit in 1736 (D1116).[17] The journey would probably have taken three or four days, giving ample time for poetic composition, nor are there any esoteric references in the poem indicating the need for bookish knowledge. Material difficulties do not appear to be insuperable. What however about the psychological circumstances?

At first sight no time might seem less propitious. One can easily conjure up a despairing figure sunk in gloom. But such a picture does no justice to Voltaire's volatile and adaptable temperament. A phase of his life has ended; even so, Cirey awaits. In a few days he will be restored to his studies alongside Emilie. For a moment he is suspended between two worlds. Despite his tribulations in Paris he must have participated too in some of its *douceurs* (Le Blanc speaks of a dinner he had with Voltaire at which they talked much of theatre, D1068; and the poet arranged to meet Baculard d'Arnaud at the Café Procope, D1090). Squalid lawsuits with Jore could not destroy the elegance of Correggio and the enchantments of the Opéra. What better moment, then, while the memories of these delights are fresh yet removed from all the late harassments?

But the ambivalences remain. The hedonist attitudes outlined in *Le Mondain*, bolder than anywhere else in Voltaire's work, do not genuinely represent his position. It is not Voltaire who follows the programme of *divertissement* but the *honnête homme*, at whom the authorial 'je' looks on (cf. vv. 78–86), with sympathy it is true but at a remove. In the end, the ideal place is not to be located on the map but rather in that more diffuse mental universe 'où je suis'.[18]

Voltaire will remain, however, convinced that the antithesis of luxury, a life based on asceticism and renunciation, is false, and this view emerges unmistakably from the poem. In keeping with his times,[19] it is not enjoyment that he is defending so much as action; hedonism has its place when the pleasure principle can be made compatible with social utility. Voltaire is to demonstrate this by his generous attitudes to others: to young authors and friends like Thieriot,[20] Linant, Baculard d'Arnaud, Marmontel, Vauvenargues, and many others;[21] to Marie Corneille, descendant of the great Pierre, when Voltaire published his *Commentaires sur Corneille* in 1764 to save her from penury and provide her with a dowry;[22] to Mme du Châtelet and Mme Denis with lavish gifts and, in the latter case, the legacy of his rich estate; to the numerous publishers and actors whom he allowed to keep profitable earnings from his books and plays instead of insisting on receiving them as was his right. He often struck hard, even harsh, bargains; but it was not his nature to be miserly.

The appearance of *Le Mondain*, as we have seen, was embarrassing. There is every reason to believe that Voltaire intended it, as he said, to be a *badinage* for the eyes of select friends. The condescending portrait of Adam and Eve, their nails long and dirty, their hair unkempt, dining on millet and acorns and sleeping on the hard ground, turns them into two brutes without the slightest sense of civility, let alone the polish of elegant Paris society. It is a rare early instance of Biblical criticism by the poet; this iconoclastic view inevitably drew down upon Voltaire the wrath of authority. The abbé Le Blanc, uncharitable as ever regarding Voltaire, dismissed the poem with contempt as worthless, not failing, however, to note that its author had badly mistreated God and Adam (D1205); while an anonymous chronicler reported the scandal it had speedily provoked by its apology for vice and hideous presentation of our first progenitors.[23] Given this latest brush with the authorities, one is unlikely to be impressed by Mme du Châtelet's protestation that Voltaire had been well-behaved ever since the *Lettres philosophiques* (D1240)! Within a few weeks he discovered to his dismay that a work which he had thought no more than indiscreet had proved outrageous, and in early December 1736 he took the painful decision to go into exile once more. On the way he changed horses at Wassy, and from there he wrote a poignant letter at 4 a.m. to d'Argental bewailing his lot. Mme du Châtelet has travelled with him thus far; now she must leave him and she is in tears: 'The situation is horrible . . . I am cut to the quick . . . what a dreadful life . . . I would prefer death . . .' (D1221). The approach of isolation and uncertainty, the renewed threat of permanent exclusion from France, once more cast his spirit into deep gloom. Emilie gives out word that he has gone to stay with Frederick of Prussia at Potsdam; in reality he makes his way through the Low Countries, eventually arriving at Amsterdam. This time the storm dies down quickly, thanks at least in part to the intervention of powerful friends like the duchesse de Richelieu with the Garde des Sceaux on Voltaire's behalf (cf. D1267); and by 1 March 1737 he is back at Cirey. But the experience confirms his horror of persecution. He will not return to Paris, he tells d'Argental, but will live either at Cirey or in a free country (D1291, 1[March 1737]). In fact he had been tempted not to return at all, according to Mme du Châtelet, whom the news had made ill with pain and anxiety (D1274).

Cirey will however retain Voltaire during 1737 and 1738. Never has he been more indifferent to Paris, as he tells Thieriot with every appearance of sincerity (D1492, 5 May [1738]). Into this world comes Mme de Graffigny at the end of 1738. She will leave two months later, her feelings a good deal more ruffled than when she arrived. The early welcome from her hosts had changed to tempestuous denunciations when, on 29 December, Mme du Châtelet and Voltaire had accused her of having sent off to her friend Devaux at the court of Lorraine in Lunéville a copy of Voltaire's poem La Pucelle. If the comparatively mild Le Mondain had given offence, no doubts existed but that this mock-heroic satire upon the sacred figure of Joan of Arc, sprinkled liberally with lubricious adornments, would constitute the most audacious of provocations. Mme de Graffigny's hosts had good reason to be worried and indignant – if indeed she had sent the poem; unfortunately for all three, she was the victim of a misunderstanding. A letter from Devaux referred to 'le chant de Jeanne' as 'charmant'. This had been taken to mean that Mme de Graffigny had sent him the poem, whereas in fact he was replying only to her description of the poem being read at Cirey. The error, natural enough in the circumstances, was however accompanied by a frightening display of anger on the part of Voltaire and especially of Mme du Châtelet. But for Voltaire's active intervention, their hapless guest reported later, Emilie would have struck her; as it was, she was subjected to verbal abuse so violent and prolonged as to leave her still sick some weeks later (D1807). Mme de Graffigny was unlucky enough to discover the full force of her hostess's fury unchained.

How had the latter come to read the offending phrase from Devaux in the first place? She had in fact been opening his letters to Mme de Graffigny, as indeed all others into Cirey at this time. To understand why is to comprehend the reason for Mme du Châtelet's wrath and the wider scene onto which Mme de Graffigny had naïvely stumbled. Emilie was interested not in her guest's gossip so much as in intercepting any incoming copies of the *Voltairomanie* before they should affright Voltaire's eyes.

This infamous work so feared by the denizens of Cirey had been written by the abbé Desfontaines. The abbé, formerly helped by Voltaire in 1725 to get out of jail at Bicêtre, where he had been incarcerated for sodomy, had repaid kindness by slandering his benefactor in writing. The feud, developing over the intervening years with many incidents on either side, eventually led to *Le Préservatif*, published in 1738 and either written or instigated by Voltaire,[24] in which this treachery is set forth. The author recounts an incident when Desfontaines, having composed an attack on Voltaire, had shown it to their mutual friend Thieriot; the latter had obliged Desfontaines to burn it, so horrible were its contents. Desfontaines, no whit inferior to Voltaire in rudeness of insult, riposted before the year was out with *La Voltairomanie*, whose very title gives a good indication of its contents. Voltaire is denounced as an 'esprit faux' in both science and artistic taste; his whole merit, properly appreciated, is 'à peu près celui d'un violon'. *La Henriade*, the *Lettres philosophiques*, the *Eléments de Newton* – these major works from Voltaire's pen are, like others, torn to shreds. Voltaire is described as the grandson of a peasant (in fact, his grandfather was a highly reputable merchant of cloth and silk). As a final blow Desfontaines announces that Thieriot had explicitly denied the story related in *Le Préservatif* concerning his actions.[25]

The *Voltairomanie* contained much to upset Voltaire's sensibilities. His most important writings, the source of profound amour-propre, are comprehensively lacerated, his critical perceptions set at naught with withering satire, his pedigree attacked and his assertions denied. Not least, the beloved friend Thieriot had been prevailed upon by Voltaire's enemy to turn Voltaire into a liar. Spirits much more phlegmatic might well have been incensed or deeply pained by the artful venom of Desfontaines's pen. Voltaire, ever vulnerable to calumny, could not but rage and suffer. Mme de Graffigny had already noted, before the arrival of this upsetting tirade from Desfontaines, Voltaire's terrible weakness in this respect; he cannot, she wrote, learn how to treat his enemies with reasoned scorn (D1700). Later, she goes into more detail about his irrational responses to barbed criticism. She observes that approbation scarcely touches him, as he already knows his true worth; but one single word from his opponents and he is at once cast down into despair and bitterness. He has so many good qualities that he deserves to be happy, yet he is 'the unhappiest man in the world' (D1807).

These perceptive comments will be of value later when we consider Voltaire's attitudes to calumny and try to understand why he was so especially sensitive in this respect. For the moment let us note other elements in the Desfontaines *fracas*. With noble disinterestedness Voltaire too, it subsequently turned out, had kept from Mme du Châtelet that he had in fact seen the *Voltairomanie* despite her precautions. She was considerably touched by his delicacy in wishing to spare her feelings; furthermore, his reaction had been much cooler and more prudent than she had dared to expect, and he had promised not to prolong the feud with another round of insults and reproaches (D1738).[26] Even so, the treachery of Thieriot was hard to bear for one who set so much store by loyalty amongst his intimates. Voltaire writes him a letter full of bitter remonstration: 'Ah my friend, my dear friend for 25 years, what have you done? . . . The tears flow from my eyes as I write to you' (D1758, 9 [January 1739]). Mme du Châtelet adds her angry denunciations in writing a joint letter with Voltaire to him (D1792). It seems that Voltaire has been more hurt by Thieriot than by Desfontaines (D1763); be that as it may, he has had a fever and fainted twice the previous day (D1712). Thieriot, for his part, temporises. It is possible, as Theodore Besterman argues, that Desfontaines's hold over Thieriot springs from a homosexual connection (D1736, Commentary), and Frederick's similar inclinations may explain his own refusal to denounce Thieriot, who was his Paris agent.[27]

The whole episode needs also to be judged in the light of Voltaire's relationship with Mme du Châtelet. The actions of each in seeking to protect the other from undue pain testify to the deep affection between them, affection that will endure until her death. But this is only one side of the picture; tensions were growing. Voltaire, we have seen, returned with some reluctance to Cirey in 1737. He confesses that Emilie is for him more than a father, a brother and a son (D1291). Yet, later that year, she writes a disenchanted letter to Thieriot disclosing that sometimes several days go by without Voltaire seeing her or at least eating with her (D1411). Voltaire's niece Mme Denis, however, visiting Cirey the following May, reports a happier scene: Emilie employs every imaginable art to please him and he seems more enchanted than ever (D1498). Such is not Mme de Graffigny's view. She finds that Mme du Châtelet has locked up Voltaire's *Siècle de Louis XIV* to prevent him from completing and publishing it; this despite Voltaire's urgent desire to get on with the historical study, as the work he says he is most happy with. She nags him to change his coat and he gets angry, flying out of the room. She ridicules his tragedy *Mérope*, which (not too surprisingly) does not please him (D1681). She persecutes him to stop him writing verse, though he passionately longs to (D1725). Yet he too taunts her so far that even Mme de Graffigny, no great friend of Emilie, feels sorry for her (D1807).

The relationship, inevitably a stormy one between two personalities so passionate, had clearly developed strains from the long years of close communion in the rustic solitude of Cirey. Despite the attentions of each for the other, the stresses of the Desfontaines episode point to the end of an era. Paris will soon beckon again, despite Voltaire's protestations of 'le paradis terrestre' at Cirey, and the 1740s will put a different face on the *rapport*: still companionable, tender, respectful on both sides, but with each one seeking for independent sources of fulfilment in private as well as public life.[28]

When Voltaire left Cirey with Mme du Châtelet for Brussels in May 1739, thereafter to go on to Paris and not return to Cirey until November, one may say that the 'Cirey period', in the strict sense, was at an end. He will return there at times in the 1740s, and it remains his base until 1749; but long residence in this rural retreat gives way to travel (mostly but not entirely with Mme du Châtelet): to Berlin, Brussels, Versailles, Fontainebleau, Paris, Sceaux, Lunéville amongst other places. Only in 1744 will he come back to the château for an extended stay of six months, and even then, despite protestations at the 'delicious solitude' of Cirey,[29] his mind is largely occupied by preparing the *comédie-ballet La Princesse de Navarre* for performance at Court. The 1740s, very conveniently for the biographer's purposes, may be seen as constituting a different period.

How then to sum up this phase of Voltaire's life now ended? The range and amount of his intellectual activity have already been indicated. Since Ira Wade's extensive researches,[30] we have ceased to regard the period 1733–49 as a break in Voltaire's evolution and come to see it as the time when he completed his education as a *philosophe*. The first section up to 1740 lays the essential groundwork, by dint of his encyclopedic reading during the long months of isolation at Cirey. Metaphysical and moral philosophy, science, history – these are the main fields of interest: the *Traité de métaphysique* (1734–7), an enquiry essentially into the nature of man; the beginnings of *Le Siècle de Louis XIV* (1735–40) where Voltaire undertakes for the first time the history of a civilisation; the *Eléments de Newton* (1736–40). Perhaps this last work commands special admiration, because nowhere did Voltaire have to make greater intellectual efforts in order to understand the nature of what he considered to be the true science. Writing to Pitot about this work, he makes a surprisingly modest confession of superficiality – the more surprising because this was already, since at least 1735, a prime element in the case brought against Voltaire by his detractors:[31] 'I am like a little stream; clear because it is shallow' (D1341, 20 June [1737]). He goes on to admit that the Newtonian calculations tire and perplex his brain, which is not made for 'algebra'. Perhaps Voltaire felt he could profess his limitations in this field because it did not seem to impinge on the rest of his activities. It is at least equally likely, however, that this uncharacteristic modesty was called forth by the man whom he set above all others, the man to whom, in the *Lettres philosophiques*, he had given the sublime phrase: 'I have discovered one of the secrets of the Creator'.[32] As he put it to the abbé d'Olivet in 1736, 'mon cher maître Newton' is the greatest man who has ever lived, so much so that the giants of antiquity are as children at play (D1174, 18 October [1736]). Newton is above all the guiding light who has demonstrated that the universe has an ordered plan, centred on the unchangeable force of gravitation. Within that cosmic design man may give some meaning to his life and infuse it with action. Reason is assured a place. Hence, as W. H. Barber puts it, the *Eléments* become for Voltaire an act of homage, a personal declaration of philosophical confidence, and a missionary work in spreading enlightenment.[33]

Contrary to the Jansenist views of Pascal or, nearer to home, of his own father and brother, Voltaire asserted a faith in man who, though compounded of both good and bad elements, has his due place in nature. Unlike Pascal who, seeing human beings as irremediably tainted by original sin, turned to religious faith as the only certain basis of existence, Voltaire exemplifies throughout this period that belief in a natural, humanist morality which he had already expounded in the remarks on Pascal in the *Lettres philosophiques*. Never again will his world-view be quite so assured.

Voltaire's activities in the world during the 1740s are largely reducible to two centres of interest: the French Court at Versailles, and Frederick in Berlin. To the latter we shall return. For the moment, let us trace the renascent attraction of French society for Voltaire. In 1739 Paris is still an intolerable 'gouffre', where peace and reflection are impossible. Life there is full of bustle, he is invited and fêted everywhere. But he feels, he says, like the old man who died from being overwhelmed by the flowers which were cast at him (D2082, [28 September 1739]). The antidote,

however, turned out to be not Cirey but Brussels, whither he repaired
in December after a short stay in Cirey. Once again, honours and
scandals intermingle in Voltaire's life. He had been planning since
October to go to Brussels (D2086), but the departure became also a
necessary measure of prudence when the police in Paris seized a *Recueil*
by Voltaire (containing *inter alia* the beginning of the *Siècle de Louis XIV*).
The pattern of illicit printing, official reaction, personal flight is repeated yet again; well might one say, anachronistically, that Voltaire's
motto of this period seems to be 'Publish and be damned'. As usual,
things eventually died down, and Mme du Châtelet, herself back in
Paris, was able to establish by October 1740 that there was no case
against Voltaire, albeit he had aroused an endless number of petty
resentments which could do him just as much harm (D2330). She was
however in a position to retrieve him. Frederick II had succeeded to the
throne of Prussia in May; she proposed to the *premier ministre* Cardinal
Fleury that Voltaire might usefully be sent on an official mission to his
highly-placed friend. It is the beginning of Voltaire's undistinguished
career as diplomat, consisting of four visits to Frederick by 1743.

   The early 1740s are years of wanderings without any clear pattern
emerging; it is as though Voltaire is in search of a new rôle. Much time
is spent in Brussels, where he and Mme du Châtelet are retained for
long periods by an interminable lawsuit in which she is engaged;
Voltaire loses any brief sympathy he may have had for the city and now
calls it a purgatory (D2437, 2 March 1741). He seeks solace in his
readings, announcing that he has found few men there but many books
(D2683, 10 November [1742]). A further attempt to gain a seat in the
Académie Française in late 1742 was defeated, the chair going to
Marivaux. Voltaire's tragedy *Mahomet* was put on at the Comédie
Française in August 1742 (after success at its première in Lille the
previous year), was much admired but considered provocative and had
to be taken off a few days later. *Mérope*, by contrast, won applause
without scandal the following February: on the success of this tragic
piece Voltaire again became a candidate for a vacant place in the
Académie Française and was once more unsuccessful. His brilliance
was well recognised, but the Académie looked for an assurance of
respectability, any hopes of which were unremittingly destroyed by a
succession of indiscretions large and small.

   However, Voltaire had highly placed friends at Court, none less so
than the duc de Richelieu who, charged with organising the celebrations for the dauphin's marriage in 1745, commanded the poet to write
a *comédie-ballet*, which would become *La Princesse de Navarre*, set to music

by Rameau, as part of the festivities. It was for this that Voltaire returned to Cirey in April 1744 for the last long stay at the château; and it was this drama which gave Voltaire his opportunity, after playing at diplomat, to play at courtier. This final spell at Cirey seems as idyllic as the early days there in 1735. It provides once again a refuge from the world's tiresome commotions, and there is work to do, banishing boredom. When the *président* Hénault visited him and Mme du Châtelet in July he found not a cloud in the sky; the two hosts were 'sated with pleasures' (D2996). But with Voltaire the distance, in Baudelairean terms, between *ennui* and *rage* was not large. If he avoided the Scylla of boredom, the Charybdis of frenzy lay in wait. The new play was required in too brief a space. Voltaire, who could in June announce to Thieriot that he had rediscovered the Garden of Eden (D2990, 11 June 1744: 'Le paradis terrestre est où je suis') has by early July gone down with a fever through overwork. The comedy is complete, but his health is in such a state that Mme du Châtelet, who must long since have learned to distinguish between real and imagined illness on Voltaire's part, is seriously alarmed (D2995). Yet here again we witness a significant aspect of his physique; though constantly vulnerable to bodily afflictions, he had a remarkable capacity for swift recovery. Two days after Mme du Châtelet had written, he was sufficiently strong to pen a substantial letter, albeit full of complaints about his health; and by the next day in a much longer letter to d'Argental he is able to refer to himself as 'convalescent' (D2999, 11 July). Doubtless, Voltaire's longevity of life owed a great deal to the resilience which his body showed under circumstances such as these.

   The poet followed his dramatic entertainment to Paris so as to be present for rehearsals, and became caught up in the vortex of preparations for the great event. *La Princesse de Navarre*, performed in February 1745, was well received. A month later the King was pleased to grant him the post of royal historiographer with 2,000 francs a year and the promise (which became actuality in November 1746) of a place as gentleman of the King's Chamber (worth 60,000 francs, according to Voltaire himself).[34] The latter did not regard his new post as a sinecure. When French forces triumphed in the battle of Fontenoy in May 1745, he at once set to work to celebrate the victory, producing the *Poème sur la bataille de Fontenoy* within a fortnight. This work received the extraordinary honour of being printed at the Louvre by the Imprimerie Royale, originally in an edition of 600 copies which, however, Voltaire's characteristic sense of enterprise managed to increase to 1,450, despite initial resistance from Maurepas.[35]

Such are the glories of Court life for Voltaire. The importunities will gradually outstrip them. From the first his attitude to the Court had been ambivalent. To his niece Mme Denis he had confessed feeling rather ashamed at giving up his philosophy and solitude in order to be a royal buffoon. He is sufficiently self-aware to realise the futility of it all, yet he cannot resist the 'honour' that has been done him. It sets him at variance with himself: 'the absurd life I am living, which is at odds with my humour and way of thinking' (D3015, 13 August [1744]). The same self-derision is displayed in a letter to Cideville several months later, when he is preoccupied with the imminent première of *La Princesse de Navarre* (D3073). Later, when he was honoured for his dramatic services to the Court, he wrote a bitter little poem contrasting these tributes with the royal indifference shown towards more serious works from his pen:

> Mon *Henri Quatre* et ma *Zaïre*,
> Et mon Américaine *Alzire*,
> Ne m'ont valu jamais un seul regard du roi;
> J'avais mille ennemis avec très peu de gloire:
> Les honneurs et les biens pleuvent enfin sur moi
> Pour une farce de la Foire.[36]

But he can neither stay nor go. He admits that his friend and fellow-writer, the marquis de Vauvenargues, will probably be surprised to receive a letter from him coming from Versailles, and his tone sounds apologetic as he adds that although the Court seems hardly suited to him, the King's favours keep him there, more out of gratitude than self-interest (D3093, 3 April [1745]). Yet there is little sign of the perfunctory in the enthusiasm with which he celebrates the victory of Fontenoy. It will take Voltaire time to accept that he is no more a courtier than a diplomat. Gradually his basic attitude becomes manifest: he is a writer first and foremost. As he tells Cideville, every night he firmly resolves to attend the *lever du roi* (one of the prestigious distinctions which he had gained by becoming gentleman of the Chamber), but the next morning invariably finds him in his dressing-gown working in his room on his latest tragedy *Sémiramis* (D3469, 9 November [1746]). Nor can he avoid indiscretions for long. A verse compliment to the King's mistress, Mme de Pompadour, upsets the Queen and causes a brief retreat to Cirey in late 1747. Voltaire and Emilie had already fled the Court earlier because he had imprudently remarked to her at the card table (where she had been losing large sums of money) that she was playing with cheats. True, the remark had been uttered quietly and in English, but it is not surprising to learn that it was overheard and repeated. The pair left precipitately that night, Voltaire going into hiding at the château of the duchesse du Maine at Sceaux for nearly two months until it was safe for him to show his face again.[37] At last, in May 1749, Voltaire resigned himself to the fact that he could not succeed at Court, and obtained permission to sell his post as gentleman (while keeping the title).

Out of this expense of spirit in a waste of shame little but sterility emerged. At least Voltaire was finally able to achieve entry to the Académie Française in April 1746; but this victory, once gained, brought him little more than satisfaction and remained a hollow triumph. It merely set a seal upon the recognition he had won as a writer of eminence. Similarly, at this time a flood of invitations to membership arrive from Academies in foreign countries – England, Scotland, Prussia and Italy, as well as from the French provinces. The honours are gratifying and appreciated, but it is more an indication of past achievements than a prognostic of further success. Voltaire sums it up, somewhat inaccurately in regard to fact but with a true sense of this period, when he says, in his autobiographical *Commentaire historique* thirty years later, that he has nothing to say about 1744 except that he was admitted to Academies.[38]

Meantime, he had fallen in love again, with his niece Mme Denis. Her husband died in April 1744, occasioning a warm letter of condolence to her from Cirey (D2958). Voltaire had expressed himself in similar terms on the death of her father in 1737 (D1379), and it is hard to say whether these feelings are simply those of an uncle who cares deeply for his family, in particular for his two nieces left orphaned, or whether already one may detect a soft spot for Mme Denis. In any event, the friendship became romance some time after Voltaire's return to Paris in October 1744. His love-letters to her deliver a final death-blow to the myth of an unfeeling Voltaire. Written largely in Italian,[39] they effectively banish any doubts as to whether Mme Denis was his mistress. Phrases like 'Baccio il vostro gentil culo', though prudishly struck out by the recipient (D3272), allow little room for ambiguity. Voltaire is even full of delighted wonderment at her expertise in making love (D3276). Equally interesting is the tenderness that permeates these letters: 'Vi amo teneramente e vi amo sola' (D3267); 'In voi e il moi riposo, e la sola vera felicità' (D3741). The first of the intimate letters Besterman tentatively dates from 28 March 1745 (D3089); the affair will go on until Voltaire leaves for Berlin in 1750; after his return to Paris following Mme du Châtelet's death in 1749 Mme Denis moves in with him.

Two themes predominate in this correspondence: Voltaire's passion for his niece and his constant preoccupation with his health. The latter betokens a deep-seated need. Though he appears to have passed through a particularly bad physical crisis in 1747–8, it is clear again how essential it is for him to tell someone close to him about it. One senses here an appeal for loving sympathy (he tells her explicitly: 'Voi fate la mie consolazione', D3651), which makes one wonder again about the effect of losing his mother while still very young. It is perhaps in part because Mme Denis could play this rôle so satisfyingly that Voltaire felt such tenderness for her. Not only was she cultivated, a lover of the arts and an author in her own right; she was intimately attentive to him in a way which, one may speculate, Mme du Châtelet was not.

At first, it seems, he brings her nothing but pleasure; doubtless too the close company and eager attentions of a man so distinguished and popular at that time at Court could not fail to gratify. But as time goes by, it becomes increasingly clear that it is he who loves and she who allows herself to be loved. He implores her not to carry out her intention of settling in Lille, where she had lived with her husband (D3730a, 8 August [1748]), and begs her to break his heart by agreeing to remarry in order that she will stay in Paris (D3841, 5 January [1749]). Meantime he reproaches her for not writing to him (D3774, 4 October [1748]; cf. also D3833, 3836), in a way that piquantly recalls Mme du Châtelet's complaints in earlier years about his failure to keep in touch with her while away, for instance, in the Low Countries in 1736–7 or Berlin in 1743. It is clear that Mme Denis is not so committed to him. A letter from her to Baculard d'Arnaud reveals that not only is she maintaining an affair with the latter, but that her attitude to her uncle is full of condescension (D3561, 14 August 1747).

Did Voltaire ever feel for Mme du Châtelet the tenderness he shows towards Mme Denis? If ever his letters to the former are recovered they might resolve the problem, but such a discovery now seems improbable. We know that they were such as to wring tears from her,[40] though that was already at a time when the emotions of which they gave token were past; Mme du Châtelet may have been weeping from melancholy and nostalgia alone. In the Voltaire correspondence which is extant his attitude towards her is often loving, full of respect and admiration; but the intimate note won from him by his niece is missing. On her side Mme du Châtelet is full of concern for him, anxious to prevent his indiscretions, desperate to stop him going to live with Frederick, whom she quickly recognises, after their first exchange of correspondence in

1736, as the main rival. When from Holland in early 1737 Voltaire hints that he will never return to Cirey and even addresses her as Madame, she is distraught (D1274). Through her own supplications and the pressure which she manages to bring upon him through d'Argental she secures his return. But Voltaire's professions of attachment to her when he arrives back at Cirey have a hollower ring. He asserts, as we have seen, that she is more to him than a father, brother or son: all masculine relations, an attitude which anticipates his comment after her death that she was 'un ami et un grand homme' (D4025). He and she are fellow-worshippers of Newton, sharing work and play together; but whereas she can write in marvelling tones of what forces love has revealed within her (D943), his more characteristic comment is one of content at enjoying 'the sweet pleasures of company and work' (D966).

Is it possible that, at bottom, he felt uneasy before her truly aristocratic background? Voltaire had set out to mingle with the nobility in his youth, and the chevalier de Rohan had inflicted an unforgettable lesson regarding his social inferiority. Later, he will be the seigneur de Voltaire at Ferney, a minor prince; certainly the aristocratic way of life never ceased to attract him. But to be a bourgeois, however well placed, wealthy and influential, seeking out the upper classes, remains different from being aristocratic without trying. Though the pair were virtually inseparable, the outside world did not necessarily confuse them socially. The chevalier de Mouhy, denouncing their conduct, is particularly severe on her; he finds it curious that 'une femme de qualité' should lead by the hand a man who has made himself the object of general scorn (D2633, 8 August 1742). Mme Denis caused Voltaire no such problems; she was of his family, of his class; whereas from early on in their relationship, Mme du Châtelet manifestly intimidated him. Having written some licentious verses to Cideville in 1735, he goes on to wonder how he can speak of the 'Sublime and delicate Emilie' after such a coarse letter, which naturally she has not been permitted to see; and he urges Cideville to burn it (D915). Later, he expresses himself as following in her orbit (D3609, 1 February [1748]), confirming the views of an observer, Mme de Staal, some months before, that Emilie was the sovereign and he the slave (D3567). He wrote to Mme Denis from Lunéville in March 1748, expressing the hope that he would return to Paris shortly to see her (D3630), but it was May before he succeeded in persuading Mme du Châtelet to leave.

As Mme de Graffigny had shown in her letters of 1738–9, rows were not uncommon between Voltaire and Emilie from the early years. In

1744 a household servant reported that they were always quarrelling, the reason being Voltaire's passion for the actress Mlle Gaussin. As no other supporting evidence has come to light for this assertion, it would be unwise to give it crucial importance.[41] More significant is Voltaire's turning to Mme Denis shortly thereafter. Whether aware of the affair or not, Mme du Châtelet must have perceived the change in his feelings. Never able to bear for long a sentimental void, she fell for the young officer Saint-Lambert at Lunéville in 1748 and devoted to him all that totality of passion which had little by little been starved of sustenance from Voltaire. Saint-Lambert it was who fathered the baby girl whose birth was to cause Mme du Châtelet's death on 10 September 1749. From Voltaire's secretary Longchamp we learn of his master's fury at discovering the liaison and how Mme du Châtelet gradually calmed him down, reminding him that for some time he had neglected her physically.[42] Persuaded by her gentle reasonableness, he accepted the new situation, remaining until her death the same close friend he had long been to her.

The birth of Mme du Châtelet's baby at Lunéville elicited good-humoured remarks from Voltaire about the ease of it all (D4005, 4006). Hence all the greater shock six days later when, with almost equal suddenness, Emilie died of a puerperal infection. Suddenly his friend of twenty years' standing has gone (D4015). Cirey revisited, that house embellished by friendship, has become a place of horror (D4020). I have not lost a mistress, he tells d'Argental, but 'half of myself', the soul for which my soul was made (D4024). Almost uniquely in his life, he cannot work; he is thinking of her day and night (D4030). Longchamp tells us that he was so stunned by her death (being with Saint-Lambert the last to leave the deathbed) that he walked out of the room unseeing, fell and struck his head. A month later in Paris he would still get up at night and call out for her from room to room; one night Longchamp came upon him fallen, icy cold and almost speechless.[43] He may not ever have felt for Emilie the quality of intimacy he shared for Mme Denis. The depth of his love can however hardly be doubted. Here for once in his letters we catch that rare phenomenon in Voltaire (other than in the love-letters to Mme Denis), direct revelation to another of intimate sentiments powerfully felt.

To the end Mme du Châtelet had been his intellectual companion. Now, back in Paris from October 1749, there is a void to fill. Mme Denis will help but only in part. Voltaire renews acquaintance with old friends like the d'Argentals and the duc de Richelieu. He puts on plays at his house in the rue de Traversière, the little theatre becoming well known in Paris; amongst the actors, he meets for the first time Lekain, who will play many a Voltairean rôle in the years to come. He quarrels with the Comédie Française and later effects a reconciliation. It is a transitional period, without any clear focus of interest save the theatre. Voltaire is disillusioned with life at Court, Paris seems to offer no anchor, even with Mme Denis's company. The long-awaited event at last occurred; free of Mme du Châtelet's restrictive control, he could now take up Frederick's invitation to go and settle at the Prussian Court. But the decision was unpopular at Versailles, where Louis XV was highly displeased with Voltaire's declared preference for a foreign monarch. When Voltaire left for Berlin in June 1750, he did so under a cloud and, worse still, full of doubts about the wisdom of his actions. From Compiègne he wrote an unhappy letter to the d'Argentals: why has he left them? He does not know, has given himself up to the 'démon du voyage'. He pleads with his friends to forgive him and to seek ministerial indulgence, for his own remorse about leaving is itself enough to endure (D4163). It is the most hesitant of departures, yet conclusive in Voltaire's life; he will not see Paris again until 1778, a mere three months before his death.

The 1740s are a period of much futility, ending in personal grief (no other death would ever matter as much to Voltaire as Mme du Châtelet's) and disillusionment. Nor had the author, in accepting Frederick's patronage, yet realised that happiness could not come from putting his trust in princes. Had he died at this point (and he was, at fifty-five, well into middle age), his life would seem incomplete, his personality only partly realised. Yet 1750 is a milestone. Voltaire's apprenticeship is over, the sources of his *philosophie* absorbed. Besides, the appearance of *Zadig* (1747) is the first major indication of his skill as *conteur*. No longer so confident of the cosmic plan or of his own place in it, Voltaire evokes the problem of evil, and finds no reassuring answers.[44]

3 Frederick, and Berlin

When Voltaire departed for Prussia in 1750, he already knew his future host very well. They had been in correspondence for fourteen years, had met on four different occasions, the last of which, in 1743, had lasted six weeks. The acquaintanceship began with a long letter from Frederick, then the Crown Prince and only twenty-four years old, to a man some eighteen years his senior, and the letter is suitably respectful, as from a young pupil to a revered master. Voltaire's works are 'intellectual treasures', whose author does honour to his century and to 'the human intellect' (D1126, 8 August 1736). Frederick encloses essays about the German philosopher and disciple of Leibniz, Christian Wolff, whom the young prince greatly admires. Thus begins a correspondence that, for all its vicissitudes, asperities and periods of silence will go on until Voltaire's death.

Frederick's first letter could not have failed to gratify the *philosophe*, who only a month before had returned from the wretched visit to Paris occasioned by the Jore imbroglio. Voltaire's recent past was full of persecutions, flights or fears of flight; he was an abiding thorn in the flesh of the French Church and State. Yet here was a young man, heir to the powerful throne of Prussia, spontaneously approaching him out of respect and admiration. Here was the dreamed-of *roi philosophe* to come. Voltaire replies promptly, in warm terms. Before the year is out, at least eight letters pass between the two correspondents and a further thirty-one in 1737, many of them of considerable length. Works are exchanged, and gifts. It is in a letter to Frederick that we first hear Voltaire announce the *Défense du Mondain*. Perhaps it was written in part with the young prince in view; at any rate, the climactic lines with their reference to Solomon fit well with Voltaire's dubbing Frederick

47

the 'Solomon of the North'. This early phase is mainly filled with literature and, above all, philosophy. Metaphysical discussion, instigated by Frederick's opening letter, reveals a certain disparity of views. Voltaire still believes in freewill (his views will begin to change as from 1738, largely thanks to his reading of Anthony Collins' *Philosophical Inquiry concerning Human Liberty*), essentially because, whatever the philosophical objections, we have an intuition of freedom, and God would not deceive us (D1432, 23 January [1738]). Frederick for his part refutes this quite cogently. All actions, he claims, have a cause, therefore men act according to laws, and besides, how does Voltaire explain away divine prescience? (D1482, 19 April 1738). To this last point Voltaire has no convincing answer. However, he insists from the beginning that metaphysics are beyond him, as the first principles of things are forever beyond human understanding (D1139, [*c.* 1 September 1736]).[1] What interests him is morality, human behaviour rather than the human soul. The debate dies away with Frederick graciously agreeing that metaphysics promises much but contains nothing (D1524, 17 June 1738). One gains the impression that in this domain at least, albeit irrelevant in Voltaire's eyes to concerns in the real world, the pupil's capacity for disputation was not at all inferior to his master's.

On literature too there is much to exchange. Frederick transmits some of his own compositions, like an Epistle dedicated to Voltaire (D1200) or an *Ode sur l'oubli*, which Voltaire praises (D1315). In return the Frenchman despatches numerous works, which Frederick is avid to obtain. The prince is quick to reproach Voltaire for any reluctance in sending him the more controversial writings, like the *Traité de métaphysique*, the *Siècle de Louis XIV* or the *Eléments de Newton*. Eventually Frederick receives Voltaire's major works of this period, including in 1739 his first-known attempt at the *conte*, the *Voyage du baron de Gangan*, which was to be published in revised form during Voltaire's stay in Berlin as *Micromégas*. One exception remains, however, to become a bone of contention: *La Pucelle*, the scabrous mock-epic poem in which Voltaire dares to make fun of that most sacred of French historical figures, Joan of Arc. Voltaire knows full well that the scandal aroused by *Le Mondain* would be as nothing compared with the storm which would burst about his head if *La Pucelle* got abroad. Frederick, guessing as much from the rumours he had heard about the poem, is all the more eager to read it, and from early 1737 his peremptory calls for it resound like a leitmotiv through the correspondence before 1750. For him it becomes a symbol of Voltaire's ultimate trust in his discretion. The latter might well have despatched it in response to such pleas; but he cannot. The prudent Mme du Châtelet has it in her possession and will not release it (D1359, [*c*. 30 July 1737]). Only several years later is Voltaire able to gratify Frederick by sending him two cantos (D2685, 14 November 1742), whereupon Frederick loudly cries for more (D2695, 2747). Eventually Voltaire obliges, as Frederick's star waxes and Emilie's wanes, informing his correspondent that he has managed to steal some pages from his mistress! (D2794, 23/24 July 1743). Even that does not satisfy the demands coming from Berlin. Voltaire is requested to bring the work with him when he comes to the Prussian capital later in 1743, and presumably Voltaire acquiesces in part, for after his arrival Frederick declares that he now has six cantos (possibly the least shocking?)[2] in his possession (D2835, 8 September [1743]). Further than that, however, Voltaire will not go during Emilie's lifetime; to be able to send more, he says, he would have to use violence (D3462, 22 September 1746). When later Frederick accuses him of having lent the notorious work to the Duchess of Württemberg (who then had it copied out during the night), Voltaire replies in injured tones that she had certainly not seen any part undisclosed to Frederick (D3511, 3514).

The evolution of this particular tussle is paradigmatic of the developing relationship between the two men. Frederick, a passionate admirer of Voltaire's work, is also, as befits his royal station, a man who expects others to bow to his will. Voltaire, flattered by his attentions to the point of dangerous imprudence, is saved from his worst weaknesses by Mme du Châtelet, who recognises in Frederick 'a rival very dangerous for myself' (D2778, 28 June 1743). That rivalry became yet more open as the years advanced. For the moment, let us consider only the intellectual relationships. In 1738 Frederick objects to Voltaire's calling Machiavelli a great man in his *Siècle de Louis XIV* (D1476). Here apparently is the seed that will germinate the following year when the Prussian announces that he is thinking of writing a book to refute Machiavelli (D1950, 22 March 1739); this Voltaire warmly encourages (D1978). Frederick is soon at work on it and has the first draft completed by the winter (D2109, 6 November 1739). Voltaire, full of enthusiasm for the views he has seen displayed therein, offers to edit it for publication and Frederick accepts, providing his anonymity is preserved. However, by June 1740 he has changed his mind and wants to buy up the whole edition (D2250). But Voltaire is determined to see the work appear, and Frederick, in a rare moment of vacillation, again decides to leave it in the *philosophe*'s hands (D2281). He thanks Voltaire warmly for all his efforts with the *Anti-Machiavel* (D2346), only to change his attitude two weeks later when, in a mood of pique, he objects to all the changes that have been made in what he wrote and insists on secrecy about his authorship (D2362).

Despite thoughts of denouncing the work and its editor, Frederick stopped short however at this point. At least he was successful in obtaining silence from Voltaire, for the latter never referred to it again in writing. The *philosophe*, in spite of great frustrations with the original publisher Van Duren (whom he was to immortalise as the rascally Vanderdendur in *Candide*), had persisted in arranging a second edition elsewhere that could be accepted as authorised; for he was intensely keen to present to the world this first written evidence that a *roi philosophe* was in the making.[3]

Why this uncharacteristic indecisiveness from Frederick? If he permitted the work to appear at all, it was probably to gratify his own pride as an author who, only a year before, had been deeply engaged in its composition. But if the earlier joy in literary creation had given way to doubts, the reason may not be far to seek. In the interim, on 31 May 1740, his father had died and the Crown Prince became Frederick II. Theoretical principles about machiavellian conduct were to be overtaken by *raison d'état*, the need to perpetuate and improve the kingdom to which he had succeeded. By September he was attacking Liège. On 16 December he invaded Silesia and conquered it, thereby adding one and a half million subjects to the two and a half million he possessed at the moment of succeeding to the throne. The *roi philosophe* of Voltaire's imaginings had disappeared, virtually in the very act of becoming king.

Frederick's accession had one immediate consequence for Voltaire. The new king, freed from his father's authoritarian ways, was now at liberty to invite Voltaire to Prussia – and did so, within a matter of days (D2233). It was part of the new king's ambitious plan to establish at Berlin an Academy of luminaries. Within a month of his father's death, Frederick announces that he has acquired Maupertuis, Wolff, Vaucanson and Algarotti, and is awaiting word from s'Gravesande and Euler (D2250). But Voltaire would obviously be the brightest star at the Prussian Court. Frederick had known from Voltaire's very first letter to him (D1139) that he could not reasonably expect to seduce the *philosophe* away from Mme du Châtelet's side for more than a brief stay. The effort was however worth making. Voltaire's reply to Frederick's invitation was little short of dismaying to the misogynist Frederick: can he, he asks the King, bring Emilie as well (D2265)? Frederick's reply is brutally straightforward: 'It is Voltaire, it is you . . . whom I want to see, and the divine Emilie with all her divinity is only the accessory of the Newtonianised Apollo' (D2281, 2 August 1740). The King must have had second thoughts about these candid phrases, for another letter followed the next day, conveying the same message but much more tactfully (D2283). There then ensued a tactical tug-of-war. Mme du Châtelet invites Frederick to Cirey (D2287): a forlorn hope. Voltaire invites him to Brussels or Paris (D2303). Frederick replies that he is not going to the French capital, but a visit to the Low Countries might be possible (D2305) and he proposes Antwerp (D2307), even suggesting that he will see Emilie there as well. But the very next day he finds himself unable to travel because of fever (D2308). Can Voltaire please meet him at Cleves?

This episode raises interesting questions. Besterman considers Frederick's conduct to be entirely cynical: the Prussian had arranged the encounter in such a way that Voltaire could not withdraw without discourtesy.[4] Mme du Châtelet would surely have agreed; she sent Frederick a curt note of regret at the way his illness had prevented her seeing him (D2309). On the other hand, the fever was real, as Voltaire makes clear in his *Mémoires*. His first sight of Frederick, on 11 September 1740, was of a little man wrapped up in a dressing-gown on a miserable bed, sweating and trembling 'in a violent bout of fever'.[5] Later, when the attack had passed, Frederick was able to get up and dine with Voltaire and others. Two theses are possible. Either, following the Besterman line, one assumes that the illness was all put on for Voltaire (which seems unlikely – everything suggests that Frederick was genuinely suffering, and over a period of some days). The alternative, a more interesting possibility and in keeping with Frederick's complex personality, is to surmise that the fever, conveniently timed though it was, had psychosomatic origins; it permitted him to do what he would have preferred to do anyway.

Frederick made a pleasing first impression upon Voltaire, judging by the latter's subsequent correspondence and later *Mémoires*; but no more than that. Voltaire's impact upon the King was however much more impressive. Frederick wrote to his own librarian Jordan that Voltaire possessed Cicero's eloquence, Pliny's gentleness, Agrippa's wisdom, uniting in himself the virtues and talents of three of the greatest men of antiquity. 'His mind works unceasingly . . . he declaimed for us *Mahomet*, the admirable tragedy he has written; he transported us beyond ourselves, and I could only admire and be silent' (D2317). He had clearly fallen under the spell of that remarkable magnetic quality to which so many other testimonies survive.[6] Not surprisingly, Voltaire was soon invited to Berlin and accepted the invitation, arriving in mid-November. Mme du Châtelet, who had some awareness of the growing attachment, wrote a despairing letter (which Besterman describes as a suicide note) to the duc de Richelieu about his departure (D2365). She had some cause. The two-week stay with Frederick considerably advanced the intimacy of their relationship, though not wholly in the direction of perfect harmony. Voltaire eventually told Frederick he must leave because Emilie was unwell (D2369); this elicited a sarcastic letter from the King about the hold she had over Voltaire (D2370). In taking his leave, Voltaire composed a poem which expresses what might well have been described as *dépit amoureux* if this had been an exchange of love-letters:

> Non, malgré vos vertus; non, malgré vos appas,
> Mon âme n'est point satisfaite.
> Non, vous n'êtes qu'une coquette,
> Qui subjuguez les coeurs, et ne vous donnez pas.

To which Frederick replied, on the same piece of paper:

> Mon âme sent le prix de vos divins appas;
> Mais ne présumez point qu'elle soit satisfaite.
> Traître, vous me quittez, pour suivre une coquette;
> Moi je ne vous quitterais pas.[7]

The lyrical tone is heightened in a poem from Voltaire a day or so later:

> Je vous quitte, il est vrai; mais mon coeur déchiré
> Vers vous revolera sans cesse;
> Depuis quatre ans vous êtes ma maîtresse,
> Un amour de dix ans doit être préféré;
> Je remplis un devoir sacré.
> Héros de l'amitié, vous m'approuvez vous-même.
> Adieu, je pars désespéré.
> Oui, je vais aux genoux d'un objet adoré,
> Mais j'abandonne ce que j'aime.[8]

(D2378)

It is almost the language of Racine's Titus saying farewell to Bérénice.

Faced with such poetic outpourings, one must ask whether, at this time, a homosexual relationship had not been established between the two. Frederick's predilections are well known; Voltaire is not however generally seen in that light. Besterman pours scorn upon Lytton Strachey for suggesting as much,[9] reminding the reader that Voltaire had satirised Desfontaines's sodomite tendencies. It is true that, in his rage against Desfontaines, Voltaire did not stint himself in excoriating what he called Desfontaines's 'anti-natural sins' (e.g., D1514, 5 June [1738]). But Desfontaines was an unmitigated homosexual, and therein lay his abnormality in Voltaire's eyes. Bisexuality by no means comes into the same category. Besides, against such an enemy Voltaire is willing to use any ammunition; he does not show the same distaste for other homosexuals, like Algarotti or, pre-eminently, Frederick himself.

The evidence for believing Voltaire bisexual is not wholly conclusive, but there is enough for it to merit some attention. A. O. Aldridge, for instance, quotes an anonymous poem addressed to Lord John Hervey, whom Voltaire met on his visit to England, and which suggests that Voltaire took to bed both Hervey and his wife.[10] Is it possible that Voltaire's remarkable patience and enduring affection for Thieriot, despite the latter's many backslidings, had originally been built upon a youthful affair? Besterman plausibly suggests that Thieriot was homosexual and that Desfontaines's hold over him in the *Voltairomanie* business may, as we have seen, have had a sexual basis, but he ignores the fact that this might equally help to explain Voltaire's strong attachment to such a scapegrace.[11] We have seen how Voltaire shocked Mrs Pope by declaring that the Jesuits had committed buggery upon him at the *collège*, adding: 'I shall never get over it as long as I live.'[12] The force of these words should not be too lightly dismissed. The same tendency towards pederasty, albeit muted, is noted in an early poem to the Regent,[13] as too in a letter to d'Argental where he reports that his teacher the abbé d'Olivet used to smack the pupils' bottoms 'out of amusement', adding ironically that if Condillac wants to use that detail in the eulogy he is composing upon d'Olivet, he will have to write a little treatise on platonic love (D15281, 2 November 1768). The same Jesuit penchant for young boys is satirised in *Candide* (Chapters XV, XXVIII).

Whatever the truth of the relationship between Frederick and Voltaire in 1740, the language which Voltaire in particular uses to express it is rhetorically heightened. If Voltaire impressed Frederick on their first meeting, it is the former who emerges the more fascinated from their second. Other poems of romantic effusion follow (D2383, 2392). Voltaire recalls how, at Frederick's court, 'I saw the reign of pleasures, of pure enjoyment' (D2493). Frederick provides a rather more detailed account of the frivolities in a letter of 21 November 1740 to Algarotti (with whom he already had a homosexual relationship). There is, he says, conversation about poetry and ideas, dancing, eating, gambling, their ears are delighted ('Nous chatouillons nos oreilles') by

languorous music which, inciting love, gives rise to 'd'autres chatouille-
ments'.[14] Possibly Frederick is enjoying the use of deliberately provocative language. Even so, given his strong sexual drives (about which
Voltaire goes into some clinical detail in his *Mémoires*),[15] his evident
attraction towards the *philosophe*, and the distinct emotional change in
Voltaire's letters during this period, the question must be asked. One
wonders too what precisely Voltaire meant when he described Frederick to Maupertuis (with singularly foolish indiscretion) as a 'respectable, singular and lovable prostitute' (D2377).

Whatever happened in Berlin during Voltaire's stay in 1740, the
parting left both men discontented. Voltaire seems torn at having to
leave, but he may also have sensed that he was in danger of being taken
over body and soul by Frederick and wished to flee to safer ground.
Even the most fulsome of Voltaire's verses to the Prussian king make
clear that he sees him as a coquette, dominating all but refusing to be
dominated; the same sense of promiscuity shows through in the striking
epithet we have just observed in his note to Maupertuis. In one
remarkable poem he compares Algarotti to Socrates, with 'le beau
Lujac' (a young French marquis attached to the French embassy) as
Alcibiades; by contrast, *he* is 'pour Frédéric seul empressé [to Frederick
alone attentive]' (D2383, 15 December [1740]). Frederick, for his part,
has quickly tired of his eminent guest and sees only his failings. Voltaire
is a madman, with an insatiable greed for gold (D. app. 60); towards
him Frederick is cool and condescending (D2419). The *philosophe* writes
an impassioned letter in March 1741, crying that 'your majesty . . .
abandons me cruelly'; Voltaire must needs love him despite himself
(D2453). But it will be a further couple of months before Frederick's
letters take on the warm tones of old.

On Voltaire's side too, it is not a simple matter of affections spurned.
Already, a fortnight after his leaving Berlin, these attitudes are mingled
with dismay that Frederick has marched on Silesia (D2383), and
Voltaire expresses himself ironically to his friend Cideville at the
discrepancy between the *Anti-Machiavel* and that invasion (D2444, 13
March 1741). To Sir Everard Fawkener he writes in English that 'the
king has altered the man, and now he relishes despotic power' (D2618,
[*c*. June 1742]). Frederick too will hear these reproaches on his war-
making and try to answer them (D2600, 2602, 2615); Voltaire must
understand, he protests, that war is ultimately the only way of obtaining justice, and if the *philosophe* had an army it too would have marched
against such as Desfontaines and Van Duren (D2628, 25 July 1742).[16]
The argument could not have been devoid of some appeal to Voltaire's

pragmatic mind, and in any case he was far from being a pacifist. His approach is rather to exhort Frederick, having made the war, now to make the peace in Europe (D2611).[17]

But this was no ordinary relationship. Both partners had expressed their spleen or disappointment in unambiguous terms to third parties, each had had comprehensive knowledge of the other's failings. One might logically expect the friendship to be at an end. But no. For all the contempt and mistrust each could demonstrate for the other, stronger ties drew them back together. This first reconciliation was to be the forerunner of many others, even after the depths of venom had been plumbed in the bitterest of quarrels.

We return in the summer of 1741 to reciprocal praises in the correspondence, and by August Frederick is enthusiastically inviting Voltaire to return to Berlin (D2534). By now Voltaire is anxious to establish that he is a good subject of Louis XV. He obtains governmental permission to visit Frederick, meets him for a couple of days at Aix-la-Chapelle in September, and reports back to the *premier ministre* Fleury on their discussions. The stage is set for a longer visit in 1743, after a preliminary stop at The Hague, whence Voltaire sends back coded messages with information about Frederick's policies which he has gleaned from contacts there. The ostensible excuse given out in Paris for Voltaire's departure is that he is annoyed at his latest failure to gain a seat in the Académie Française and the refusal of permission to stage his tragedy *La Mort de César*. In this way, it was hoped, Voltaire would enter Frederick's Court under a persuasive 'cover story'. At any rate, some well-placed people in Paris were taken in by it (D2778, Commentary).

Frederick, however, was not so easily deluded. During Voltaire's stay (from 30 August to 12 October 1743) he achieved nothing on the diplomatic level. Perhaps the gift of six cantos from *La Pucelle* was intended to sweeten the relationship. If so, it had no effect at all on Frederick, who unerringly knew where to discriminate between his private and his public rôles. His only interest was to trap Voltaire once and for all in Prussia as some prize trophy. He wrote to the *philosophe* before the visit, asking Voltaire how he could stand all the ignominy and disdain he was suffering in Paris (D2770). But Voltaire, whose hopes of favour at the French Court were as yet unsullied, was not ready to be persuaded by that argument. At the same time Frederick was trying, though without success, to discredit Voltaire behind his back in France so thoroughly that he would have no recourse but to flee (D2813). A strange complex of attitudes, in which the Prussian was striving so ruthlessly to have beside him a man whom in many respects he despised! A remarkable double letter survives from Voltaire's visit, in which he pleads with Frederick to give him some agreeable news to take back to the French Court; Frederick disdainfully replies that he has no links with France, not even hostile ones, and it would be ridiculous to offer advice to France except to conduct itself more sensibly in future. He will however write a panegyric of Louis, in which not a single word would be true (D2830)! The chilling flippancy is characteristic of Frederick at his most cynical.

So Voltaire fails to get any intelligence, and Frederick fails to get Voltaire. The relationship has run its course for the time being. Frederick writes 'Adieu' (D2953) as he realises that Voltaire will not come to stay permanently in Berlin so long as Emilie needs him. After November 1744 there is a silence for nearly two years, followed by a mere half-dozen letters during the next two. Only when in 1749 Voltaire realises that Mme du Châtelet, now pregnant by Saint-Lambert, might no longer be the centre of his life does the old friendship resume.

It is easy to deride Voltaire's diplomatic naïvety with Frederick and to observe that he entirely lacked the cool detachment necessary for espionage work of any kind. Nor was Voltaire himself unaware of his limitations: a letter to Richelieu in 1752 telling of his success in bringing the abbé de Prades to Prussia adds: 'I think this is the first time in my life that I have been adroit and successful' (D5084). More useful for our purposes is it to note that he is looking for an identity. The poet wishes to be more than poet; he seeks *engagement* in the public life of his time. All the zeal, flair, energy that will establish his renown as the defender of Calas is already on display before the eyes of Fleury and Frederick. But the occasion is misjudged, the time unripe; and Voltaire still has to learn through harsh experience that his own form of commitment will come through a stance independent of government rather than service on its behalf.

When the friendship resumes, it is because both sides want it – indeed, Frederick perhaps more so than Voltaire. The former writes on 29 November 1748 complaining that he has not heard from the *philosophe* for a year (D3814: the last previous letter from Voltaire to Frederick extant dates in fact from more than twenty months earlier) and sends him some of his latest verses. With it comes the almost inevitable reissue of an invitation to Berlin. To all this Voltaire replies in gracious terms, while not failing to remind Frederick that the latter's *Ode sur la guerre*, expressing weariness of wars, comes strangely from the man who started it all (D3856). The king responds plaintively that

Voltaire no longer offers real criticism as of old (D3866). Revived by these more winning tones, Voltaire's own friendliness returns to his correspondence with Frederick, and he talks of going to see the King the coming summer. Indeed, he envisages a stay of six or eight weeks, during which they could work together on Frederick's compositions (D3914). Frederick readily agrees (D3929); but then Voltaire realises that Emilie's coming confinement might well take a fatal turn, so he cannot leave her till it is over. He will come in October (D3952). The subsequent tragedy to Mme du Châtelet causes a further postponement. All this was an affront to Frederick's impatient possessiveness, and the castigations of old returned to his letters. But eventually a *modus vivendi* was found, Voltaire reassured that he will be welcome and provided (after he had himself asked for monetary reimbursement) with 16,000 francs (D4149, Commentary). In a state of some bewilderment, unsure of his motives, probably still disorientated by the loss of Mme du Châtelet and particularly of her guiding hand, Voltaire set forth, arriving in Berlin on or about 22 July 1750.

As he makes clear in the *Commentaire historique*, he had left after six months of battling with his family and all his friends, who had strongly urged him against this migration.[18] The *Mémoires* indicate, however, the compelling force of a man who was a conqueror, poet, musician and philosopher, and who in addition claimed to love him. Voltaire adds rather pathetically: 'Je crus que je l'aimais.'[19] Though later, as we shall see, Voltaire advanced many excellent reasons for this major decision, the step when taken has such a somnambulistic quality about it that the real motive, one feels, must be affective. These few words of the author himself have the ring of truth. Voltaire, loving his hero, wants to idolise him, if only perhaps as one sure anchor in a shifting world. One of his last letters before setting out conveys the same impression: 'You are the man of all times, all places, all talents. Receive me among your worshippers' (D4156). More than just conventional flattery is involved here.

So there is the feeling of waking from a dream to cold reality once Voltaire has reached Berlin. As he writes in October to Mme Denis, who would have thought all this possible seven or eight months before, when he was setting up house with her in Paris? But after so many years of flirtation with the King of Prussia, he could not avoid saying Yes to marriage: 'Will it be a happy one? I have no idea' (D4240). As René Pomeau puts it, Voltaire had hoped to find at Frederick's court the Versailles of Louis XIV complete with operas, tragedies and tournaments, but a *philosophique* Versailles to boot.[20] For in attendance upon

Frederick there were such eminent men of letters as Maupertuis and Algarotti, both old acquaintances of Voltaire and ardent Newtonians, and the audacious materialist La Mettrie. Furthermore, the King had made Voltaire a chamberlain, given him the medal *Pour le mérite* which he had previously sought unsuccessfully (D4001, 4019), and a pension of 20,000 francs. The *philosophe* has virtually everything he could wish for, he tells the d'Argentals in his very first letter from Potsdam; but he misses them, he hungers to know what they are doing (D4174). The plangent tones of the homesick exile are unmistakable.

So it will be for a while. Voltaire is cosseted and wretched; he realises with remorse that he has perhaps committed the irredeemable act and may never see Paris again. He is in torture, ill, cannot sleep (D4192, 4205). He seeks to rationalise his motives, citing the persecution he has suffered (interestingly enough, it is the troubles he had encountered over *Le Mondain* in 1736 which remain the most bitter memory), the French King's coldness toward him, his exclusion from the Académie des Inscriptions et Belles-Lettres; whereas Frederick warmly welcomes him, has afforded him total freedom and excellent company (D4201, 4206).

Even so, he is haunted by the sense that he has missed the way. From afar Lord Chesterfield sums up the situation with that simple objectivity which perfect detachment can provide. Why, he asks wonderingly, has Voltaire, a member of the Académie Française, Royal Historiographer and Gentleman of the King, given up all this for Germany (D4226, Commentary)? Voltaire himself writes that he had meant to come for six weeks; now it looks like a stay for life (D4201). For Frederick had effectively compromised him by writing to France asking official permission for the move from Louis XV, and the French King's formal approval had, as Voltaire knew, sealed his fate (cf. D4184, 4194, 4196, 4240). What, therefore, was there left for him to do, to keep the bridges open with Paris?

From his first letter in Prussia, Voltaire had recommended himself through d'Argental to influential political figures like Chauvelin and Choiseul. Shortly afterwards, we find him asking the marquis de Puisieulx to let Louis know that he is serving him loyally and to preserve all his French rights and privileges (D4182). But the marquis is soon to send word that Voltaire cannot remain as the Royal Historiographer if he is absent from France (D4204); Duclos is to replace him (D4243), though Voltaire is allowed to retain his pension of 2,000 francs accruing from the post (D4239). It would seem that during these early months in Berlin Voltaire's situation at Versailles stood on a knife-edge. Not surprisingly, he decided that he must return in the autumn of 1750 in order to re-establish himself (D4219). Not the least fascinating aspect of Voltaire's correspondence at this period lies in the dramatic irony surrounding his countless announcements of an early departure for France. No one coming to the letters of 1750–2 for the first time and knowing nothing else about the man could guess that in fact he will not re-visit the French capital before 1778. In September 1750 he plans to be in Paris in three weeks (D4223), in October he has hopes for November (D4248), then he realises that the roads are so muddy he must wait for them to freeze over (D4250); thereafter he finds he must await better weather before returning (D4365). And so it goes on in an ever-deferred sequence. Like Godot, Voltaire will not come today, but he will surely come tomorrow.

It is possible to argue that during these months Voltaire mortgaged his future in Paris. A situation still fluid at the moment of his departure gradually hardened against him. D'Argental, for instance, urges him in August 1751 to return while he is still missed (D4539). Why then, after being poised for flight, did he neglect to flee? The weather, as so often his illnesses, can hardly be more than a façade for the real reasons. In fact, after a couple of months the miserable sense of separation from all he held dear (except Frederick!) begins to diminish, though it does not entirely disappear. Voltaire has commenced work on the *Siècle de Louis XIV* and, always a further precious therapy for him, organised productions of his plays, notably *Rome sauvée*. A remarkable affirmation from him, he gratuitously admits that it is doing his health good (D4220, 14 September [1750])! Soon it is a question of completing the *Siècle* before he comes to Paris (D4450), then of revising it and seeing it through the press (D4549). Truth to tell, during the year from September 1750 to September 1751, Voltaire had settled down to life in Germany.[21]

This should not surprise us. Professor Pomeau rightly points out that this capacity for flexible adaptation is one of Voltaire's most striking qualities; in a new climate, he feels himself renewed and regenerated;[22] and M. Pomeau aptly cites Voltaire's letter to Mme du Deffand of 1754 ('I had become English in London, I am German in Germany', D5786). Without such chameleon-like adaptability (Voltaire himself uses the image in this same letter), his energy would scarcely have survived the assaults of fortune past and future to find a harbour at Ferney.

So a daily round is established. An hour is given by Voltaire to improving Frederick's writings. The rest of the day is his own, ending up with a delicious supper (D4251), just three steps away, in the

company of a man full of wit and imagination (D4241) and a very select
company of special favourites. Near the end of his life, Voltaire was to
assert that he had never enjoyed pleasanter suppers in Paris[23] and, in a
Horatian ode, to sing the praises of Frederick's witty words during
these meals.[24] Voltaire has perfect conditions for work, an asylum from
persecution and the most agreeable society in the evenings. It sounds
like a calm routine at last. But such was never the tenor of Voltaire's
life. Tensions had quickly begun to make themselves felt in his new
environment.

There was first a clash over Baculard d'Arnaud, a young poet
formerly a protégé of Voltaire (and probably a lover of Mme Denis).
Frederick had already aroused Voltaire's jealousy of Baculard by
inviting the latter to Berlin and comparing him flatteringly to Voltaire
at Voltaire's expense (D4166).[25] Squabbles broke out between the two
soon after Voltaire arrived; Voltaire appealed to Frederick, who had no
recourse but to dismiss the lesser adornment to his Court in November
1750.[26] But the troubles over Baculard were momentary, compared
with the drawn-out, complex and sordid quarrel concerning Abraham
Hirschel. Hirschel was a Jewish banker who had facilitated Voltaire's
speculation in buying certain bonds in Saxony to which Voltaire had
no right, not being a Prussian subject. Against the money Voltaire had
lent him Hirschel deposited jewellery as security. But the transaction
collapsed, there were complications over the return of Voltaire's money
and the jewellery proved to be of inferior value in his eyes. So he
brought a suit against Hirschel, who was arrested on 1 January 1751, and
eventually Voltaire gained a technical but pyrrhic victory, Hirschel
being fined with infamy and ordered to make restitution to the
Frenchman. Voltaire, in a false position to start with, incurred further
ignominy by his pursuit of the banker and the particular scorn of
Frederick, who wrote to his sister Wilhelmina, the Margravine of
Bayreuth, that it was 'the affair of a scoundrel who wants to cheat a
rogue' (D4358). Voltaire was excluded from the King's presence until
the case had been completed in February 1751, and Frederick took the
opportunity to deliver him a monumental reprimand (D4400), not only
over Hirschel but over several contentious matters besides; he is not
prepared to see Voltaire unless the latter can resolve to live *en philosophe*.
It is for Voltaire to wax humble, and his apologies are abject: 'I have
had a mania for wanting to prove that I was right against a man with
whom it is not even permitted to be right . . . I have never felt pain so
deep and bitter' (D4406). Once again, the absence of Mme du
Châtelet's prudent wisdom is almost palpable.

So life was re-established on a more even keel and Voltaire resumed his engrossing labours on the *Siècle de Louis XIV*. His world had been enhanced too by the charms of Countess Bentinck, to whom his letters reveal an intimacy that strongly suggests she had become his mistress. There is not the closeness of his correspondence with Mme Denis, and Voltaire rarely departs from a tone of respectful gallantry. Besides, the affair seems to change into a simple though still warm friendship by early 1752. Still, in the Countess he finds a sympathetic companion, and perhaps no better evidence exists that they were lovers than that in a large number of the letters Voltaire complains of his health, just as he had done so often in those to Mme Denis in the late 1740s.

In August 1751, then, the *philosophe* is impervious to the passionate pleas of d'Argental to return to Paris, even though the latter has assessed the situation shrewdly in pointing out that Voltaire is isolated in Berlin, with the King as his sole consolation (D4539).[27] Voltaire tells his niece Mme de Florian during the same month that he is eating better, he has never been happier and more tranquil (D4548); and his reply to d'Argental's urgent letter shows that his friend's exhortations have fallen on deaf ears (D4557). At this moment, Voltaire's latest 'paradis terrestre'[28] is invaded by the serpent. The calamity is reported to Mme Denis on 2 September. La Mettrie has conveyed to him the cruel words Frederick had used on Voltaire's account: 'I shall need him another year at most; you squeeze the orange and you throw away the peel [*l'écorce*]' (D4564).

Things would never be the same again for Voltaire at Frederick's Court. At first he is thunderstruck. He describes the poignant scene in which he had La Mettrie repeat the fateful phrases and plied his companion with questions while the latter swore over and over that it was all true. How could Frederick say it, after all his protestations of love to Voltaire? He is utterly at sea: 'I am totally confused, I don't understand anything of it.' A painful revision of his whole relationship is forced upon him: perhaps Frederick has never meant any of his compliments and caresses? The King has been totally hypocritical with others; why should Voltaire remain an exception to that rule?

André Delattre makes the point that Voltaire is extremely reticent about personal feelings, transporting them into mockery on the rare occasions when he touches on them.[29] Excellent observation though it is, this instance shows that it is not universally true. Here, for once, is Voltaire naked, defenceless and utterly shaken by the revelation of basic falsity in one whom he admired and loved. His immediate thought is of flight.[30] At the moment he cannot leave, with the editions of the *Siècle* and of his collected works to be seen through the press; but the thought of doing so has entered his head and will never again leave it until he actually departs some eighteen months later.

One must assume that La Mettrie was telling the truth. The trenchant cynicism has all the hallmarks of Frederick's style, and La Mettrie had no particular axe to grind against Voltaire, nor was he, it seems, given to lying calumny for its own sake. Did Frederick, then, mean what he said? In one sense, yes. Literally, he is referring to the limited need he has of Voltaire's professional advice on his writings. But Frederick was never one to moderate his comments about the *philosophe* to third parties. Already in 1749 while eagerly urging Voltaire to join him, he could write in equally cynical terms to Algarotti: 'I need him for studying French elocution. You can learn good things from a rascal. I want to know his French; what do his morals matter to me?' (D4011, Commentary). But these harsh sarcasms are but one side of the coin. At the same time, Frederick wanted Voltaire's company for more than his knowledge of French, and was to bear the latter's indiscretions, over Hirschel and later over Maupertuis, in a way not wholly devoid of patience and moderation. Frederick, in brief, could never resist the wounding gibe, as for that matter Voltaire rarely could, though he does not often reveal the dismissive cruelty of the Prussian King. Besides, reported observations made to a third party often carry an extra venom which would be neutralised if they were uttered face to face. It may be somewhat Olympian to criticise Voltaire for failing, hurt as he was, to see the remark in this context and in the light of his intimate knowledge of Frederick by this time. The truth remains, however, that in such a situation he shows a limited awareness of the complexities of human nature.

The *écorce d'orange*, then, is the crucial turning-point of Voltaire's stay with Frederick, rather than the Maupertuis affair which provided the *dénouement*. A hiatus intervenes, during which the intimate suppers go on as before. But in his letters to Mme Denis (the only ones from Berlin in which he is consistently able to disclose his feelings unguardedly) Voltaire returns in later months to ruminate on La Mettrie's awful disclosure. In November the latter died of a surfeit, thereby removing himself for ever from any further probing; but Voltaire feels that he spoke the truth, even though Frederick has just paid the poet a compliment which does not fit at all with the *écorce d'orange* (D4628, 24 December 1751). Friendly letters pass between the two men, and by the spring Voltaire is even beginning to refer again to the amenities of life with Frederick. But talk is revived of returning to France and, in his first allusion to the Maupertuis quarrel, Voltaire tells Mme Denis that he will do well to depart for the banks of the Seine (D4895, 22 May 1752).

Voltaire's definitive farewell to Berlin was precipitated by a dispute between two members of the Berlin Academy, its president Maupertuis and a mathematician, Samuel König, who had been Mme du Châtelet's tutor for a period at Cirey. The quarrel turned upon the dispassionate question of the 'least quantity of action', by which Maupertuis thought to establish as fundamental a principle to the laws of movement in the universe as had Newton. König read Maupertuis's demonstration in 1749, found it unsatisfactory and published a courteous refutation in Latin in 1751, while also citing a letter by Leibniz which, he claimed, had stated the Maupertuis principle long before him. Unfortunately for König, when requested by his opponent to produce the original letter he was unable to comply;[31] at which Maupertuis accused him of bad faith and succeeded in obtaining from the Academy on 13 April 1752 a condemnation of König's methods. The latter riposted with an *Appel au public*; a subsequent series of published letters from various hands proved generally favourable to König, though without any rancour. But at this point, the *Bibliothèque raisonnée* (July–September 1752) published in Amsterdam articles by Voltaire in which he accused Maupertuis of lacking scientific method and, worse, of having abused his position to persecute an honest, innocent man. Not content to stop there, Voltaire referred to Frederick as Maupertuis's protector. Frederick could not now forbear to lend his weight to Maupertuis, despite the preponderance of scientific weight on the other side; Maupertuis required his support as President of his Academy. In a *Lettre d'un académicien de Berlin* of November 1752, printed complete with Prussian eagle, crown and sceptre on the title page, Frederick praised Maupertuis and attacked, without naming him, Voltaire. The latter was not disposed to accept Frederick's polemic as the final word in the affair. He responded with the satiric *Diatribe du docteur Akakia*, ridiculing Maupertuis savagely. Frederick, incensed by this direct challenge to his own authority, ordered the work to be lacerated and burned on all the public squares of Berlin on 24 December.[32]

So the wheel had turned full circle. Voltaire, who had gone to Prussia to escape persecution, had now suffered exactly the same condign punishment to his work in Berlin as his *Lettres philosophiques* had undergone in Paris in 1734. It may well be that Voltaire had challenged Maupertuis because, like Baculard d'Arnaud, he was in a privileged position at Frederick's court but far more importantly placed than Baculard ever was. It may also be true that as the frictions grew he seized, consciously or not, the opportunity of a quick challenge and a dramatic exit. But one should not overlook either that, here again, we see Voltaire acting in a style anticipatory of the Ferney years, defending the personal rights of a blameless disputant against the arrogance of office and arbitrary authority. Having made arrangements for financial security after his departure (through an annuity bought with the Duke of Württemberg, which allowed him to transfer funds out of Prussia), he had purchased independence and with it the right to speak his mind even against a king.

Frederick's oppressiveness, writes Voltaire, lost him at about this time three other men of letters as well, one of them Algarotti.[33] It is hard to know how far to credit this statement literally, but the row seems to have acted as a deterrent upon other possible candidates for the Berlin Academy. After the *Akakia* was burned, the marquis d'Argenson noted in his *Journal* that no one wanted now to go to Berlin, preferring freedom to money.[34] Yet here again we must beware of over-simplifying Frederick's personality. Though moved to burn Voltaire's satire publicly, he made no attempt to imprison or otherwise oppress Voltaire personally, as the French authorities would have done in 1734 if they had caught the writer. As Duvernet puts it, a king who was being simply a king would have crushed Voltaire.[35] The latter handed in to Frederick his chamberlain's key, medal and pension on 1 January 1753, but these symbols of status were returned to him the same day along with a placatory letter from the King, saying that he preferred to live with Voltaire than Maupertuis. Voltaire sums up Frederick's predicament acutely in quoting an old epigram by Martial: 'I cannot live with you nor without you' (D5184); it admirably conveys the impossible nature of their relationship. But this time the *philosophe* feels no such ambivalence. He wants and means to go, bides his time till a favourable moment, then pretexts a visit to take the waters at Plombières in the Vosges (D5229). Frederick, defeated by his persistence, coldly gives him leave.

Even now, however, the separation was not clear-cut. Voltaire came to see Frederick for the first time in two months, spent a couple of hours with him and, reports Voltaire's secretary Collini, emerged completely reconciled.[36] Six more days passed with them supping together each day before Voltaire departed on 26 March 1753. Duvernet recounts a similar tale of camaraderie,[37] and Collini asserts that Voltaire promised to return from Plombières. Such had been the extraordinary resilience of this friendship, that a future to it was even yet a possibility. Countess Bentinck writes a warm letter to Voltaire in May, urging him to swallow his pride, admit his past provocations and renew his loyalty to Frederick; he will see how swift the King will be to respond (D5296).

But this time the inertia of events had already ruined any such hopes. With Voltaire departed, Frederick's old suspicions were revived. Besides, the *philosophe* had taken with him Frederick's *oeuvre de poésie* and the King's imagination left him in little doubt as to what the author of *Akakia* could make of those conscientious verses. The work must be recovered; orders were sent to intercept Voltaire at Frankfurt, search him, and remove papers from his luggage (D5254). The stage was set for what was arguably the most humiliating episode in Voltaire's life. Arriving at Frankfurt on 4 June, he was detained by Frederick's minister Freytag until the poetic volume had arrived with his luggage. The book was returned to Freytag on the 17th, at which point Voltaire thought he might be free to go. Not so. Freytag, executing his orders slavishly, would not give permission for Voltaire's release until he had written authorisation from Frederick. Meantime Mme Denis had joined her uncle, and Voltaire decided on the 20th that the two of them would, accompanied by Collini, try to escape. The plot was discovered and this time all three were put under close arrest in a dreadful inn. Each was deprived of his effects, including money and jewels, and locked up in a separate room with three or four soldiers (accounts vary) at the door bearing guns and bayonets. Worse still befell Mme Denis, the officer in charge, Dorn, deciding to spend the night brutishly in her room. Eventually the prisoners were released but obliged to pay for their imprisonment, and Voltaire was kept under detention until a letter arrived from Frederick on 6 July. The next morning, as they were preparing to leave, Voltaire caught sight of Dorn and, according to Collini, rushed up to him with a pistol. Voltaire himself claims variously that he was cleaning or taking it to be repaired – an unlikely act as he was leaving – when Dorn appeared and took fright; the coincidence sounds slightly improbable, and Voltaire had good grounds for bitterness at Dorn's actions with Mme Denis. At all events, Dorn fled and made an official complaint. The trio were allowed to go, but Voltaire's confiscated moneys were only partially restored to him. In the end, he later wrote, he paid dearly for Frederick's book of poetry, about as much as the King spent on him to bring him to Berlin and keep him there. 'Consequently, we were quits.'[38]

A simple if arbitrary action initiated by Frederick for the recovery of his verses had turned, through an excess of zeal and stupidity on the part of his lieutenants, into an outrage. Frederick acknowledged as much privately (D5362, 5372), but publicly, as with Maupertuis against König, he was determined to uphold his officers. Besides, his patience had worn thin with Voltaire and his niece, who had bombarded him and other relevant authorities with complaints, and he was persuaded that Voltaire had tried to kill Dorn (D5464). Yet the King had acted *ultra vires* in the first place. Frederick's writ did not run in Frankfurt, a free city under the Holy Roman Emperor.[39] Furthermore, whatever grounds for action he might have against Voltaire, he had none with Mme Denis, an innocent companion. Yet in reality she suffered at least as much as her uncle, and Voltaire claims with every appearance of sincerity that it was the atrocity of what she underwent which horrified him most (D5413, 5475). According to her own account, she was so distraught at the time that she suffered convulsions for thirty-six hours afterwards (D5342). Her uncle's passion for her had clearly revived at their meeting, which made the way she was treated in his presence, because of him and without his being able to intervene, all the more intolerable. But the Venerable Council of Frankfurt, under Frederick's protection effectively if not legally, would do nothing for fear of upsetting him, and so the principal agents went scot free (D5438, 5458). Eventually, to Mme Denis's relief, Voltaire abandoned the action and accepted that nothing could be rescued with honour from this affair.

It remained only, then, for Voltaire to find a new home. He left Frankfurt for Mainz, then Mannheim, home of the Elector Palatine, who welcomed him and took him to his country home at Schwetzingen, then on to Strasbourg, arriving in mid-August. Thence he removed in October to Colmar, where he spent the winter in almost total retreat. His stay there was passed in isolation, without leaving his room for eight months (D5829), his time divided, as he put it, between illness and work (D5767). Yet this way of life, wretched for most men, is not so for him. True, he has suffered much from the breakdown of all his hopes with Frederick and his future is quite obscure. But, as so often before, withdrawal and work are his salvation. His vocation, he writes to Mme Denis, is to be a monk, for he loves the cell (D5821). This is not the whole truth, for it excludes the sense of commitment which will be more fully realised in the years ahead, but it is an important part. A letter to Mme Denis of 12 April 1754 (D5767), after months of this lonely life, is a veritable profession of faith. How futile and vain is society! Only work can console the human species for existing. Most, even of the wisest, need to seek help elsewhere against the 'emptiness of their souls'. But he, thanks to his ill-health, is lucky. He is alone, he can work, and he always has an aim in view in his studies; he is fulfilled. It affords a remarkable glimpse of the man for whom, in one form or another, 'cultivating one's garden' is the way to salvation.

But after Colmar, what? It had been made clear to him by early 1754 that his presence in Paris would be unwelcome to the French King (D5664, 5682). Incredibly, even after the débâcle of Frankfurt, Voltaire apparently tried to return to Berlin (D5574). This time it was Frederick who turned reluctant; but even now the way was not totally blocked, for the King agreed to allow Voltaire to stay at Bayreuth with his sister the Margravine (D5804) – from which, presumably, he might yet be restored to favour in Berlin after a probationary period. When all hope of reconciliation seemed at an end, yet one more flicker had appeared against all expectation. However, Voltaire's thoughts began to turn elsewhere. He left Colmar in June but returned to it, with Mme Denis, a few weeks later, staying until November. By then the outline of the future was taking shape. She would come and look after him (D5888), in spite of his tender warnings of how dull she would find it (D5779, 5804); and he began actively looking for a property in the area of Geneva or Lausanne (D5904). In early October 1754 it was still all in suspense (D5946), but negotiations were actively going forward in the next few months, and in January 1755 Voltaire bought on the outskirts of Geneva a property to which he gave, hopefully, the name of Les Délices. At this elegant house (today the home of the Institut et Musée Voltaire), accompanied by Mme Denis, he began to settle down in style as a Genevan citizen, as the marquis d'Argenson noted in his diary on 26 February (D6184, Commentary). The same hope of better times to come is revealed in the Epître he wrote in March to celebrate the new life:

> Liberté! liberté! ton trône est en ces lieux:
> . . . .
> Descends dans mes foyers en tes beaux jours de fête.
> Viens m'y faire un destin nouveau.[40]

In future years Voltaire was to be reconciled with Frederick once more and praises for each other's activity in the cause of *philosophie* would be resumed. In 1766 Voltaire would consider setting up a colony of enlightened men in Frederick's territory and with his blessing at Cleves, but others, most notably Diderot, were not persuaded by the efficacy of work in exile.[41] Voltaire tried hard to incite Frederick to action by comparing him with his hero Julian the Apostate. Frederick however was not disposed to be persuaded by such flattery, and in the end Voltaire had to settle for what he calls a 'Julien minor' (D20925).[42] As Peter Gay maintains, Voltaire's disapproval of Frederick was ultimately personal rather than political, and he did not appreciate that the Prussian King's absolutism 'was an authoritarian defense against constitutionalism and civil liberties, rather than a transitional step toward them'.[43] For Voltaire Frederick is, until the Prussian experience goes sour, a hero, a *philosophe* and an *honnête homme*, capable of winning battles, creating a new Athens, working on his writings each day: an epic, stylised figure telling us more about Voltaire than Frederick, as Christiane Mervaud has well observed.[44] When, as she shows, he changes his mind, an equally unrealistic picture emerges, of a heartless, false tyrant. Never, in the correspondence, is the *philosophe* able to appraise Frederick in balanced manner. He is too close to the events, and only in poetry will he produce a complex and realistic picture (in variant lines to the *Poème sur la loi naturelle*) of 'Mon Patron, mon disciple, et mon persécuteur'.[45]

How far did Frederick help or hinder Voltaire's intellectual development? The *président* Hénault had expressed the fear that the *philosophe* would lose his talent if he stayed in Berlin (D4641). Voltaire's own view was different; as long as life was tranquil in Germany, he had perfect conditions for working, whereas back in Paris he would have so much trouble with 'les sots, les dévots, les auteurs' that he would have to give up writing (D4940). The hyperbole of that statement does not destroy its essential truth. In the late 1740s Voltaire had wasted his substance in courtly living. By contrast, Berlin was to see the completion of his great historical work the *Siècle de Louis XIV* and the appearance with the publisher Walther of an important new edition of his works.[46] Frederick too played an important role in the genesis of the *Essai sur les moeurs*,[47] while the *Dictionnaire philosophique* was probably the product of a supper-time conversation at Frederick's table in 1752, Voltaire setting to work on it the very next day.[48] Besides, though Frederick might not have wished to take credit for it, Voltaire's ironic view of the universe developed apace from the experience of Prussia. It shows in the bitterly brilliant *Histoire des voyages de Scarmentado*, written probably in 1753–4. It is discernible in the *Mémoires* through the speedy recital of events, the swift concatenation of incongruous circumstances.[49] The black humour carries through to the opening, 'German sections of *Candide*. The Baron of Thunder-ten-tronckh, like Frederick's father, combined despotic arrogance with wealthy barbarism.[50] Candide's punishment, to pass thirty-six times through the bastinado, is reminiscent of that precise discipline handed out by Frederick to his soldiers.[51] Indeed, the King of the Bulgares comes along in *Candide*, just as Frederick was a witness to the same punishment in Berlin, but in the *conte* he is merciful and saves the hero any further beatings. The reference to Bulgares is surely a reminder of Frederick's homosexuality, 'Bulgare' being linked etymologically to 'bougre'.

The quarrels between Voltaire and Frederick have a heroic quality, as befits two personalities so vigorous, so complex and so enterprising. Each recognised in the other a great man, for all the faults. Frederick's energy inspired the *philosophe* to work; Voltaire had never, he said, seen a man so industrious (D4483). Frederick, for his part, was to continue to see Voltaire not merely as a rascal, but also as a god.[52] Beneath the rancour, contempt, jealousies, lay an enduring reciprocal esteem. As John Morgan noted on his visit to Ferney in 1764, Voltaire kept a snuff box containing a miniature of Frederick;[53] and he did not miss the opportunity of sending greetings to Frederick via Lord Percy six years later, on learning that the latter would pass through Berlin on his way to Russia.[54] But, no more than Frederick, could Voltaire endure calumny or outrage. Apologise as he might after the Hirschel affair for instance, his needs must riposte. Sadly, it has to be concluded that no place could house them together for long, the more so because the one was born to command and the other to seek his independence. Yet the paradox remains. Voltaire, writing the *Commentaire historique* at the end of his life and with greater detachment than the earlier *Mémoires*, remarks that their row at Frankfurt was soon forgotten by both partners: 'It was a lovers' quarrel: the harassments of courts pass away, but the nature of a beautiful ruling passion is long-lasting.'[55]

4 Geneva, and *Candide*

In Geneva, Voltaire's social life developed an ample style it had not known before. He was at last master of his own house, independent and free. The leading citizens of the city flocked to his doors. People came to dinner almost daily, writes his secretary Collini in 1756 (D6797); Voltaire himself speaks of inviting seven or eight people on most days (D7004). At first he put on plays at Les Délices. But this soon incurred the displeasure of the puritanical pastors of Geneva, and so Voltaire transferred his theatrical performances to Montriond, the other house he had bought, in Lausanne. Here, he writes in 1757, people came from thirty leagues around to see his production of his tragedy *Zaïre* (D7179). At last, in his own words, he was leading the life of a patriarch (D6214). He had also become a gardener, and the correspondence of the Geneva years resounds with Voltaire's assumption of this new rôle. He does not, he says, like to live in holes or palaces (D6307). Now he can enjoy a life of wealthy independence, with his six horses, four carriages, a coachman and several other employees (D6797).

In this fine new house at Les Délices he claims he will live and die in peace, if Fate permits (D6218). But not everyone is convinced. His old friend Countess Bentinck wonders to an acquaintance whether he will remain quietly living the simple life in Geneva, as his Délices *Epître* has proclaimed, or need once again to be involved with kings and their vicissitudes (D6530, Commentary). It is a shrewd question. The answer however appears to be reasonably clear. Though Voltaire does not neglect opportunities to keep his name in favour with Louis XV (e.g., D7016), he seems to feel quite genuinely the contentment he professes at being removed from the world of courtly intrigue. As we shall see, that situation will change in mid-1758; but until then, Voltaire is to enjoy three years of relatively peaceful acceptance of his new situation. The ambivalent mixture of repulsion and attraction for Paris that was so strong during the 1730s is seldom apparent; indeed, its supposed effect upon the whole genesis of *Candide* has sometimes been exaggerated. Only in the later months of 1758 does it become an important factor. Paris is for Voltaire the city where for instance the fanatical consequences of the ancient quarrel between the Jesuits and Jansenists can still be seen in the appalling attempt by Damiens to assassinate the King in 1757 (D7118, 7180); Voltaire for his part wants none of it.

Swiss Protestant pastors had been among those natives encouraging Voltaire to settle in Geneva. When he arrived he was full of goodwill towards them, and eager to be as conciliatory as possible. He was persuaded that the Genevan theologians were more *philosophiques* than those in Paris and that the number of people 'thinking reasonable thoughts' was increasing daily, as he told his friend Thieriot in April 1756 (D6824). A year later he informed d'Alembert that there were very few Calvinists left in Calvin's old city; all the *honnêtes gens* were Christian deists (D7357). Not that irritations failed to arise. The refusal by the Genevan Consistory of clergy to allow local participation in the theatrical performances at Les Délices was officially pronounced on 31 July 1755. Voltaire, though he may have had grounds to feel that he had been promised immunity,[1] accepted the order without demur. When Jacob Vernet, one of the most conservative of the pastors, urged him on his arrival to cooperate with them in discouraging the youth of Geneva from impious libertinage (D6146), Voltaire in reply expressed his respect for the religious laws of Geneva (D6149). When *La Pucelle* appeared in Geneva in a pirated edition, Voltaire intervened to disavow the poem, asking the Petit Conseil (the ruling executive and legislative body in Geneva) to proceed against it and claiming that many offensive remarks against religion and respectable people were not by him. The Petit Conseil obliged by burning the work on 5 August 1755 (D6393). There is an evident readiness on the part of the exile to settle down in his new home and live peaceably with his neighbours.

But as time passed Voltaire became convinced that the aid of the liberal pastors must be invoked in the fight which he was beginning to wage more directly against religious superstition. Writing to one of the most progressive, Jacob Vernes, in January 1757, Voltaire provocatively congratulates Geneva on the fact that it has been possible to print in the city the statement that Calvin was a barbarian, adding: 'You are not Calvinists, you are men' (D7119); he is referring to remarks he had made in his historical work the *Essai sur les moeurs* relating to Calvin's condemnation of Servetus to death. Enlightened Protestant opinion did not, however, extend to criticising Calvin so harshly. Voltaire's compliment was not well received, even less so when he wrote to Thieriot a letter which appeared in the *Mercure* in May, to the effect that Calvin had, along with an enlightened mind, 'une âme atroce' (D7213). The Consistory, meeting that month, requested the Petit Conseil to show its disapproval of these audacious remarks. However, peace was restored, the Council indicating that no more should be written on the subject,[2] while Voltaire for his part also graciously agreed after a while to drop the matter (D7364).

Meantime, Voltaire had decided to defend the reputation of Joseph Saurin, a Protestant minister who had fled Switzerland in 1690, settled in his native France and abjured the faith. He wrote to Saurin's son in January or February 1757 expressing his support (D7137), which is articulated in the *Siècle de Louis XIV*.[3] But Saurin had done more than renounce Protestantism, for he was reputed to have fled after confessing to a number of crimes. Because of the notorious reputation which he had left behind him, the Saurin affair in its own way touched a nerve as sensitive as did the reputation of Calvin. Voltaire was attacked in the *Journal helvétique* in October 1758 and his good faith impugned; he replied in the December number in similarly thunderous terms.

But by late 1758 the early hopes of cooperation with the Swiss Protestant leaders had already vanished definitively. The crucial episode was surely the appearance in November 1757 of Volume VII of the *Encyclopédie*, containing the article 'Genève' by d'Alembert. In order to prepare this article, d'Alembert had come to stay at Les Délices in August 1756 and met many of the city's leading figures. Voltaire had obviously played a vital part in its preparation, and when the scandal broke, following its appearance in print, he was accused of being in close league with d'Alembert (D7512). The attitudes expressed in the article follow closely Voltaire's own views about the trends towards deism amongst the Genevan pastors, its author claiming that the ministers were often pure Socinians, believing (like the supporters of that heresy) in neither the divinity of Christ nor the eternity of hell.

Though Voltaire had played a decisive role in the genesis of the Geneva article, the composition itself belonged entirely, it would seem, to d'Alembert, who was always to claim total responsibility for it. Indeed, as Naves shows, the views expressed are six months out of date in Voltaire's thinking, antedating the unfavourable reception of his comments on Calvin.[4] Already he was aware that the city's pastors were not as far advanced on the road to deism as he had hoped; the uproar at the end of 1757 merely confirmed his disillusionment. As has been shown, in doctrinal terms Voltaire and d'Alembert had made a shrewd assessment of the situation.[5] Voltaire was therefore all the more angered that the pastors would not leave the shelter of Calvinist orthodoxy and come out to join hands with him in the cause of true enlightenment. They on their side feared his compromising embrace. When he decided to leave Geneva at the end of 1758, it was largely because the republican freedom he had thought to find had been ruined for him by clerical authority. Already a year earlier, during the crisis after the article 'Genève' had appeared, he had denounced Calvinist fanatics alongside papist fanatics in the same abusive tones (D7512).

This crisis also marks a turning-point in Voltaire's relations with the Encyclopedists. When Diderot and d'Alembert had begun their great Dictionary, Voltaire had looked on from Berlin, sympathetic but personally uninvolved (D4990, 5005). Closer contact was established later, but only at Les Délices did Voltaire's part develop apace as d'Alembert commissioned an increasing number of articles; Volume VII alone contains eighteen by his hand (out of a total of forty-six Voltaire probably contributed to the *Encyclopédie* altogether)[6] not to mention others where he was the intermediary between the editors and Swiss pastors. Voltaire's letters during the Geneva period carry numerous references to his collaboration in this enterprise. Although bewailing the lack of reference books in the city, which exacerbates his problems in compiling articles (D6731), he is actively *engagé*. But in late 1756 he still does not know the *Encyclopédie* and asks for the existing volumes to be sent him (D7018). A little later, with greater knowledge of the work, he has some serious criticisms to express of it. There are too many private opinions, not enough method and objective truth (D7055); should the editors not have issued guidelines to the contributors (D7093)? D'Alembert admits that some articles are weak but stresses the necessary compromises that have to be made in a work appearing under an official privilege to print (D7320).

Already before the troubles over Volume VII, then, Voltaire has doubts about the *Encyclopédie*. Warmly though he supports the idea of a collective philosophic crusade, he dislikes the unevenness of quality and the moderation that must never be forgotten by editors whose work has to incur the scrutiny of the royal censor. By living on the periphery of France Voltaire had purchased greater artistic freedom. His bolder writings appeared anonymously or ascribed to others. If accused of authorship, he disclaimed all knowledge of the work, or alternatively as with *La Pucelle* asserted that the version which had appeared was a deformation of what he had actually written. As his anti-Christian attitudes grew more militant in the late 1750s, it seemed inevitable that he would sooner or later have broken off with the *Encyclopédie* as too tame for his purposes.

The appearance of Volume VII accelerated that separation. For the article 'Genève' itself, one of the boldest in the whole dictionary, he had warm praise, feeling that it told the simple truth about the Genevan ministers; but he expressed grave dissatisfaction to d'Alembert at the puerility of many of the rest (D7539). When the storm clouds multiplied around the editors' heads, Voltaire showed sympathy for them in being unable to publish in a free country (D7561). Then d'Alembert announced his intention of leaving the enterprise. Voltaire appealed to him not to give up (D7564, 7592), but when d'Alembert replied that the situation was hopeless and Voltaire learned from him that the opposition to the work was coming not from the Jesuits as he had thought but from the Court (D7607) he changed his tune and urged all the Encyclopedists to imitate d'Alembert and resign *en bloc* (D7631, 7632). Diderot answered rather caustically that they must carry on and in Paris, as they had a responsibility to their subscribers and the publishers (D7641); Voltaire told d'Alembert that he considered Diderot's letter shameful (D7651). They must withdraw, until in three months' time the weight of public opinion summoned them to return in triumph (D7653). But gradually Voltaire saw that such a course was unrealistic and returned to urging d'Alembert not to abandon Diderot (D7708); in May 1758 he was himself still actively engaged in supporting the *Encyclopédie* (D7727, 7729). However, his interest in the dictionary had virtually run its course, and when the work lost its privilege to print in March 1759, the event merely confirmed Voltaire's beliefs that open publication of a *philosophique* writing was useless. The moment of breakdown coincided with the great popular triumph of *Candide*, itself a production written and published in conditions of profound secrecy. Voltaire could scarcely have wished for a better indication that his future way was not that of the *Encyclopédie*.

The Geneva article had had other consequences too. Not only had d'Alembert made controversial assertions about the city's clergy, he had also expressed regret that regular theatre was forbidden in Geneva. At first the virulent reaction by the ministers caused the remarks on theatre to be overlooked, only one public reply appearing, in May 1758. But one Genevan citizen, Jean-Jacques Rousseau, fervently disagreed with d'Alembert, and by early March he had completed his *Lettre à M. d'Alembert sur les spectacles* in a state of exalted emotion, as his *Confessions* make clear.[7] Rousseau found distasteful the manipulation of Genevan affairs by French intellectuals for their own interests, assisted by upper-class Genevans betraying, as he saw it, their country's future. He knew full well Voltaire's close links with such Geneva patricians as the Tronchin family and was aware of the former's rôle in the article 'Genève'.[8] For Rousseau, it is clear, theatre-going is *ipso facto* a matter for censure. The need indicates a lack of inner resources; the experience merely leaves the playgoer dissatisfied. Theatre cannot improve morality. Quite the contrary; the spectacle of passions on the stage is likely rather to debase the audience. The social consequences of introducing theatre are likely to be even more pernicious than the moral ones. A hard-working community will become prey to idleness, boredom and luxury.

Rousseau's Letter appeared at a key moment in the debate over establishing a theatre, which had been going on ever since 1617. A fairly clear-cut social distinction had developed between the opponents of theatre, mainly drawn from the less privileged classes, and its supporters, who were especially to be found among the more aristocratic sections of the community and who looked towards Paris and the *mores* of French polite society as their norm. The cause of theatre became central to the whole Genevan policy towards France during the eighteenth century.[9] In 1737 a company of players had been set up, but the enterprise quickly foundered. The Consistory of pastors, for its part, resolutely opposed any development of theatre in private houses, objecting even for instance to a performance of Corneille's *Polyeucte* in 1748, though, as they admitted, it had been played with perfect decorum.[10] As we have seen, Voltaire was greeted with the same unyielding opposition on this matter when he arrived in the city.

Rousseau's essay helped to ensure the continuance of the *status quo*. A further attempt by the French in 1766 to introduce a theatre was defeated and it was 1782 before the local aristocrats won their point.[11] On this question too Voltaire was to find no gratification in Geneva. He disagreed completely with Rousseau, claiming to d'Alembert that the city was wildly enthusiastic for plays and describing theatre as the third sacrament of Geneva (i.e. after the only two recognised by the Calvinist faith: baptism and communion) (D7842, 2 September 1758). Here too were grounds for disillusionment with what Voltaire saw as a clerical oligarchy.

The *Lettre à d'Alembert* had other larger results as well. It marked the definitive parting of the ways between Rousseau and the *philosophes*, especially as it came at a moment when the latter group were already on the defensive over the mounting opposition to the *Encyclopédie*. Voltaire found Rousseau's intervention unforgivable when Diderot and d'Alembert were already in disarray. In the same letter to d'Alembert quoted above, he compares Rousseau to Diogenes sitting in his tub barking at them. Rousseau was no longer, in Voltaire's eyes, merely an eccentric; he was also a traitor.

Thus emerged into full view Voltaire's quarrel with his greatest enemy. Yet the fundamental differences had been becoming apparent for some time. Rousseau claimed that they had once met, and this appears to be true; though as it was in a crowded room in 1743, when Rousseau was unknown but Voltaire already famous, it is hardly surprising that Rousseau remembered the occasion but not Voltaire.[12] Their first letters to each other date from 1745, a perfectly courteous exchange of correspondence arising from the task Rousseau had been commissioned to undertake at Court in revising *La Princesse de Navarre*, on which Voltaire and Rameau had collaborated, for a new performance. When Rousseau's first important work, the *Discours sur les sciences et les arts*, appeared in 1750, Voltaire's reaction was generally unfavourable to its argument, though he had not yet had a chance to read it. Only with Voltaire's coming to Geneva did the relationship take on more substance. Soon afterwards, Rousseau sent him a copy of his *Discours sur l'inégalité*, that diatribe against contemporary culture and description of how natural man had become corrupted by society. Voltaire attempted politely to find some common ground in writing to thank him.[13] Agreed, the arts and sciences can cause harm, as he realises when he reflects on the sufferings undergone at the hands of persecutors by himself and fellow-writers; but these misfortunes are of no consequence compared to crimes like the Saint Bartholomew Day Massacre. 'Literature nurtures the soul, corrects it, consoles it; it constitutes your claim to fame even as you are writing against it.' But the temptation, he says humorously, is to go on all fours after reading Rousseau's work (D6451, [30 August 1755]). Rousseau replies in well-mannered terms, accepting some of what Voltaire says but arguing, as in the *Discours*, that arts and sciences are linked to an internal vice in a nation. True, he enjoys literature and owes to it 'le peu que je suis'; but he would doubtless have been happier as an illiterate. For Rousseau the prime source of social disorder nowadays is not ignorance but rather overweening pride, error, the mania to know all (D6469). Rousseau, one feels, would have understood the Faust myth better than Voltaire.[14]

The basic difference of opinion about the nature and value of society is already clear in these two letters and will merely receive further exemplification from the arguments over the article 'Genève'. For Voltaire, improvement could come about only within the existing social context, but enhanced by cultural refinement, greater freedom and tolerance; the specific means by which this might be achieved were to preoccupy him more intensely than ever during the Ferney years. For Rousseau in 1755 the way to achieving a purer society had still to be discovered. Beyond the awareness that a return to the state of nature was quite out of the question, much else remained unclear and would not be fully outlined until his *Contrat Social* (1762). But he already felt that there must be some radical revision of human conduct in order to attain that integrity for which he longed. It will not do simply to tinker with the society man has created for himself; a fresh start in keeping with what Rousseau considered to be the true nature of man would have to be made.

The two thinkers were equally at variance with each other on the question of divine providence. Voltaire's concern over the problem of evil had its origins well before the Geneva period, but during these years it evolved as a major preoccupation. The first important landmark occurred in late 1755 when he learned of the dreadful earthquake that had shattered Lisbon on 1 November, a catastrophe in which tens of thousands died. Voltaire's immediate reaction was to write his famous *Poème sur le désastre de Lisbonne*; within ten days of his first mentioning the news on 24 November the poem, though well over two hundred lines in length, was in his publisher Cramer's hands. The work is an anguished cry such as many a sensitive person makes in face of a particularly awful disaster: why did it have to happen, to the innocent as much as to the guilty? In Voltaire's case it takes the form of an assault on the philosophical Optimism of such as Pope, who had proclaimed in his *Essay on Man* (1733–4):

> All Nature is but Art, unknown to thee;
> All Chance, Direction which thou canst not see;
> All Discord, Harmony not understood;
> All partial Evil, universal Good:
> And, spite of Pride, in erring Reason's spite,
> One truth is clear, 'Whatever is, is RIGHT'.[15]

This doctrine of 'Tout est bien' is specifically attacked by Voltaire as early as the fourth line of his poem. In his distressed state of bewilderment, he rebels against the fatalistic assumption that things must be the way they are. Gradually his vision widens, to embrace not only natural catastrophes but the awful spectacle of universal war on this earth:

> Eléments, animaux, humains, tout est en guerre.
> Il le faut avouer, le *mal* est sur la terre.[16]

How can this be reconciled with a good God? Either we are guilty and He must wish to punish us in the perspective of a future life, or He is totally indifferent to our lot. In either case, His ways are inexplicable to us, and the philosophers can offer us no more useful advice than teaching us to doubt. Whatever our future destiny, our fate in this world is to suffer; the only remaining resource to us is hope.

When he arranged in June 1756 for his new poem to be distributed to d'Alembert, Diderot and Rousseau, Voltaire (D6879) wrote to Thieriot that he thought his colleagues would understand him. In Rousseau's reaction at least he was to be disappointed. Rousseau delivered himself of a weighty 'Lettre sur la Providence' (D6973), dated 18 August 1756. It is Rousseau's solution to the problem of evil, just as, in its way, the *Discours sur l'inégalité* had been.[17] Man himself, free to abuse his situation and therefore to become corrupt, is the source of moral evil. As for physical evils, they are inevitable, and man has only added to them by crowding into cities like Lisbon. The question is not so much Why evil? as Why existence at all? The *philosophes* are far too busy balancing good and evil to remember the simple pleasure of being alive. Furthermore, the existence of God justifies everything, for it offers promise of immortality, which makes earthly life of no importance. Providence therefore, in Rousseau's eyes, emerges acquitted of all responsibility for human misfortunes.

Voltaire courteously accepted Rousseau's letter, telling him he would reply at another time. In the event he did not, and Rousseau was later to claim that the true reply was *Candide*, but the evidence for this is limited, as Professor Leigh has shown after investigating the assertion. The essential difference in their attitudes, as Leigh makes clear, is that Rousseau believes in the immortality of the soul.[18] Voltaire merely flirts with the idea, whereas for Rousseau it is an existential reality, the very ground of his being: 'I feel it, I believe it, I wish it, I hope for it, I shall defend it to my dying sigh . . .'

During the Geneva period we witness the actual break between Voltaire and Rousseau. The full virulence of their hostility will however be reserved for later years. By 1760 Rousseau could write to Voltaire stating explicitly that he hated him (D8986). Voltaire for his part

denounced the Genevan to d'Alembert for being a hypocritical moralist
(D9682) and cast aspersions upon his novel *La Nouvelle Héloïse*.[19] The
quarrel degenerated into abuse, Voltaire being convinced that Jean-
Jacques was mad as well as dishonourable (D12296). Above all, the
latter had put himself out of court by attacking the cause of *philosophie*,
which is where his talents might have made an important contribution
to the cause (D14048). Behind the slander and personal idiosyncrasies
lie however two major views on the world, irreconcilable even though
both writers are now thought of with justice as major figures of the
Enlightenment. For all his pragmatism, which has rightly received
greater recognition in recent years, 'one of the springs of Rousseau's
political thought', as Franco Venturi puts it, 'lay in [the] very contrast
between reality and vision . . .'[20] Voltaire's gaze was more hard-
headed.

Let us return to an examination of Voltaire's own attitudes as they
evolved in the period immediately preceding *Candide*. That *conte*, considered by general consent to be Voltaire's masterpiece, is a kind of
summation of Voltaire's views in the late 1750s on the human condition, beset by suffering and wickedness yet not wholly without scope for
initiative and improvement. This is not the place for an analysis of
Voltaire's tale;[21] but no biography of the *philosophe* can reasonably
neglect a close look at the way his mind came to absorb and shape
materials from the world around him and from his own reading. Such a
consideration, involving as it does a careful review of detailed, even
minute, matters, inevitably calls for a certain rigour of attention; yet
without it we cannot hope to understand very much about the genesis of
Voltaire's greatest work.

As we have seen, the news of the Lisbon earthquake in 1755 played
an important rôle. Voltaire's immediate reaction is one of horror: 'One
hundred thousand ants, our neighbours, crushed all of a sudden in our
ant-heap, half of them perishing doubtless in inexpressible anguish.'
The sole consolation is that the Jesuit Inquisitors of Lisbon will have
disappeared with the rest. That, concludes Voltaire, should teach men
not to persecute men, 'for while a few confounded rascals are burning a
few fanatics the earth is swallowing up both' (D6597, 24 November
[1755]). Already the ironic perspective that informs Chapter VI of
Candide on the Lisbon auto-da-fé has been glimpsed. Such expressions
of horror resound through letters of succeeding days. The very size of
the catastrophe is 'a terrible argument against Optimism' (D6605).
Confronted by it, Voltaire feels his own problems shrink to such petty

dimensions that he is ashamed of them (D6605, 6607). This attitude is somewhat reminiscent of the way his hero Zadig in an earlier *conte* had forgotten his own miseries in contemplation of the infinite heavens.[22] But there is a sombre difference; Zadig's vision was sublimely consoling, whereas Voltaire's merely confirms the awful destructiveness latent in physical nature.

It is clear that the *Poème sur le désastre de Lisbonne* constituted an almost instinctive response. However, less attention has been paid to the fact that once the poem is completed Voltaire's attitudes are swiftly transmuted into a rather different stance. In a letter to the Protestant pastor Allamand on 16 December 1755 he writes: 'I pity the Portuguese, like you, *but men do still more harm to each other on their little molehill than nature does to them*. Our wars massacre more men than are swallowed up by earthquakes. If we had to fear only the Lisbon adventure in this world, we should still be tolerably well off' (D6629: my italics). Two new notes are struck. Despondent alarm at the earthquake has given way to a more detached attitude; and the physical evils of the universe are set in a context in which man's wickedness to man, particularly in wars, looms far greater. Even in his very first letter after learning of the earthquake (D6597) he had, as we saw, found space to think also of the persecutions inflicted by the Inquisitors. It is this kind of consideration which, with more time for reflection, becomes paramount. Physical suffering, it is true, is a sufficient refutation of the belief that 'all is well'; but the true horror lies in the spectacle of what men do to one another. The same evolution of attitudes can also be glimpsed in the *Poème sur le désastre*, which begins with the actual catastrophe at Lisbon but then opens out onto a wider scene in which 'tout est en guerre'.

Reasons to support this new-found awareness that war is the supreme evil were soon to be sadly abundant in the world around. On 29 August 1756 Frederick the Great invaded Saxony, thereby precipitating the Seven Years War. It accords well with Voltaire's darkening mood. In early 1756 he had passed from specific concern with the Lisbon earthquake to a more general brooding on the problem of evil. He tells Elie Bertrand (another of the Genevan clergy) in February that the myth of the Fall of Man, whether Christian or otherwise, is more reasonable in human terms than the Optimism of Leibniz and Pope,[23] which beneath the disguise of a consoling name simply removes all hope: 'if *all is well*, how do the Leibnizians admit of a better?' (D6738: author's italics). It is the fatalistic quality of Optimism that is so cruel, for it invites man to acquiesce and therefore give up all striving for improvement. As we have seen, in the desolate picture Voltaire paints of the human condition, he allows man one single consolation: hope. Otherwise, the pessimism is general, and indeed increasing in the author's view of the world. He begins to become more interested in Manichean beliefs, according to which evil has a life of its own quite independent of the forces of good in the universe. A letter to Mme du Deffand in May 1756 talks of Jupiter's two casks, one for good and another, bigger, for evil. Not only does he pose the basic question – Why so? More daringly, he wonders whether the evil cask could have constructed itself. Here are the seeds of an outlook voiced in *Candide* by the self-styled Manichean Martin.

However, this increasingly sombre view of the world does not relate to a personal crisis as is sometimes claimed. Apart from worries over such matters as the widespread circulation, despite his efforts to the contrary, of his notorious mock-epic *La Pucelle*, Voltaire is by and large happily established in Geneva. Les Délices has needed some improvements and from the early weeks he is busy planting, furnishing, building. Claude Patu, a visitor in autumn 1755, speaks wonderingly of Voltaire's vigour: 'Imagine, together with the air of a dying man, all the fire of first youth, and the brilliance of his attractive stories!' Never has one seen better fare or more engaging manners; the whole of Geneva is delighted to have him there and is doing all it can to keep him (D6562). The picture, in short, is not far short of idyllic. True, Voltaire looks like a corpse, as another visitor confirms (D6646). But the sense of returning vitality and purpose flows from the correspondence as it must have done at the dinner table. In 1758 Mme d'Epinay was also to find the *philosophe* full of gaiety and cheerfulness (D7704). Even the references to ill-health become less common. Voltaire has found 'a port after weathering so many storms' (D6842). To Thieriot he makes the touching confession that he is writing about the sufferings of his fellow-men out of pure altruism, for 'I am so happy that I am ashamed of it' (D6875, 27 May [1756]).

Yet this state of personal contentment in no way precludes a total divorce with the philosophy of Optimism, and from its outset the Seven Years War is invoked as a decisive refutation (e.g., D7001). To his friend the Duchess of Saxe-Gotha, who is to find herself in the thick of the battle, he never ceases to point up the absurd horror of it all, using the War polemically to express disagreement with her adherence to Optimism (e.g., D7023). To his more intimate acquaintance Thieriot, he voices an attitude of indifference: 'Happy is he who lives in tranquillity on the edge of his lake, far from the throne, and far from envy' (D7028). To the duc de Richelieu, also a friend but more distant as being of high rank and politically influential, another side appears. Richelieu being in charge of the larger of the two French armies, Voltaire turned to him to advocate his invention of an armed chariot which, he reckoned, would kill many Prussians, indeed would knock out everyone it met, so that two of the machines would be enough against a battalion and squadron combined (D7043, 7293). This particular notion (which the French Government did not take up) should of itself dispose of two long-standing myths about Voltaire: that he was a total pacifist, and lacked all sense of patriotism. Generally pacifist in outlook, he nevertheless was forced to accept the realities of preparing a military defence against the aggression of Prussia on land and the British at sea. Both countries fill him with consternation, though for rather different reasons.

He is appalled by the desolation wrought by Frederick's armies in central Europe, once they had won the decisive engagement at Rossbach on 5 November 1757. But prior to that he had been moved by compassion for the Prussian King, who had intimated that he was contemplating suicide (D7373). Voltaire replied in urgent tones dissuading him from such a course, pointing out that it would dismay his supporters and give joy only to his enemies. Instead, Frederick should seek an honourable peace (D7400), show he is a *philosophe* and live for all the good things still remaining to him: possessions, dignities, friends (D7419). A further plea follows on 13 November (D7460). Ironically, it is written after Rossbach, which is Frederick's contemptuous reply to Voltaire's advice (the King had already expressed his scorn in a letter to his sister Wilhelmina, D7414, Commentary). The news of that Prussian victory reverses Voltaire's attitude. A despairing Frederick gains immediate access to his warm sympathy. Yet at the same time he is hoping for revenge over Frederick for the humiliating moment at Frankfurt when four bayonets had menaced Mme Denis, and he is disappointed when Frederick triumphs (D7471).[24] His feelings towards the Prussian King are as strongly ambivalent as ever. Richard Phelps, a British visitor at this time, acutely observed: 'He was the most inconsistent, whenever he talked of the King of Prussia.'[25]

By contrast, Voltaire's views on the British Navy are unequivocal. He fears their superior numbers (D7210) and wants to see their piratical ways punished (D7491). The British were exercising a direct influence upon Voltaire's life. Not only were they likely by their hostile actions and blockades to cause the price of sugar to rise (D7131, 7901). They were, more gravely, capturing French vessels in which the writer had considerable investments, especially the fleet sailing from Cadiz

(D5719), and at times the Cadiz mercantile trade was to give him much cause for concern (e.g., D6811). Besides, the British Government had provided one of the more signal instances of horrible folly during the Seven Years War by the execution of Admiral Byng for failing to relieve Minorca against the duc de Richelieu's forces at Port-Mahon in May 1756. Voltaire and Richelieu had both intervened on Byng's behalf in the court-martial following the engagement, but to no avail; Byng was sentenced on 27 January 1757 to be shot, the sentence being carried out on 14 March. André-Michel Rousseau, providing a comprehensive account of the affair,[26] sees it as Voltaire's baptism as champion of the oppressed. This time he was to gain nothing, save the achievement of making Byng, through his appearance in *Candide*, far more famous in death than he ever was in life and of turning the ironic remark that he had been executed 'pour encourager les autres' into one of the very few phrases from French literature to have gained a proverbial currency in the English language.

After the outbreak of the Seven Years War, Voltaire's sense of the absurd aspect of warfare evolves considerably. Tales in that vein from the Duchess of Saxe-Gotha (D7040) might have heightened that impression, just as the Byng episode undoubtedly did. By February 1757 the acid tones of *Candide* are evident in a letter to the Englishman George Keate when Voltaire writes à propos of Byng: 'Your sailors are not polite', going on: 'If you want to see some fine battles, Germans killed by Germans and a few towns pillaged, it is up to you to enjoy this little entertainment in the spring' (D7162). In June 1757 the same spirit of sarcasm appears in a letter to the Duchess of Saxe-Gotha. There would be much unhappiness, he tells her, if the warring armies did not destroy at least fifty towns, reduce some fifty thousand families to beggary, and kill four or five hundred thousand men. 'We cannot yet say "All is well" but it is not going badly, and with time Optimism will be conclusively proven' (D7297).

In early 1757, then, the essential tone of *Candide* is already present in Voltaire's mind. Other details too are beginning to appear in his letters. The final destination of Candide and his little band in the garden outside Constantinople is already foreshadowed in March 1757, when Voltaire cites a comparison between the view he has over the lake from Lausanne with a similar outlook in Constantinople (D7213). The writer who had drawn this parallel, so suggestive to Voltaire's imagination, was the seventeenth-century explorer Jean-Baptiste Tavernier, who had travelled widely in the East before retiring to Switzerland not far from Voltaire's house in Lausanne. Louis XIV had been offended that Tavernier had settled in Switzerland, to which he had replied that he wanted to own something that belonged entirely to him. Not surprisingly, Voltaire felt a kinship with this earlier Frenchman who had also shaken the dust of France from off his feet in order to find genuine independence; he adds that 'I am finishing up as he did' (D7215). One sees here a complex interweaving of elements. Lausanne view = Constantinople view, thanks to Tavernier. As Voltaire is retired and free outside France, so too Candide in his final retreat in Turkey. Whether yet consigned to paper, the lineaments of the *dénouement* to the *conte* are all mentally in place by March 1757.

On 26 October 1757 Voltaire laments the death of Patu, who had visited him two years before. His obituary notice is simple and touching: 'il aimait tous les arts, et son âme était candide' (D7434). Thus appears our hero's name. When Voltaire introduces it at the beginning of the *conte* the conjunction is much the same: 'Sa physionomie annonçait son âme...on le nommait Candide'.[27] A vital step in the creation of the *conte* is prefigured here. Shortly afterwards on 9 November 1757 Thieriot is writing to Voltaire saying that they are as ignorant as 'des souris dans un vaisseau de l'intention de ceux qui le conduisent' (D7456).[28] This, as we have seen, is not the first time the image has come to Voltaire's mind, as he had himself used a similar expression to Frederick in 1736.[29] But Thieriot probably refreshed Voltaire's memory at a crucial moment, and his influence is seen in one of the most trenchant observations in *Candide* about divine Providence: 'Quand Sa Hautesse envoie un vaisseau en Egypte, s'embarrasse-t-elle si les souris qui sont dans le vaisseau sont à leur aise ou non?'[30]

Another important detail is added to the genesis of Voltaire's *conte* at the end of November 1757 when he receives a letter from the Margravine of Bayreuth describing the battle of Rossbach. She wrote:

Cette armée [i.e., prussienne] . . . fut rangée en ordre de bataille sur une ligne. Alors l'artillerie fit un feu si terrible que des Français . . . disent que chaque coup tuait ou blessait huit ou neuf personnes. La mousqueterie ne fit pas moins d'effet. Les Français avançaient toujours en colonne pour attaquer avec la baïonnette . . . L'infanterie . . . fut taillée en pièces et entièrement dispersée.

(This [Prussian] army was drawn up in battle order along a line. Then the artillery laid down such a terrible barrage that Frenchmen say . . . each shot killed or wounded eight or nine people. The musketry was no less efficacious. The French were still advancing in columns to attack with the bayonet . . . The infantry . . . were cut to pieces and totally scattered.)

(D7477)

This must surely be at the origin of Voltaire's account in *Candide* of the battle between the Bulgares and the Abares:

Rien n'était si beau, si leste, si brillant, si bien ordonné que les deux armées. . . . Les canons renversèrent d'abord à peu près six mille hommes de chaque côté; ensuite la mousqueterie ôta du meilleur des mondes environ neuf à dix mille coquins qui en infectaient la surface. La baïonnette fut aussi la raison suffisante de la mort de quelques milliers d'hommes.

(Nothing was as beautiful, as sprightly, as well ordered as the two armies. . . . The cannon first of all knocked over about six thousand men on either side; next the musketry removed from the best of worlds around nine to ten thousand rascals who were infecting its surface. The bayonet was also the sufficient cause of the deaths of a few thousand men.)[31]

The order of details is the same: the military line-up, the artillery, musketry, bayonet. Voltaire simply transforms an honest and poignant account into a display of ironic brilliance. The rôles are similarly distributed in both passages, and the overall effect of utter devastation is the same. But at Rossbach only the French were routed. It is part of Voltaire's strategy to ensure that both sides in his absurd and horrible battle are shot to pieces. The Margravine is able to offer further help a week later when writing to Voltaire about the starving soldiers who have fled after the defeat at Rossbach and are now wandering about everywhere (D7483). This time the impact upon *Candide* is less impressive, but it is true that Candide too flees without direction and runs out of food.[32]

Such are the details that have begun to accumulate by the beginning of December 1757. At the turn of the year the number of parallels increases strikingly. Voltaire's bitter memory of the Frankfurt incident where his niece had 'Four bayonets . . . in the stomach' (D7521) is renewed, as we have noticed, after Frederick had triumphed at Rossbach. This may be the starting point for the knife wound which the heroine of the *conte* Cunégonde receives in the side (Chapter VIII) or the account of her disembowelling by Bulgarian soldiers (Chapter IV). Voltaire advises the Genevan clergy not to react to the *Encyclopédie* article 'Genève': 'Que faut-il donc faire? Rien, se taire, vivre en paix . . .' (D7536, 27 December [1757]). The similarity is close with the dervish's brusque reply to Pangloss, who wants to know the truths of metaphysics: 'Que faut-il donc faire? dit Pangloss. – Te taire, dit le derviche.'[33] In January 1758 Voltaire is telling the Duchess of Saxe-Gotha that Prussians and the like are 'the children of the evil principle'

(D7554); we see here a further premonition of the Manichean Martin in *Candide*, who believes that God has abandoned this world to some evil being and cites war as one of his strongest arguments for believing so.[34] At the same time Voltaire is working on his history the *Essai sur les moeurs*. The topics to which he specifically refers include the English colonies in America and the Jesuits in Paraguay (D7559). Both enter into the make-up of *Candide*, Paraguay directly (Chapter XIV) and the State of Pennsylvania in the disguise of Eldorado (Chapter XVIII), that Utopia where, as in Pennsylvania, there are no judges, doctors or priests.[35] Just as, in Eldorado, the natives build a machine 'pour guinder [to hoist]' Candide and his companion Cacambo out of Eldorado,[36] so too does Voltaire on 26 January 1758 use the same somewhat uncommon verb in writing that 'we would hoist' a visitor over the mont Cenis to Turin if he should wish to pass by Geneva (D7603).

On 8 January 1758 a reference to the efficient manoeuvres of Frederick's troops, including 'le pas redoublé [at the double]' (D7565), compares with the well-drilled Bulgare in *Candide* who also knew how to 'doubler le pas' (Chapter II). Reference to the auto-da-fé recurs in a letter of 12 January (D7579). On the 15th mention is made of the mosques in Constantinople, as too of the Sultan's officers with the exotic title of 'azamoglans' (D7584); Cunégonde's brother is sent to the galleys for being found bathing with 'un jeune icoglan', and Pangloss for making advances to a pretty girl in a Constantinople mosque (Chapter XXVIII). On 29 January Voltaire sympathises with d'Alembert's problems over the *Encyclopédie*, adding that his colleague is a victim of the publishers: 'Vous avez travaillé pour des libraires' (D6708). So too in *Candide* has Martin suffered, and acquired his gloomy outlook on life, as the 'pauvre savant qui avait travaillé dix ans pour les libraires...'[37] Just as the 'Protestant ministers' of Surinam persecute Martin because they take him for a Socinian,[38] so too d'Alembert suffers persecution because his article 'Genève' had suggested that the Genevan pastors were Socinian. On 12 February Voltaire writes that the War is a labyrinth from which one can hardly escape except over dead bodies, and he expresses regret that the nations must fight so ruinously for 'quelques arpents de glace en Acadie [a few acres of ice in Acadia]', a reference to the battles between the French and English in North America (D7630). Candide leaves his own battle by crossing over heaps of dead (Chapter III), while Martin represents Voltaire's feeling of folly that England and France are at war for 'quelques arpents de neige vers le Canada'.[39] The next day Voltaire compares working on the *Encyclopédie* to rowing in the galleys (D7632); this latter occupation is what we find Pangloss and Cunégonde's brother doing near the end of the *conte*. Finally, Voltaire refers on 3 March to 'La canaille de vos convulsionnaires' when writing of the odious Jansenist fanatics who went into convulsions (D7660); 'la canaille convulsionnaire' is known to Martin also.[40]

These details, by their nature fragmentary, need to be assembled if one is to obtain a comprehensive view of Voltaire's state of mind during the period between late October 1757 and early March 1758. His letters, we can see, are full of allusions that are taken up, often without any virtual reworking, in *Candide*. The *conte* must have been taking shape in his mind during those months. More specifically, the passages cluster around certain areas of the story: the opening, and particularly the battle; the Eldorado episode; the appearance of Martin soon afterwards; and the concluding sections in and around Constantinople. Equally interesting, direct echoes of *Candide* more or less vanish from Voltaire's correspondence after the beginning of March 1758 and do not reappear until he pays a visit to the Elector Palatine at Schwetzingen four months later.

This visit, which takes him away from Geneva in July 1758 for about five weeks, appears to coincide with a change in Voltaire's mood that has not been sufficiently noted by his biographers. Until his departure he had led a relatively contented existence. A visitor to Geneva just before he left remarks on how he seemed younger, happier, healthier than before his stay in Prussia (D7784). But even so, a period is coming to an end in Voltaire's life. The disappointments with the Genevan clergy have had their effect and he wishes to leave the territory where they hold sway. The search is on once more to find a property which combines the maximum of security and independence. He thinks of Lorraine, which he had last seen at the time of Mme du Châtelet's death; as he writes to Saint-Lambert from Schwetzingen, he would like to place himself under the protection of King Stanislas (D7795). But though the latter appears to have been personally sympathetic to the proposal, he was well aware that he could not afford to sanction it without first seeking the approval of his son-in-law Louis XV (cf. D7787). The latter was to reply in August to Stanislas, clearly intimating his coolness on the matter (D7787, Commentary); and Voltaire thereafter was to look elsewhere for a home.

The visit to Schwetzingen, reluctantly undertaken, was made apparently with business in mind in order to invest money for optimum benefit.[41] Perhaps Voltaire's maritime losses through the activities of the British Navy had made the excursion indispensable. However, the journey permitted him also to sound out a number of influential people about returning to Lorraine or France, and this in the end may have been the more important reason.[42] Whatever the precise motives, it is clear that uncertainty about his future has re-entered Voltaire's life. For a period he is transported back to the climate of insecurity that prevailed during the years immediately preceding installation at Les Délices. Hopes of a return to Paris flicker briefly, and for that he is willing to do obeisance to the French King (e.g. D7762). But the nomadic life no longer brings him any pleasure at all. Although well fêted at Schwetzingen, he is also miserable and lonely. One of his letters to Mme Denis is a *cri de coeur* such as has not been heard in his correspondence for some years: 'No letters from you, it is heart-breaking, it is abominable. I write to you daily, and you abandon me. I have never missed you so much and never been so angry with you' (D7803). It is the eloquent complaint of a man homesick for Les Délices and above all for the one person there whose company is essential to him.

Was *Candide* elaborated under such unhappy circumstances? Did Voltaire perhaps take with him a sketch, drafted out some months before, such as we now know preceded the composition of *L'Ingénu*?[43] If so, he had probably written at least some sections in greater detail, as we have seen. But the composition of *Candide* may essentially date from the visit, when ample leisure time would have been available for it. It seems quite possible, as Voltaire's secretary appears to have made the first copy of the *conte* while at the château, the author then presenting it to his host.[44] But the work was not necessarily finished even then, and one biography of Voltaire recounts an incident, which must remain unverifiable, to the effect that it was completed in three days' concentrated work back at Les Délices.[45] However, Schwetzingen would seem to mark an important milestone in the genesis of the tale. When Voltaire wrote to Countess Bentinck in mid-August on his return journey that he had much to tell her when he saw her, adding that 'notre roman est singulier' (D7825), he may well have been referring obliquely to *Candide* as much as to personal experiences. At any rate, the phrase he uses: 'nous reprendrons le fil de nos aventures [we shall pick up the thread of our adventures]' is echoed by Voltaire's observation in *Candide* about Cunégonde's narration of her own troubles: 'Elle reprit ainsi le fil de son histoire.'[46]

Unless *Candide* were virtually finished before Voltaire's visit to Schwetzingen, which appears unlikely, one must view it as written not simply in a state of ambivalent feelings about Paris and Geneva nor as a work of detached irony by a happy man but as the composition of someone who was once more plunged into despairing gloom. When he returned to Geneva he received definitive news from d'Argental that Mme de Pompadour had declared him *persona non grata* at Court. Besterman rightly notes: 'it is from this moment that can be dated his spiritual severance from his fatherland' (D7836, Commentary). A genuine sadness prevails in this letter, betokening the same kind of personal vulnerability as he had shown at Schwetzingen regarding Mme Denis. The buoyancy which had been uppermost even when he was deploring the horrors of the War has vanished. Comments are more direct, less ironic: 'tout le monde est ruiné. . . . Ah quel siècle!' (D7842, 2 September 1758). 'Quel triste siècle' (D7846, 3 September 1758); 'Le naufrage paraît universel' (D7848, 5 September 1758). To the theme of shipwreck is added the despairing note: 'Une planche, vite . . . !' (D7839, 2 September 1758). It is the dark mood of the Lisbon storm, when the one selfless man in *Candide*, Jacques, is drowned, while the sailor who murdered him swims to safety (Chapter V).

One general factor must also not be overlooked in this pessimism. Voltaire is disheartened by the decline of French prestige and influence in the world. Concern is often expressed about cultural and military affairs together, as in a letter to d'Argental in March where he bewails the fact that since the battle of Rossbach 'everything has been in decline in our armies, as in the fine arts in Paris' (D7676). The *philosophe* had long been persuaded that *belles-lettres* in France were degenerating and that the French were living on past credit.[47] This kind of comment proliferates in 1758. Voltaire notes that every French play now is hissed in Europe (D7836). The observation about living off the glory of the previous century returns in a letter where the author links together a series of charges against the French: a shortage of talent in every field; a profusion of writings on war, the navy and trade, yet French ruin and defeat on land and sea; a plethora of mediocre minds who possess a little wit, but not a genius anywhere; persecution and calumny as the lot of any man of merit who appears in France (D7846). Voltaire's professed response is to turn his back on all these lamentable happenings and enjoy the asylum he has discovered. But the very intensity of his reactions indicates a man who once again feels the need to be *engagé*, even if as yet he has no clear idea whether or how he will achieve it. When he eventually undertook negotiations to buy the Châteaux of Tournay and subsequently of Ferney, both just outside Geneva on the French-Swiss border, was his only idea, as he put it to the vendor of

Tournay (President de Brosses), 'to die perfectly free' (D7871)? Or did he already have some inkling of what his new life would bring?

Be that as it may, the depressed tones of August and early September are closely related to the search for a new home. Voltaire approached de Brosses about Tournay on 9 September (D7853). A month later he has bought that château and, more important still for his future life, is about to buy the one at Ferney (D7896). He has taken a new decision, to renounce urban life (D7936). The tone of contentment begins to return to the correspondence. To his friend Formont he writes: 'I do not know of any situation preferable to mine' (D7888, [c. 3 October 1758]). True, he protests perhaps too much in his fulminations against a Paris that he can no longer hope to see; but elsewhere, too, the sense that the life of philosophers is much better than that of kings (D7936) and that he can now cultivate his garden in tranquillity (D7943) emerges clearly.

Thus far one might say that Voltaire is merely repeating in 1758 the search previously undertaken in 1755. But a remarkable letter of 18 November, the importance of which Besterman has rightly stressed, marks the beginning of a new and final period in Voltaire's life. He has been inspecting his new estate at Ferney and finding that there is more involved than the cultivation of plants. He has acquired peasants who depend on him. What is the state of the community? Half the land lies fallow, the *curé* has celebrated no marriages in seven years, the countryside is depopulated as people rush to nearby Geneva. Taxation (especially the salt-tax) destroys those who remain; either the peasants pay and are reduced to abject poverty, or they evade payment and are clapped in jail. 'It is heart-breaking to witness so many misfortunes. I am buying the Ferney property simply in order to do a little good there. . . . The prince who will be my liege lord should rather help me to drag his subjects out of the abyss of poverty, than profit from his ancient feudal rights ['du droit goth et visigoth des lods et ventes']' (D7946, 18 November 1758).

This is a new voice in Voltaire's letters. We have seen how many times he had sought to intervene on the social or political scene and been frustrated. Here at last the right opportunity in time and place comes to hand. By acquiring seigneurial rights he is freer, he says, than when he possessed only his house in Lausanne and his 'country cottage [guinguette]' in Geneva, where the people were 'a little arrogant' and the priests 'a little dangerous'; Ferney and Tournay have added 'deux grands degrés' to his happiness (D7976). The rôles of 'maçon' and 'jardinier' which he has long since arrogated to himself are now supplemented by a new one: 'seigneur' (D7985). Once again, as in 1755 (D6214), he claims that he is becoming a patriarch (D7970); this time the claim will have a firmer grounding. Already before he is even installed at Ferney he has taken up the cudgels against the *curé* of Moëns, who is the malefactor extorting moneys from Voltaire's peasants and forcing them to sell their own lands. His appeal to the diocesan bishop at Annecy (D7981, 16 December 1758) marks the beginning of a long campaign against the priest.

This note of social concern enters into *Candide*, but only just. From late August 1758 another spate of parallels with the *conte* is to be found in the correspondence: Westphalia (D7838); shipwreck (D7839, 7848, 7862); the earth covered with corpses and beggars (D7852) reminding us of Chapters III–IV; the cultivation of pineapples in India (D7875), as in Turkey in Chapter XXX; *te deums* as thanksgiving after battle (D7890, 7908, 7928): these and other phrases reminiscent of the *conte* suggest that the latter was in the forefront of Voltaire's mind up to early November. But most of these are not new and indicate no more than elaboration of the finished product. However, one episode, that of the black slave in Chapter XIX, is more important, because we now know that it did not figure in the earliest manuscript version of *Candide*.[48] René Pomeau has shown that the source for this passage lies in Voltaire's reading of Helvétius's *De l'esprit*, which contains strikingly similar references to slavery, around 18 October 1758 (cf. D7912).[49] Not that Voltaire was unaware of the horrors occurring to blacks in the colonies; he had already written about them in the *Essai sur les moeurs* the previous January.[50] But Helvétius recalled the institution of slavery to mind as one of the horrors which no comprehensive account of the world's evils should ignore. It also linked up for Voltaire with his new experiences as *seigneur de Ferney*.

This passage in *Candide* is surely the one where the most direct assault is made on the reader's conscience: 'This is the price you pay for eating sugar in Europe.'[51] It also leads to one of *Candide*'s few impassioned outbursts against Optimism.[52] But it is poorly integrated into the plot, as was almost inevitable given the date of its interpolation, and has no direct impact upon anything subsequent to it. An element of hesitation can be discerned on the author's part. It relates to the ambiguity of Voltaire's views on social commitment in the *conte*. The Ferney epoch with all its glorious activities in social protest and reform is only just opening after virtually the whole of *Candide* has been completed. One of the reasons for the unique tragi-comic quality of the tale must surely be sought in its period of gestation: the relative contentment of the Geneva years is beginning to dissolve as Voltaire begins work on it, a sharp decline in morale accompanies the Schwetzingen phase when it is generally thought to have been for the most part composed, and the prospect of a new era opening out, as yet full of possibility but of uncertainty too, is descried as it is finished. No biography of a writer can, or should, attempt to explain his art through his life. Voltaire's *Candide*, infinitely complex, savagely lucid, is the author's most brilliant of his innumerable attacks on the strongholds and methods of obscurantism. Like all such creations, it will not yield its ultimate secrets. The biographer, confronted by such mysteries, has but one useful function. By delineating the area where echoes from the world of *Candide* overlap into the world of Voltaire's daily life, he may hope to catch an element that went into the amalgam of forces creating the *conte*.

At the end of 1758, Voltaire tells d'Argental with pride that he has created for himself 'a rather nice kingdom' (D7988). At last he has his own principality: he is now both *roi* and *philosophe*. His installation at Tournay on Christmas Eve 1758 was of fitting dignity and pomp, with sound of cannon, fife and drum, all the peasants bearing arms and girls presenting flowers to his two diamond-bedecked nieces. 'M. de Voltaire', writes a spectator, 'was very pleased and full of joy . . . He was, believe me, very flattered' (D7998). Henceforth rank and authority will be used to advance social good. By the New Year Voltaire sees this as involving the overthrow of superstition (D8029); it is the tone of 'écrasez l'infâme', and the famous phrase itself will make its appearance in 1760 (D9006).[53] As *Candide* begins to enjoy, a few weeks later, the success which has never since deserted it, so too does Voltaire enter at last into his kingdom. In his sixty-fifth year, François-Marie Arouet has finally realised himself as M. de Voltaire.[54]

Plates

Voltaire frequented the Société du Temple while still a schoolboy, meeting there a circle of free-thinking epicureans

LEFT: Voltaire at 24 years of age, by Largillière. With his first play *Oedipe*, Voltaire was just beginning to establish himself as the leading tragic playwright of his day

BELOW: Voltaire spent two periods in the Bastille, the first (1717-18) lasting nearly a year

Frederick II of Prussia, by Antoine Pesne

Voltaire at 41 years of age, by La Tour

Mme du Châtelet, Voltaire's companion and collaborator for the last sixteen years of her life

Title page and frontispiece of the first edition of Voltaire's greatest scientific work

ELÉMENS
DE LA
PHILOSOPHIE
DE NEUTON,

Mis à la portée de tout le monde.

Par M^R. DE VOLTAIRE.

A AMSTERDAM;
Chez ETIENNE LEDET & Compagnie.
M. DCC. XXXVIII.

The château of Cirey, in
Champagne: Mme du Châtelet's
home, and also Voltaire's in the
period 1734-39 particularly

Voltaire moved to Les Délices on the outskirts of Geneva in 1755. The house is today the home of the Institut et Musée Voltaire

Voltaire's view of Geneva from Les Délices. *Collection Musée d'Art et d'Histoire de Genève*

Ferney, Voltaire's home from 1759 until his return to Paris in 1778: view from the west side

Voltaire in his study: oil painting after an original drawn by the Chevalier de Boufflers on a visit to Ferney in 1764-65

D'Alembert, by La Tour: founder, with
Diderot, of the *Encyclopédie* and one of the
leading *philosophes*

Rousseau, by La Tour

'Le Déjeuner de Ferney': the original was drawn by Denon during a visit to Ferney in July
1775. Mme Denis is seated at Voltaire's side; an engraving of the Calas family hangs on the
wall. Voltaire complained at being made to look like Lazarus at the rich man's feast, and
Denon later apologised

Voltaire being crowned at the Comédie Française, 30 March 1778, in the presence of Mme Denis and the Marquise de Villette

The return of Voltaire's remains to Paris on 11 July 1791. The house where he died is to the immediate left of the bridge

5 Ferney, and *L'Ingénu*

With Voltaire ensconced at Ferney the high tide of his career as a writer is reached. René Pomeau's dictum that he lived in order to write and publish[1] acquires its full meaning during these last twenty years. Voltaire's biographer is condemned to labour after him, marvelling and constantly frustrated. The need for rigorous selection of material now becomes imperative.

We shall take up the main narrative again in the autumn of 1765. Voltaire, frustrated by squabbles with President de Brosses at Tournay, has given up going there and let out the property to others. Ferney is now his true and only home. Not that Les Délices had been abandoned as soon as Ferney and Tournay were acquired in 1758; Voltaire kept on using it for many years and definitively quitted it only in December 1764. But Les Délices suffered from the close and suffocating attentions of the Genevan clergy. Ferney, geographically close but part of France and therefore not subject to the authority of the Republic, yet well removed from Paris and near the border if sudden flight became necessary, was a different world. Here Voltaire could launch the crusades that were to make him the most famous of all Frenchmen in his lifetime.

It is the campaign against *l'infâme*, especially as waged on behalf of persecuted French Protestants like Calas and Sirven, which has ensured Voltaire a permanent place in the annals of great fighters for justice. But other projects, not crucial to life and limb though equally ambitious and consuming, must not be forgotten. One such was the aim to edit the plays of Pierre Corneille, his distinguished predecessor as tragedian in the previous century. When in 1760 Voltaire discovered that Marie Corneille, descendant of the great playwright, was living in poverty, his susceptibilities were affronted at this latest proof that the French public cared not a whit about their cultural heritage. Once aroused he acted with characteristic decisiveness. Marie was invited to live at Ferney and Voltaire looked around for ways and means of assuring her future through a good marriage and handsome dowry. The practical problem coincided with the author's desire to see her ancestor properly remembered; thus it was that with Marie under his roof he began the monumental edition, adorned with lengthy commentaries.

The subsequent *Commentaires sur Corneille* proved a spectacular success. Techniques employed long ago during his English stay to find subscribers for *La Henriade* were once more put to use, to such effect that the whole of enlightened Europe, including twenty-one royal houses (among them that of France) was numbered among its patrons. Twenty-five hundred copies were printed for the first edition (1764), grossing 180,000 francs in receipts, of which 52,000 in clear profit went to Marie Corneille. It is a signal instance of Voltaire's generosity towards someone in need. As David Williams makes clear in his excellent critical edition of the work,[2] Voltaire's triumph bears ample testimony to the range of social contacts which he now enjoyed throughout Europe, as also to his subtle powers of persuasion and limitless energy. No episode in his life better illustrates his capacity to combine cultural activities with business flair.

Voltaire's decision to invite Marie to live in his house, though motivated by the most disinterested of impulses so far as she was concerned, did not escape the strictures of captious gossip. Amongst those who viewed the journey of Marie Corneille to Ferney with a hostile eye was the journalist Elie Fréron. It would have been surprising to find matters otherwise. Since 1749 there had existed between the two writers a feud such that, in course of time, it conferred upon Fréron the honour of perhaps outranking all other contemporaries as the object of Voltaire's implacable hatred. From 1749 until his death in 1776 Fréron was editor of an influential journal; from 1754 he ran the *Année littéraire*, appearing on average three times a month. The continuity of such a literary outlet, the vigorous expression of its editor's views, the omnivorous curiosity he displayed, the inexpensive cost of the review and the degree of its penetration throughout France and Europe, all these factors provided Fréron with a position of immense influence. It has been justifiably argued[3] that the *Année littéraire* rivalled the *Encyclopédie* and its group for two decades, evolving from about 1770 into a sort of alternative French Academy, the established body having by then become the preserve of the *philosophes*.

Fréron, like Voltaire, championed many enlightened causes: inoculation, commerce, scientific development, religious toleration. But his support of Christian absolutism necessarily placed him in the opposite camp, and he came increasingly to epitomise for Voltaire the whole movement of *anti-philosophie*. Were this all, however, it would not suffice to explain the magnitude of the feud, which lasted as long as did the two opponents, inducing each to commit acts of demeaning malignity at his opponent's expense. With Desfontaines Voltaire's fury had been briefer, with Jean-Jacques Rousseau and Frederick more equivocal because he could not altogether ignore that each had a measure of genius in him. But the quarrel with Fréron, lacking such restraints, took on with time a quality of personal obsessiveness. In 1760 Voltaire published a number of *Anecdotes sur Fréron* so scurrilous that before the end of his life he would himself admit how disgusting they were (letter to d'Alembert, D20626, 8 April 1777). True, Fréron emerges even more badly from the duel which, to his discredit, he had been the one to initiate. But our particular interest must be to enquire why Voltaire, even when at the height of his fame and in no serious danger from Fréron's sallies, could not treat his opponent with the Olympian scorn one might logically have expected of him.

Naturally, Fréron's malevolence was itself an important causal factor. The former's carping, ungenerous approach is well exemplified in the Calas case. When Voltaire had succeeded in 1765 in gloriously rehabilitating Jean Calas's memory (alas! too late to save his life), Fréron undertook to argue that the *philosophe* had acted too precipitately without concern for all the facts, implying that Voltaire was moved only by considerations of personal glory. Not only did he forget that if the circumstances of the case were as ambiguous as he himself conceded, the presumption must be one of innocence; his initiative smacks too of a grudging parasitism, which can only call in question, without any supporting evidence, a noble and courageous crusade. By bespattering his opponent, his act of sophistry is in danger, as M. Balcou sees, of bespattering the dead victim and his persecuted family as well.[4] Such a negative attitude could hardly fail to outrage, especially so volatile an opponent as Voltaire.

But the grievances go deeper than this. For Fréron is almost an alter ego to Voltaire; like his enemy he possesses an untiring commitment to his cause, an unremitting aggressiveness towards the institutions and people he attacks, a propensity for the critical thrust. Above all he shares Voltaire's gift for satire and irony, and this, directed at Voltaire, is unforgivable. The latter was not one to take kindly, for instance, to being described in witty terms as a courtesan, displaying all the graces and talents but also the total lack of principles revealed by the 'femmes galantes'.[5] We have seen the distress occasioned by Desfontaines's diatribe *Voltairomanie* when it reached Cirey in 1738. Fréron was to inject similar poison, but with a consistent regularity that spanned nearly thirty years.

Such calumny Voltaire could never tolerate. Throughout his life he referred in sombre terms to the fickle public. Why, he writes to Formont in the 1730s, does one bother to please in order to win its empty accolade? And yet, 'what would we do without this pipe dream? It is as necessary to the soul as food to the body' (D526, [c. 12 December 1732]). He cannot but seek for praise; and so he cannot but suffer when instead he receives blame. As a liberal he wanted the censor to act with tolerance – except for defamatory works; for such writings were criminal.[6] Mme de Graffigny had glimpsed at Cirey the vindictiveness of Voltaire's hatred for those like Desfontaines who had attacked him: 'I have just emerged from a terrible conversation on the subject in which we tried to persuade him to scorn them. Oh human frailty! he is beyond reasoning when he talks of them . . . as soon as you cross him he is ill' (D1700, [?20 December 1738]). A little later, she concludes that he is the unhappiest man in the world: 'he knows his own worth and approval is almost a matter of indifference to him; but for the same reason one word from his opponents puts him into what is called despair; it is his sole preoccupation and plunges him into bitterness . . .' (D1807, [c. 20 January–8 February 1739]). Voltaire's Genevan doctor Théodore Tronchin was to make similar observations nearly twenty years later, albeit more acidly:

He has become the slave of his admirers, his happiness has been dependent on them . . . he has grown used to praises. . . . Habit has taken away from them any illusory value, since it is vanity which sets store by them, and vanity which then discounts what it possesses, and overrates what it does not; from which it follows in short that La Beaumelle's insults give more pain than the acclaim of the groundlings has ever given pleasure.

(D6985, to Jean-Jacques Rousseau, 17 September 1756)

Roland de la Platière carried away the same basic impression from a visit to Ferney in 1769, expressing scepticism at Voltaire's profession of happiness because the latter made it too closely dependent upon society.[7] All these witnesses concur in glimpsing a dark side to Voltaire's soul (Tronchin links it to fear of death), a void never wholly filled by public admiration, no matter how great. Even as early as 1733, he links calumny and envy to a dark vision of internecine warfare throughout the animal world,[8] while in 1732 he had already yearned for the ideal colony of three or four men of letters, all living together without jealousy (D493). Do these attitudes relate to his hypochondria, a crying out for comfort and reassurance as we saw demonstrated in the love-letters to Mme Denis? Certainly, a melancholy sensitivity formed an essential element of Voltaire's make-up. Indeed, without a sense of the vanity of all things, one basic aspect of *Candide* would have been missing.

But it would not do to reduce Voltaire to a Hamlet forever brooding on whips and scorns. Such a man would have been incapable of rallying his fellow-*philosophes* to crush *l'infâme*. This note sounds loud and clear, explicitly repeated during 1761 in particular. Voltaire will, for instance, advocate ardently, though always unsuccessfully, the admission of Diderot to the Académie Française. His relations with the Encyclopedists remain, however, detached though benevolent. He is persuaded that the *Encyclopédie* will not prove to be the philosophic instrument of victory against the Establishment. It is too large, too unwieldy, too expensive, he tells d'Alembert: 'never will twenty folio volumes produce a revolution; it is the portable little books at 30 sous which are to be feared. If the Gospel had cost 1200 sesterces, the Christian religion would never have been established' (D13235, 5 April [1766]). Besides, the great Dictionary is fatally compromised in Voltaire's eyes because it is edited and published in Paris; we shall shortly witness an abortive attempt by him to lead his fellow-*philosophes* into a free colony in exile. His perspective of the battle from Ferney was necessarily different, and it distorted his relationships with his Parisian *confrères*. When the dramatist Palissot satirised the Encyclopedists in his play *Les Philosophes*, which enjoyed a *succès de scandale* on its first performance at the Comédie Française on 2 May 1760, Voltaire (whom Palissot had been careful to exempt from his attacks) was slow to rally to their defence; he wrote to the playwright refuting his strictures point by point, but in a generally indulgent and friendly tone (D8958). Only on 23 June does he act in full awareness of his position in the philosophic movement, when he composes a letter of rebuke to Palissot for allying himself with the most ardent enemies of the *Encyclopédie* (D9005), and it was several weeks more before he made public his total disagreement with the spirit informing *Les Philosophes*, when he produced his *Recueil des facéties parisiennes*. But essentially it was not Voltaire's fight, as it was Diderot's; the former's energies were directed elsewhere.[9]

These energies found an effective focus in the persecuted French Protestants of the Midi. Voltaire's views on Protestantism, as we have seen when they concerned its British or Swiss adherents, were complex, ambiguous and generally doomed to frustration if he became tempted to view them as the vanguard of the Enlightenment. But judicial murder was horrible to him, wherever it occurred and for whatever reason, as his intervention in the Byng affair had demonstrated. From 1761 Catholic intolerance towards Protestants in the Toulouse area developed a new virulence, largely in reaction to the social and economic conditions created by the Seven Years War.[10] In September 1761 a Protestant minister, François Rochette, was arrested in a village near Montauban and found guilty of having carried on his pastoral duties within the Huguenot assemblies; he was publicly hanged in Toulouse on 19 February 1762. Voltaire, appealed to for assistance by a local Protestant, intervened with his friend the duc de Richelieu, who was then governor of the neighbouring province of Guyenne, but nothing could be done to save Rochette.[11] It was however a significant curtain-raiser to Voltaire's activities when he learned of the execution of Jean Calas.

Jean Calas, a respected Huguenot tradesman in cloth goods in Toulouse, had four sons, of whom the eldest, Marc-Antoine, was found dead in the shop beneath the family home on 13 October 1761. The circumstances were suspicious; a rope mark around the dead man's neck indicated that he had either hanged himself or been strangled. The family added to the suspicion by at first agreeing that it was a case of murder – not too surprisingly, as the public humiliations visited upon the body of a suicide were savage, the corpse being dragged through the streets and then thrown onto the municipal dump, while the dead man's property was confiscated. It has to be added that the precise reason for Marc-Antoine's death remains uncertain even today, though the weight of evidence suggests suicide.[12] Unfortunately for the Calas family, the deceased was reported to be ready for conversion to Catholicism, and it was tempting to believe, in a city where sectarian passions were running high, that he had been killed to prevent this. The family's earlier prevarications only reinforced this belief. Jean Calas was condemned to be broken on the wheel after previously being tortured. He went to his death on 9 March 1762 maintaining total innocence; the rest of the family was dispersed.

Voltaire learned of this execution before the end of the month; the news of Rochette's execution had also reached him during March. At first he believed Calas guilty (D10382, 22 March 1762), but soon he

became aware of the condemned man's heroic death, of the complicated circumstances surrounding the alleged murder of his son, of the
fact that the judges had voted for the capital sentence by the narrow
majority of eight to five (D10387, 10389). By early April he concluded
that a terrible injustice had been perpetrated (D10406). Thereafter,
the fight to clear Calas's name would occupy Voltaire's close attentions for three years, until the victim's memory was rehabilitated by
the royal body of the *maîtres des requêtes* at Versailles on 9 March 1765,
the third anniversary of his death. It was to prove the greatest of all
Voltaire's individual triumphs.

From 1762, *tolérance* becomes one of his key words.[13] In 1763 appears
his *Traité sur la tolérance* (written in 1762), which moves from Calas's
assassination to an eloquent plea for religious toleration. By 1764 he is
involved in another case of French Meridional intolerance with many
similarities to that of Calas. Elisabeth Sirven, a new convert to Catholicism, was found dead in a well in January 1762. Her Huguenot family
were accused of having murdered her and a warrant was issued for their
arrest. Her father Pierre Paul Sirven did not wait to encounter the same
fate as Jean Calas; he gathered together his wife and two other daughters and fled to Switzerland. In their absence the local judges sentenced
all but one daughter to hanging, the sentence being executed in effigy.
From the start Voltaire knew that this case would be more difficult. The
public, he recognised, tires quickly of repetition (D12923, 8 October
1765) and, as he put it ironically, 'unfortunately no one was broken on
the wheel' (D12969, 7 November [1765]). This time the campaign was
more drawn-out, less satisfyingly dramatic; but Voltaire eventually
succeeded in obtaining an acquittal in 1771 and rehabilitation of the
Sirvens in 1775.

So, although the fight for enlightenment is arduous, victory seems
certain. Books are appearing now, he tells d'Alembert, that could not
have been circulated in manuscript form to friends forty years before;
what is more, they can run through six editions in the brief space of
eighteen months (D12937, 16 October [1765]). He clearly has in mind
his own *Dictionnaire philosophique*, first published in 1764, that *vade mecum*
of devastating criticism of the doctrines and practices inherent in the
Catholic Church and in the Ancien Régime which allowed such an
institution independent sway. No one was better attuned than Voltaire
to the mood of the times, and he rightly judged that the success of such a
bombshell meant that *l'infâme* was on the defensive if not in retreat. As
he well knew in recommending the *Dictionnaire* (though careful as usual
with such combustible material to attribute its authorship elsewhere),

the work was so easy to read because of its many brief entries, and was therefore all the more dangerous (D12939, 16 October 1765). He accepts that he will not succeed in obtaining complete religious toleration in France during his lifetime, but he will at least have laid the foundations and helped *philosophie* to gain the upper hand over barbaric superstition (D13224, 28 March 1766). Indeed, he is more hopeful of the French provinces than of Paris itself, where there is too much dissipation and too little time for reading and learning. In ten years, he says, he thinks it quite possible that toleration will be established in that centre of reaction Toulouse (D13369, 22 June 1766). So the *philosophes* must work in unity. Voltaire exhorts d'Alembert: 'preach and write, fight, convert, render the fanatics so odious and contemptible that the government is ashamed to support them' (D13374, 26 June [1766]). It is the voice of leadership and dedication to the struggle.

In its intellectual honesty Voltaire's attitude is explicitly different from that of his free-thinking predecessor Fontenelle who had reportedly stated in a famous phrase that if he held the truth enclosed in his hands he would not open them. For Voltaire such an approach is cowardly and useless; by following it his generation would still be subjected to the most horrible fanaticism (D13355, [c. 15 June 1766]). Yet even so, he did not advocate universal enlightenment. The *peuple*, by which he meant those engaged in manual labour, could not in his opinion find the time for education; 'it seems to me essential that there should be ignorant beggars'. It is not the labourer whom one should teach, he tells his friend Damilaville, but the *bon bourgeois* who is a town-dweller (D13232, 1 April 1766). Does this argue a cynical indifference toward the masses? Surely not. For Voltaire the advance of progress is slow and hesitant; to extend education indiscriminately without proper deliberation is to risk opening Pandora's box. Cultural improvement should filter downwards from the top, beginning with the little band of *philosophes* and philosophic monarchs. But this does not bring him back to the position of a Fontenelle, who regarded enlightenment as an aristocratic fief. Voltaire did not wish to keep the populace in a state of brute ignorance. On the contrary, the lower orders should be weaned away from the kind of unthinking fanaticism that produced would-be assassins like Damiens; they too should be taught a religion devoid of superstition and based on the principle of a good God who offers rewards and punishments. As he goes on to add in the important letter to Damilaville cited above, one should teach virtue to the people but not whether, for example, the Jesuits or the Jansenists are right. The masses should be trained to become good workmen rather than theologians.

Much of this may sound cautious and even an apology for the propertied classes. But one must never forget Voltaire's empirical realism. He fought for specific reforms within a foreseeable future against a régime that committed scandalous injustices. Much more liberal are the theories of Diderot, Condorcet and d'Holbach, who wished to make education available to all. Yet in practice it was the apparently less radical Voltaire who had indulged in political activity and become *l'homme aux Calas*, who showed the way to freedom of the press by the very fact as well as tenor of his innumerable writings. Voltaire dreaded any sudden upset of the *status quo* that might precipitate bloody revolution; but the whole trend of his advocacy of legislative equality, more humane taxation, reform of the criminal code, constituted an irreversible movement towards social betterment for all classes of Frenchmen.[14]

An admirable instance of his interest in the common man appears during this period around 1765. Voltaire, still fascinated by Geneva, was drawn into the city's political troubles as they began to increase from about two years earlier. The city's inhabitants were divided into five groups, of whom only two, the Bourgeois and the Citoyens, enjoyed the right to vote, while the Citoyens alone could hold political office; the rest of the community, amounting to well over ninety per cent of the population, were completely disenfranchised. Within this self-perpetuating oligarchy existed an even smaller group of influential families who effectively controlled the little republic through the Petit Conseil, consisting of twenty-five members. Constitutional quarrels had occurred earlier in the century, but a settlement mediated from outside by representatives of France, Berne and Zurich had been reached in 1738, and this established peace for a whole generation though, as we have seen, d'Alembert's *Encyclopédie* article 'Genève' had aroused controversy in the interim on religious and social grounds. The appearance of Rousseau's *Emile* and *Contrat Social* in 1762 led to their condemnation by the Petit Conseil as being seen to be critical of the *status quo*. The following year a representation was made by a group protesting against this decision and resurrecting the old claims for a more democratic form of government; it was quickly rejected, the Petit Conseil being unwilling to concede any compromise arrangements whatsoever. The quarrel developed apace through 1764, with important statements of the aristocratic and *représentant* positions respectively by Jean-Robert Tronchin and Jean-Jacques Rousseau. Voltaire, despite his aversion for the latter and long friendship for the former, found himself gradually shifting his political stance. By October 1765 he is writing to the d'Argentals that he is now leaning towards the democrats; the Petit Conseil, he feels, are losing all sense of reason (D12933); the magistrates are ever seeking an extension of their power, he tells d'Alembert, whereas the people try only to avoid oppression (D12937).

This new alignment was accompanied by new gestures. The *représentants*, made aware of Voltaire's sympathies, came to consult him at Ferney. Writing to Jacob Tronchin, a member of the Petit Conseil, he rejected the suggestion that he had been provocative, claiming that his sole aim was reconciliation and that he would like to invite members from both sides to meet together over dinner at his table (D12976, [13 November 1765]). The Petit Conseil replied politely but intransigently that no discussion was possible on the Genevan constitution, hence such a dinner party would be futile. But Voltaire continued to hope that he had a rôle to play as conciliator, quite opposite to the inflammatory part which Rousseau had taken while still in Geneva (D12988, 13001). He became involved in technical questions, drawing up a plan of pacification. What number of people, for instance, should be necessary to oblige the Petit Conseil to summon a Conseil Général of all the Bourgeois and Citoyens? Voltaire proposed seven hundred, arguing that the Conseil Général would itself number no more than thirteen hundred at most (D13006).

But Voltaire's aid was not to be invoked. Hennin, the new French Resident arriving in Geneva in December 1765, was soon reporting to the duc de Praslin, France's foreign minister, that Voltaire was unduly involved in Genevan problems (D13048, Commentary). At the end of the month, the Petit Conseil rejected the *philosophe*'s scheme for pacification, repeating their assertion that there could be no compromise on the constitution (D13065, Commentary). Hennin felt that Voltaire had become too close a supporter of the Bourgeois (D13094, Commentary).

Thus far, Voltaire had not advanced beyond identifying himself with the propertied classes, albeit on the liberal side. But when in 1766 the Petit Conseil decided to invite France, Berne and Zurich as in 1738 to mediate, another group appealed to Voltaire, the disenfranchised Natifs through their leader Georges Auzière (D13240). In response, Voltaire composed for them a *compliment* to the mediators and helped them to draw up their *mémoire*. This *compliment* was then printed with characteristic Voltairean celerity and a thousand copies run off. The authorities were not pleased at this publication of an address that should never even have been pronounced, and the printer was arrested and briefly imprisoned.[15]

In the event, the Natifs were too unskilled in the ways of diplomacy to register any effect upon the outcome. Voltaire's advice has a touchingly paternalist air about it; they must keep their *mémoire* brief to avoid tedium and maintain the possibility of adding new arguments later if the mediators find their first initiative sufficiently modest (D13263, [22 or 23 April 1766]). But when the delegation of four Natifs who had approached the arbitrators confessed that Voltaire had been their literary adviser, the chevalier de Taulès (secretary to the French mediator) conveyed to Voltaire the mediators' displeasure at his interference and the threat that the French foreign minister would be informed if he continued. If Taulès is to be believed, Voltaire was thunderstruck at this show of force (D13274, Commentary). By 30 April Auzière was in prison, and Voltaire could do no more than plead for mercy on his and the others' behalf (D13275). Thus the attempts of the Natifs to secure some representation for themselves in the government of Geneva proved stillborn, Voltaire, feeling that he had angered all parties in the city, withdrew from active participation in their affairs (D13294).

At the time, this intervention in Geneva represented the wrong kind of commitment for the *philosophe*. Part of his land lay within Genevan territory, which offered some justification for his expressed desire to maintain peace within the republic. But in general his actions have a gratuitously meddlesome quality about them, serving only to exasperate those possessing a direct stake in the future of Geneva. Even so, there were to be later occasions when he could demonstrate his genuine concern for the Natifs. The mediators failed to find an acceptable formula, their peace plan being decisively rejected by the Conseil Général in December 1766. Unrest continued, breaking out into violence involving some of the Natifs in 1770 and leading to the flight of a number of them from Geneva. Some came to settle at Ferney, where Voltaire furnished them with homes and work, notably in the watchmaking and silk industries. Here is the practical man of action seen at his truest, when he has the capacity to affect fortunes, turning the masses, as he had put it, into good secular workmen rather than priests.

The expressions of confidence in the progress of *les lumières* that we have been noticing in Voltaire's letters during 1766 run consistently through the first half of the year. When he writes to Mme d'Epinay on 6 July, he has the usual message to proclaim: 'True knowledge necessarily brings tolerance. . . . In many things we are the disciples of the

English, we shall in the end equal our masters' (D13393). The very next letter in the Besterman Correspondence, written the following day to Damilaville, strikes a different note: 'My dear brother, my heart is stricken. . . . I am tempted to go and die in a foreign land where men are less unjust. I hold my peace, I have too much to say' (D13394). The dramatic change occurs because he has just learnt that the chevalier de La Barre had been put to death.

In February 1766 the nineteen-year-old chevalier had been convicted of certain acts of sacrilege in Abbeville, including the mutilation of a wooden crucifix, failing to remove his hat when a religious procession bearing the Sacrament passed by and uttering blasphemies, and was condemned to be burned at the stake. Despite appeals to the Parlement of Paris the verdict was upheld, and on 1 July La Barre, after being tortured at length, died courageously. His companion d'Etallonde, similarly accused, avoided a similar fate through taking flight. This case was in some respects more terrible than the Calas affair, as Voltaire was himself to argue (e.g., D15044, to Beccaria, 30 May 1768). For one may at least concede that the evidence in the Calas case was confusing and that, if Calas had really been guilty of murder, the implementation of the capital penalty would in no way have been incompatible with eighteenth-century justice. The La Barre sentence cannot be justified along these lines. It was the relationship of the punishment to the crime which was so particularly odious.

Voltaire appears to have heard about the case from Hennin on 21 June. At first he was hopeful that the Paris Parlement, by delaying the signing of the sentence, was giving the parents time to obtain a commutation of sentence from the King (D13371). But La Barre was also rumoured to have confessed that he had been influenced by the Encyclopedists, and this too was worrying. When the news came through that the sentence had been carried out, Voltaire's immediate reaction was to seek more information from his niece the marquise de Florian. Who were these men, how old, what did they do for a living? Had they a record of lunacy? Were they drunk when they committed their acts of sacrilege (D13396)? By a week later, he has discovered that the punishment was even more horrible, as family jealousies in Abbeville had also played a part (D13409). The poor chevalier was badly defended in court, the King had not known the facts on which he would surely have based a pardon, the defendant was condemned for no offence covered expressly by law, and no fewer than ten of his twenty-five judges had not voted for the death penalty. Should a majority of five be enough to destroy in horrible torments a young gentleman guilty only of folly

(D13410)? The correspondence resounds with shock and horror; La Barre becomes for a time as obsessive a theme as had been the Lisbon earthquake. The clock seems to have been put back to the worst days of barbarism; even the Inquisition would not have been so cruel (D13428, 13516). When d'Alembert writes to Voltaire using a black irony worthy of *Candide*, the latter rounds on him: 'Ah my dear friend, is this the time for laughter?' (D13440, 23 July [1766]). The same day he writes to the actor Lekain that his indignation is so strong he cannot settle down to reread the tragedies in which the latter is playing (D13444). As with the first reaction to the Lisbon disaster, Voltaire's attitude is one of unmediated pity and horror. One might well argue that he was not primarily an ironist by temperament; the detached view took time and distance to elaborate when he was deeply moved.

France, then, was not so far advanced towards the light of reason as he had thought. The French are monkeys who frequently change into tigers (D13428). Both frivolous and cowardly, they 'groan, keep silent, go to supper, forget' (D13485). So Voltaire begins to regret that he has settled in a country where such barbarous acts are committed in cold blood by people on their way to dinner (D13420). Flight from French soil seems the only practical solution. Indeed, a week after hearing of the chevalier's death Voltaire had moved to Rolle, on the shores of Lake Léman halfway between Geneva and Lausanne; a rare journey for him of such length in the 1760s. But this time he does not seem to envisage solitary exile. It is consistent with his attitude of recent years towards his fellow-Encyclopedists that he should want them to follow him into a *philosophe* society in a freer land. A possible place for such a colony exists at Cleves, to which Frederick warmly welcomes him (D13402). There they could publish and export without hindrance their views to the world. Voltaire appeals to Damilaville, arguing in impassioned terms that two or three years of such an existence would be enough to bring about the great revolution in ideas (D13449, 25 July 1766). To d'Alembert he points out that the latter's comfortable existence in Paris is dearly bought: 'You have connections, pensions, you are in chains' (D13485 [*c*. 10 August 1766]).

But the key figure to be persuaded was Diderot, who had recently seen through the *Encyclopédie* single-handedly to the end after d'Alembert's withdrawal in 1758. Voltaire approached him on 23 July; Diderot, who saw matters differently, took his time about answering, and his reply did not arrive until 7 November. Although Voltaire kept alive the idea a little longer, Diderot's letter when it came crushed any real hope of a move to Cleves. Diderot eloquently acknowledges all the arguments for quitting Paris, he admits his inertia in staying, as also his delusive sense of security; besides, he has a wife, daughter, friends. It is a gracious, self-deprecating letter, but it closes the door upon Voltaire's utopic appeals. For good or ill Diderot is fated to live his life out with all the compromises enjoined by a social existence in Paris. Voltaire, by contrast, has become the philosophic king in exile, whose intellectual and literary way of life is now geared to the audacious firebrand literature which he can dare to publish from afar. Diderot's letter destroys his last expectation of a concerted attack upon *l'infâme*. His fellow-*philosophes* will continue to prefer their comforts, their connections and their chains.

In these circumstances one of Voltaire's most important *contes*, *L'Ingénu*, came to be written. This tale of a naïve and uncivilised young man, who arrives in France in 1689 after being brought up by the Huron tribe in Canada, allows its author full play in depicting the contrast between a healthy man of nature and sophisticated but corrupt French society. Being of French blood, he is baptised into the Catholic faith by his Breton relatives, with the beautiful Mlle de St Yves acting as his godmother. The two fall in love; but a woman may not marry her godson, and St Yves is placed in a convent beyond his reach. The Ingénu decides to go to Versailles and plead his case there. On his way he falls in with Huguenots at Saumur. They eloquently describe their oppressed situation and the Huron promises to take up their cause as well. But at Versailles he falls foul of authority and is himself placed in the Bastille. St Yves, now released from the convent, follows him to the Court and succeeds in obtaining his freedom, but only by giving herself to the governmental minister in charge; and the knowledge of this deed destroys her, even when the Ingénu is restored to her side. She dies; the Ingénu, though strongly tempted to commit suicide, survives to become an excellent officer.

The *conte*, as can be seen, deals with the effect of persecution upon someone endowed, because of his special background, with exceptional determination to pursue his own rights as a free individual. Though set nearly a hundred years earlier, it clearly has contemporary relevance, springing from Voltaire's experiences of many judicial scandals in the 1760s, but notably the Calas and Sirven trials and most strikingly of all the La Barre affair. Memories of La Barre's execution were still very painful at the time of writing *L'Ingénu*, and many details of the La Barre case have been integrated into the story.[16] Though Calas and Sirven were Protestants while La Barre was, at least nominally, a Catholic, they were all alike in being persecuted, and Voltaire lumps them together in this regard when writing to the duc de Richelieu (D13560, 15 September 1766). Echoes of *L'Ingénu* begin to occur in the correspondence from late July 1766. In two letters of 25 July Voltaire writes that according to report La Barre would have become 'un excellent officer' (D13448, 13449), which is the phrase that appears in *L'Ingénu* about its hero's eventual destiny.[17] In August Voltaire enquires about La Chalotais, the Breton *parlementaire* who had been imprisoned for rebellion (D13498, 16 August 1766); here may be the seeds that helped to give the Ingénu a Breton background. But these are fragmentary details. One may feel that more of the mental climate of the *conte* is revealed in the letter of 15 September to Richelieu already mentioned, when Voltaire talks of being 'necessarily surrounded by the persecuted who merge together around me'. Indeed, perhaps the truly seminal notion is stated in a letter written apparently a little later: 'Could one not write some book that might be read with some pleasure, by the very people who do not like to read, *a book which might conduce hearts to compassion?*' (D13641, [October–November 1766]).[18]

An interesting series of references occurs from October 1766 that does not seem to have been noticed by previous commentators on *L'Ingénu*. On 8 October Voltaire tells Richelieu that the latter's young protégé Claude Gallien has arrived at Ferney, and that he finds him 'vif mais bon enfant' (D13602).[19] This description would fit well the eponymous hero of the *conte*, who has a mind both 'vive' and clear because formed by nature alone.[20] On his side, Voltaire asks Richelieu for help with Despinasse, one of the Protestants who had grievously suffered for his faith, having spent twenty-three years in the galleys for giving hospitality to a pastor. If Voltaire's mind, particularly when writing to Richelieu, was running much on mitigating the oppressions visited upon the Protestants, it would not be too improbable to see in Richelieu's protégé a model for the hero of his tale about persecutions. The resemblances are heightened when Voltaire next writes to the duke on 28 October. Although Gallien has little taste for Christianity, he has 'infiniment d'esprit, une grande lecture, une imagination toute de feu, une mémoire qui tient du prodige, une pétulance et une étourderie bien plus grandes. Mais il n'est question que de cultiver et corriger. Laissez-moi faire' (D13632).[21] All these characteristics fit the Ingénu, and in some cases the resemblances are textual: the hero has 'un grand fond d'esprit',[22] 'une mémoire excellente',[23] quickly learning almost the whole New Testament by heart; just as Voltaire was educating Gallien, so the Ingénu's Breton relatives felt that 'il fallait l'instruire'.[24] As with the Huron, Gallien's face and wit gain him easy access to a stranger's house. Above all, the two are candid in the same way. Voltaire tells Richelieu that Gallien 'me dit tout ce qu'il pense'. The Ingénu has acquired his name, he himself says, because 'je dis toujours naïvement ce que je pense'[25] and the phrase is repeated in much the same form later.[26] Even Gallien's reading has a bearing on L'Ingénu. The sole book he has brought with him from Paris is the Amours du Père La Chaise. This Jesuit father makes several appearances in the tale; in one of them he is found to be closeted with his mistress.[27] It may seem presumptuous to suggest that Voltaire needed to depend upon a chance visitor to Ferney to provide him with some of the seminal inspiration for the hero of a major conte. Yet the parallels are so suggestively close as not to be easily dismissed. As André Delattre pointed out, Voltaire had a weak capacity for aesthetic creation and never truly animated anything tragic, epic or critical.[28]

A further point of interest about these resemblances is that they almost all relate to the early chapters of the conte and serve to confirm two hypotheses put forward by S. S. B. Taylor, that the Breton section was composed in the autumn of 1766, and that although the tale is 'a general commentary on the individual in an absolutist state', a distinct Protestant colouring informs it.[29] It may well be, as he suggests, that the conte was then put aside for several months. Only in February 1767 does one begin again to pick up isolated echoes: a phrase to the d'Argentals ('Je ne dis que trop ce que je pense' – D13931, 9 February 1767); a reflection on the state of mind in which one commits suicide (D13995, 26 February 1767), reminiscent of the Ingénu's temptations in that direction when St Yves is locked up in the convent and later when she dies; a reference to Hercules ridding the world of brigands and Catholic superstition (D14012, 3 March 1767), which reminds one that l'Ingénu is baptised as Hercules.

But it is only from late April that the comparisons become more substantial, beginning with a reference to Protestants deprived of their rights by the Jesuit Fathers La Chaise and Le Tellier, and of going to Versailles to intercede on the Huguenots' behalf (D14140, 24 April 1767), just as the Ingénu promises the French Protestants at Saumur that he will do.[30] When Voltaire writes to Marmontel on 16 May denouncing the absurdity of the Sorbonne in condemning a proposition from the latter's Bélisaire (D14184), he follows exactly the line of argument he takes in L'Ingénu.[31] The same day he comments to the Protestant pastor Paul Rabaut on the absurd paradox that everyone in France ridicules the claims of the Pope, yet persecutions continue of the Protestants who were the first to overthrow that idol, and a host of

Huguenot merchants who might enrich France are kept in exile out of the country; he also rejoices at the destruction of the Jesuit Order (D14185). Precisely these points arise in Chapter VIII of the story, where the Protestants at Saumur, who are mainly merchants, point out that Louis XIV is a declared enemy of the Pope, yet they are persecuted by the Jesuits under the leadership of Père La Chaise for not recognising the Pope; however, they hope that one day the Jesuits will be banished from the kingdom as the Huguenots have been. It is difficult to resist the conclusion that at that date in mid-May 1767 the composition of *L'Ingénu* was very much on Voltaire's mind.

The factors affecting the genesis of *L'Ingénu* are highly complex, probably more so than for *Candide*. A substantial number are covered in Professor Taylor's article and by Jacques Van den Heuvel,[32] and it has long puzzled the commentators of this *conte* as to which details should claim priority. Taylor is doubtless right to stress the importance of the Collonge affair,[33] not so much for any direct reflection in *L'Ingénu* as for the thoughts of flight it had aroused in Voltaire. The crisis had occurred when Mme Le Jeune, wife of d'Argental's valet, was caught by French officials smuggling dangerous books into France from Geneva after being a guest at Ferney. Voltaire realised that he might well be implicated, that he might once again have to flee; he tells d'Argental that the alarm has caused him to suffer an apoplectic attack (D13839, 13 January [1767]). Once more he is reminded that his situation is far from secure, that he cannot hope to make war on *l'infâme* with complete impunity. We find ourselves again, as at the time when Voltaire was writing *Candide*, in a period of uncertainty about where he is to see out the rest of his days.

As we have seen, the news of La Barre's execution had caused him deep distress and shame six months earlier at the legal injustices of which France was still capable. Alarming too had been the report that he might be implicated in the La Barre affair, seeing that a copy of his *Dictionnaire philosophique* was publicly burnt in the flames that consumed La Barre's corpse. In removing himself so speedily to Rolle, was he perhaps already poised for flight to Cleves? In any case, the following months witness his vigorous campaign to found a colony of *philosophes* in Frederick's territory. No sooner has that hope died down than the Collonge affair comes along to resurrect anxieties. Nostalgic recollections in a letter to Frederick at this time, in which he assures the King that his years in Berlin were the most pleasant of his life, are coupled with explicit regret that he has made his home in France (D13805, 5 January [1767]). By the end of January he is talking of moving to

Holland for the rest of his days (D13892). It is a particularly difficult winter, for after the breakdown of the Geneva mediation French forces have been sent to blockade Geneva, and Voltaire at Ferney is cut off from his source of food supplies. In February 1767 he talks of going to live in Lyons (D13946), and this possibility is still alive in April (D14151). But by early May Voltaire is resolving that his community at Ferney requires his presence in order to prosper (D14159) and by 16 May (when, as we have noted, he appears to be actively engaged on *L'Ingénu*) he has decided to stay (D14181), even though the hesitations continue a while longer. By June he sees clearly that the pays de Gex in which Ferney is set enjoys virtually unique privileges, which he had himself negotiated with Choiseul, in paying no taxes to the French Government and in being completely independent except in the judicial domain (D14237). An important corner is turned; Voltaire's destiny is to stay at Ferney.

These existential experiences of personal insecurity and menace from an absolutist government surely make a significant contribution to the tragic tone of *L'Ingénu*. If the irony is much more muted than in *Candide* when suffering is portrayed, the reason may also be sought perhaps in Voltaire's failures with a tragedy, *Les Scythes*, upon which he lavished unavailingly much time and devotion. One must never forget how deeply sensitive Voltaire always remained to comments upon his tragic dramas; he was sufficiently classical in taste to maintain to the end that a writer's literary reputation rested essentially upon the noble *genres*, among which tragedy was for him pre-eminent. By November 1766 he was acclaiming the play, now completed, with touchingly naïve enthusiasm to the d'Argentals (D13676, 13685, 13686). But it did not find favour with his friends, and although Voltaire went on amending tirelessly it received a cool reception when put on by the Comédie Française in March 1767, being given only four days' performance. Voltaire continued the losing struggle to have it revived, his comments sometimes revealing a remarkable vulnerability: '[*Les Scythes*] hastens the end of my days; it is killing me. . . . I had an extreme need of success with this work' (D14197, 25 May 1767). But by early June the lamentations are almost over, and one suspects that a new work has taken hold of his imagination.

Was this work *L'Ingénu*? Not only does the date fit reasonably well; there are close resemblances between the description of its hero and of Athamare, hero of *Les Scythes*.[34] At the time *L'Ingénu* was being written, Voltaire's little circle was giving several performances of the play at Ferney (cf. D14186, 18 May 1767; 14194, 23 May 1767); it was therefore in the forefront of his mind. The tone which the *conte* possesses, so different from that of all the other major *contes* by Voltaire, may well arise in part from a compensatory reaction to the disappointments Voltaire had suffered over the failure of *Les Scythes*.

But *L'Ingénu* and *Les Scythes* have the same ultimate aim. Both make propaganda for advancing the progress of Voltaire's natural morality, based as it is essentially on pity and justice. Justice must be tempered with compassion or charity; this is the theme of Voltaire's polemical writings of 1760 like the *Avis sur les Calas et les Sirven* or the *Relation de la mort du chevalier de La Barre*. The correspondence resounds with the same message. After a while, the shock of the La Barre execution is absorbed and Voltaire rediscovers a qualified measure of the optimism which he had felt before July 1766. Even by 22 July 1766 he is able to take the larger view and see that in Europe generally a great revolution has occurred in men's attitudes (D13437). By September, he can tell the d'Argentals that he feels humanity and philosophy to be gaining ground in France, despite fanaticism in Languedoc (D13551, 13 September 1766). Gradually the optimistic note returns, though more rarely heard and generally more cautious.

Social progress and mental equilibrium are both achievable, as ever, through hard work. The letter to the d'Argentals just mentioned contains references to two such enterprises: the Sirven case, and the *Commentaire sur le livre des délits et des peines*. The Sirven case is proving difficult; Voltaire has found that a *rapporteur* (spokesman) must be found, and he has to obtain the right man. It is a technical problem typical of many that caused the Calas and Sirven affairs to require such attention and energy. The *Commentaire,* however, is an original composition, based on the influential treatise by the Italian thinker Cesare de Beccaria, *Of Crimes and Punishments,* which appeared in 1764 and, translated into French in 1765, quickly achieved great renown in France. Beccaria had attempted to establish a firmly rational approach to penology. His work is also informed by deeply humanitarian attitudes: punishment is always a necessary evil, an admission of defeat; it is the prevention rather than the punishment of crime which should be society's basic concern. In order to achieve that, the law must be codified and written down, so that men may guide their lives by its fixed principles, applicable to all without exception. The accused should be presumed innocent until proved guilty, suicide should not be regarded as a crime, the death penalty should be abolished, the practice of judicial torture should cease. Here is the blueprint for a liberal code based on purely secular criteria. As such it commanded widespread

praise among the *philosophes*, none more so than Voltaire, who greeted
the essay with enthusiasm when he received it in October 1765. He
soon set to work to compose his Commentary, supporting Beccaria's
aims and relating them to the need for judicial reform in France.

Voltaire was aware that torture had been practised on Jean Calas,
that the fear of declaring his son a suicide had led the Toulouse
merchant into fatal lies, that the magistrates, lacking conclusive evidence, had allowed an agglomeration of vague pieces of hearsay to
condemn the man; that La Barre had been punished for a religious
offence, not a crime; and that Sirven, like the others, was sentenced to
death on insubstantial evidence. He calls for an end to such arbitrari-
ness, fully aware now as a result of his recent judicial campaigns that an
attack on the *infâme* necessarily requires an onslaught on the system of
criminal justice itself. The *Commentaire* is a typical weapon from the
Ferney armoury, allying itself to the reformist mood which was getting
under way in France in the late 1760s. Voltaire will return to the
subject, amplifying and extending his views on criminal law in a work
written near the end of his life, the *Prix de la justice et de l'humanité* (1777).

So the *philosophe* will not leave Ferney. He settles down again to
conducting the battle from his château. In 1767 and 1768 there is to be
the fight, already hinted at in *L'Ingénu*, to defend Marmontel's *Bélisaire*
against the Sorbonne. This latter novel, a didactic account of how a
king should govern, had by its support for civil toleration aroused the
objections of the Sorbonne when published in February 1767, and the
work was publicly censured. Voltaire quickly became involved, his first
Anecdote sur Bélisaire circulating by the end of March. The affair ended in
defeat for the Sorbonne who were forbidden in January 1768 to deliber-
ate or make any further pronouncement on the matter. The Church
was thereby effectively prevented from discussion of toleration, a subject where previously it had felt that it held a proprietary right. Marmontel himself not only retained his seat in the Académie Française but
continued to garner important posts, including that of Royal Historiographer.[35]

We may suitably conclude here with this further triumph by Voltaire. It exemplifies the *philosophe*'s capacity for decisive intervention
and practical support through the pen. Once again he is to be found
where the forces of obscurantism are arrayed against expression of the
new enlightenment; once again he leads on to victory. Courage is all;
the struggle continues unabated. The essential tone of the correspondence during these years, for all the alarums and despondency, is surely
caught in a simple phrase that arises within a letter to Damilaville full

of sundry mundane details: 'Oh, how I love this philosophy of action and goodwill!' (D13212, 19 March [1766]). The remark springs up unbidden, joyful. Happiness lay at the heart of these multifarious campaigns, and the Voltaire of Ferney knew it.

6 Ferney, and the Patriarch

During the last decade at Ferney the drama of Voltaire's life subsides. The revulsion at La Barre's death, the projected flight to Cleves, mark a high point in his career;[1] thereafter he settles in to Ferney as his permanent home and turns it into a principality ruled by a *patriarche philosophe*.

We shall presently see what had become of that community by the final years of his life there. Let us first briefly review the intervening years. In March 1768 Voltaire's world was rudely shaken when he discovered that Mme Denis had left him, entirely without warning. The immediate shock was considerable. A letter to her on the same day speaks of his despair, knowing that the parting would have been painful in any case but that it was so much more terrible that she should have left without saying goodbye.[2] As ever, the only antidote is to be found in work; during that day thirteen letters flowed from his pen, a characteristic response by Voltaire to personal suffering. But Mme Denis's departure could not have come as a total surprise. The visit of a young writer, La Harpe, had led to tensions. Voltaire had accepted him warmly and treated him as he had treated many another disciple. But Mme Denis had become involved with La Harpe and, it would appear, given him some of Voltaire's manuscripts to take with him to Paris the previous October. Voltaire seems not to have noticed the loss of his writings until February 1768, when he gave vent to anger at such a breach of hospitality and taxed his niece with complicity. A break had become well-nigh inevitable.[3]

Voltaire's early reaction to his niece's departure was to declare Ferney for sale and say that he was retiring to Tournay (D14834). This may well have been to some extent a bluff; at any rate Mme Denis was not slow to urge that the sale of Ferney be prevented (D14914), and by May it is clear that the château will not be sold (D15027). Meantime she mounts a campaign to bring her uncle to Paris. But he will not be drawn, urges her to stay in the capital while he remains at Ferney. Soon the shoe is on the other foot. It is Mme Denis who wants to return. But Voltaire, though still affectionate towards his niece, is no longer as dependent emotionally upon her as he was. He encourages her to settle in Paris, assuring her that he will provide for her adequately (D15464, 15491); Paris and its pleasures are starkly contrasted with the Siberia that is Ferney (D14897). He briefly considers visiting Paris, only to plead ill-health and financial hardship as excuses for putting off the journey (D15853). In the end Mme Denis wins one part of the argument, but only to the extent of persuading Voltaire to take her back at Ferney, whither she returns on 27 October 1769.[4]

1768 had been notable for another event of dramatic impact, though this time it was the outside world which registered surprise, as it was initiated by Voltaire himself. On Easter Day the *philosophe* took Communion in his own church at Ferney and afterwards preached the sermon, inveighing against the evils of drinking and thieving. Had the foremost anti-Christian of his day fallen into the arms of the Church? It seems unlikely. Voltaire mutiplied explanations of his act in the following weeks (e.g., to d'Argental, D14973; to d'Alembert, D14983), but the most probable reason for this typically impulsive gesture lies, as René Pomeau argues,[5] in fear: a sudden attack of panic at the thought of what his enemies might do to punish him for his audacious writings. Rumours of the indiscretion quickly reached the capital where, reported Grimm, everyone was scandalised, the *philosophes* just as much as society people or the devout.[6] The action seemed to embrace a remarkable number of failings; it was diversely judged hypocritical, sacrilegious and dangerously provocative. But Voltaire escaped scot-free from any serious consequences, despite the attempts of the bishop of Annecy (under whose spiritual jurisdiction the church at Ferney lay) to compromise Voltaire seriously with the government and perhaps even have him expelled from Ferney (D15659). In 1769 Voltaire repeated the offensive act of taking Communion, despite the bishop's insistence that he must sincerely repent his sins first. This time a stratagem was necessary. Voltaire, taken to his bed, asserted that he was dying. The village curé hastened to the château, confessed his parishioner and administered the sacrament, on obtaining Voltaire's signed profession of faith. If the Communion of 1768 was solemn, at least in ceremonial appearance, that of 1769 descended to pure farce.

Voltaire, perhaps feeling momentarily more secure than in the previous year, had simply found irresistible the opportunity of an anti-clerical triumph. In its own way it too was an assault, in pure derision, upon the *infâme*.

But the attack on *l'infâme* lost momentum from the early 1770s. From 1767 Voltaire, recovered from the La Barre incident, indulged in an onslaught that would last five years. The *philosophe*'s crusade reached its height in an outpouring of works of every kind: *contes*, satires, *épîtres*, tragedies, dialogues, dictionary articles, pamphlets.[7] However, in 1770 appeared a work which far outdistanced Voltaire in freethinking, d'Holbach's *Système de la nature*. The *Système* is a thoroughgoing treatise of materialist determinism. The 'system of nature' is made up exclusively of matter and movement. Like all else, consciousness is material in origin, based on experience. Man is not free but determined by his own unremitting search for happiness; self-interest must therefore be the criterion of all morality, as society itself arises out of a collectivity of human needs, all of them originating in personal interest. As for God, that concept is a human invention, designed to free man from evil and explain all incomprehensible phenomena. Religious belief is attacked at its very base.

Thereafter, Voltaire feels he must fight on two fronts, against *l'infâme* and against atheism, with the threat from atheism by no means the lesser danger. His deist beliefs, too radical for the comforts of orthodox Christianity, were also too conservative for materialists like d'Holbach. The *Système de la nature* itself posed a direct threat to thinkers like Voltaire who argued the existence of God from the cosmic design; any such design is, in d'Holbach's view, apparent not real, the necessary consequence of material laws acting blindly. Indeed, the author of the *Système* argues that deism is closely akin to religious superstition; the deist has only to feel ill, for instance, and he is ready to believe anything.[8] Voltaire was forced onto the defensive; within a few weeks he was denouncing the work with vigour, complaining of the harm it was doing to the cause of the *philosophes* (e.g., to Grimm, D16693, 10 October [1770]). The treatise comes in for repeated attack in his published works as in his letters. He fears the social effects of unbelief, serving merely to strengthen the unbridled lust for power in the atheist prince or to precipitate anarchy among the atheist populace. But the impetus of the attack on *l'infâme* is sapped and the intellectual revolution in which men will be freed from the bondage of superstition seems to be postponed indefinitely. However, it is not in Voltaire's nature to give up half-heartedly. The fight will continue against *l'infâme* as before, albeit in more muted form. Between 1770 and 1772 Voltaire brought out the final version of his personal *Encyclopédie*. Entitled *Questions sur l'Encyclopédie*, it contains 423 articles, running to nine octavo volumes in the first edition. It is, considered quite separately from all of Voltaire's other writings and activities, a prodigious enterprise. When the comte d'Antraigues visited Voltaire with Princess Potoska in 1776, the patriarch enthusiastically undertook the task of trying to convert her from her atheist views: 'there was not a single argument that he did not employ to win her over', albeit without success.[9] No greater Valiant for Truth ever existed than Voltaire, though his truth was very different from Bunyan's.

With Diderot Voltaire's relations remained polite but distant. The latter had long since concluded that little would be gained for the cause from a man who did not dare to speak out in public and preached only to his friends who were already converted; such is the burden of a letter to Diderot in 1776, though couched in polite terms (D20255). Of the *philosophes* in Paris it was with his old acquaintance d'Alembert that Voltaire was closest in touch, and with the young Condorcet, fifty years his junior. Condorcet, today generally considered the last great *philosophe* of the French Enlightenment, came to occupy a special place in Voltaire's affections. The patriarch confided to a Parisian visitor, Amélie Suard, that Condorcet's humanity, love of truth, sensibility and reason merited that he be preferred above all her other friends.[10] Condorcet was loyal and honest; he candidly warned Voltaire soon after this compliment that the latter was creating disunity in the philosophic ranks by so loudly opposing the atheists and weakening the combined forces of enlightened thinkers, in face of the threats from the Church and Parlement (D19603, 12 August 1775). Voltaire took the reproach with equanimity (D19617) and the exchange of letters between the pair continued with unabated warmth.

Particular cases of injustice still occupied Voltaire's attention during those last years of his life. He fully recognised now the atavism of French justice, a survival of tyranny and superstition liable to inflict any family at any time with lawsuits both absurd and iniquitous (D19493). The laws are an arbitrary patchwork, the government, like the city of Paris, is a mixture of palaces and hovels (D19635). This latter remark, in a letter to Frederick, is related to the La Barre case. The chevalier's accomplice, d'Etallonde, had fled to Prussia and made a successful career in the King's army. In 1775 Voltaire was still seeking to clear d'Etallonde's name as well as that of the dead victim and hoping to get the sentence quashed in the Conseil du Roi, as he tells

Condorcet and d'Alembert (D19301); it would make, he felt, a fitting end to his career (D19303). D'Etallonde was given an extended leave of absence from Prussia while Voltaire pressed his case, but when it became clear that all they could hope for was a free pardon, the *philosophe* accepted that it was much better for the young man to return to Frederick's service, in which the King gratified Voltaire's wishes by making d'Etallonde a captain and one of his engineers, and endowing him with a pension (D19549). Frederick had in the end proved a useful ally; Voltaire was convinced that it was an attempt to compensate for the harsh treatment to which he had formerly been subjected at the King's hands.

The *philosophe* was also involved in a larger struggle, more complex and with less immediate appeal than the championing of individual victims like Calas or La Barre. At Saint-Claude, not far from Ferney, he discovered that a chapter of twenty monks was holding twelve hundred peasants in conditions of serfdom. These peasants were obliged to pay a tax to their feudal lords on every sale of property and indeed were dependent upon the monastery's goodwill as to whether the sale could be effected at all. The right to inherit was also strictly governed. The heirs had to remain in the same house, otherwise the will was null and void. If a peasant died intestate, his property reverted to the monastery, as too it did if the serf left the community. Freedom could be obtained, but only by moving elsewhere, and that meant total destitution of one's wealth. The plight of these tenants aroused the sympathy of a young lawyer living in Saint-Claude, Charles Christin, who in 1765 wrote to Voltaire to acquaint him with the situation. The defender of Calas was to receive during his later years many such appeals for help over cases of injustice. This one particularly touched him, probably because the spectacle of oppressive feudal rights being exercised by a community of monks represented an especially notorious instance of *l'infâme* at work.

From the late 1760s, with the help of Christin on the spot, he waged the battle for the serfs' liberation. *Requêtes* were addressed to Louis XV, the aid of powerful patrons invoked. But Choiseul's fall from power in 1770 removed a central ally in the government. Although further efforts were made to gain ministerial support, the case was referred back in 1772, as Voltaire had feared, to the local Parlement of Besançon, where it hung fire interminably in accordance with the best principles of legal delay. In 1774 fresh hopes were kindled when Turgot, the great hope of the *philosophes* and a noted thinker and writer himself, was made a minister, and this seemed to promise better prospects. The Parlement at last pronounced in August 1775, but unfortunately it found for the monastic chapter. There remained only one hope, to appeal to the government, counting on the favourable intervention of Turgot's liberal views within the Conseil du Roi. In February 1776 Voltaire inaugurated this phase of the campaign, providing a comprehensive account of the appalling situation in which the twelve hundred 'spectres' enslaved by the abbey found themselves obliged to contribute one-sixth of their crops to their noble lords, who took what they pleased of their tenants' property when these poor wretches died (D19946). A typical Voltairean crusade was under way. Alas! Turgot was to fall from power in May and with him went any remaining hope of winning this particular battle, as Voltaire sadly acknowledged to Christin (D20143). Even so, the *philosophe* did not completely relinquish the struggle, and as late as 1778 he was considering a new *démarche* with the French Government. The victory was destined however to be only posthumous; the following year Louis XVI signed an edict abolishing serfdom not only at Saint-Claude but in all the other places in France where it had lingered on. But the monks of Saint-Claude made a stubborn defence of their rights, and it was not until 4 August 1789 that their privileges were removed along with all other remaining feudal rights in France.[11]

The Saint-Claude case, therefore, lacks the exemplary qualities of the Calas affair. It was long, tedious, and ultimately indecisive. But it amply illustrates those elements of Voltaire's personality which elsewhere led on to victory: energy, persistence, humanitarianism, shrewdness, skilful intervention. Besterman justifiably considers it the most important of all the *philosophe*'s campaigns in its wider political significance.[12]

In 1769 Voltaire received a visit from one Roland de la Platière. The latter returned four years later and was impressed by the change that had come over Ferney in the interim. It had been transformed since his first visit into a small town. He reported that 'apart from the wheelwrights, joiners, carpenters, masons, tailors, shoemakers, innkeepers, etc.', the community contained more than two hundred workers in the watchmaking industry.[13] According to President d'Hornoy, Voltaire's great-nephew, Ferney consisted of only seven or eight cottages when the *philosophe* acquired the château. Voltaire gradually attracted more people to live there and increased the community to twenty or so houses. (Already in 1765 John Wilkes had reported that he was adored by all the inhabitants because he had established a thriving community out of a desert.)[14] But it was when the Natifs in Geneva began to suffer oppression from about 1770 that the attraction of Ferney as a place of refuge became fully manifest. At that time the only industry was one engaged in a crude preparation of watch parts. But when the Genevan watchmakers saw that they could work just as well in Ferney, Voltaire realised that he could establish a complete watch-making industry to rival Geneva's. The number of immigrants increased, the business becoming important enough to warrant the presence at Ferney of representatives from the main watchmakers in Paris, Marseilles and Bordeaux. In four years the establishment was built up, to the point where by 1775 the trade was about a half-million francs yearly and no longer dependent on Voltaire for financial sup-port. Under Voltaire's highly active promotion (in which important acquaintances at home and abroad like Louis XV's mistress Mme du Barry, Frederick of Prussia and Catherine of Russia were eagerly solicited to become customers), watches were being exported as far abroad as India and Russia, and in particularly large numbers to Spain and the Levant. The industry in its turn attracted ancillary trades such as enamel painting and jewellery mounting. By 1775 Ferney could count twelve hundred inhabitants and over seventy houses, almost all of which were owned by Voltaire and rented out (D19711, 17 October 1775).[15] D'Hornoy's report, favourable though it is, seems if anything to understate the situation, for in the following May François Tronchin wrote that Voltaire was then building his ninety-fourth house, having spent over a million francs on housing his workers at Ferney (D19807, Commentary). According to another local resident, the rate of building in June was such that the community was scarcely recognisable from three months before (D20152). The actor Lekain, visiting Ferney in August 1776 to inaugurate the new theatre which Voltaire had also put up, wrote to d'Argental that the inhabitants were all well housed, well fed, living at peace with one another in complete religious toleration, busily engaged and prosperous (D20239). Even the poorest of the houses, noted the Genevan pastor Moultou, was better than the best villages around Paris (D19281).

   Given these well-nigh idyllic pictures of a thriving community, it need come as no surprise to find Voltaire telling d'Argental that the inhabitants want to call Ferney Voltaire (D19658, 15 September 1775). Besterman points out in his Commentary that this is not mere self-congratulation, for a letter survives from 1780 date-stamped Ferney-Voltaire. (The township was not to receive this title officially from the French Government until the centenary of Voltaire's death in 1878.)

The devotion shown by the workers to their generous patriarch was exemplified by the fêtes which they put on in 1775, first in May to celebrate Mme Denis's recovery from a serious illness and then on 4 October to commemorate the feast of Saint François and thereby Voltaire's name-day: cavalcades, illuminations, fireworks, troops under arms, cannon, bands, dancing, grand suppers – by such rejoicings the citizens expressed their delight in their *seigneur* (D19476, 19486, 19693). Wagnière, Voltaire's secretary, makes it explicitly clear that the latter fête was put on not by Voltaire but by his people.[16] As Hennin, the French Resident in Geneva, wrote to his minister in Paris the comte de Vergennes after attending the May festival, it was extraordinary to see a show which many towns in the kingdom could not match, put on in a community where only twelve years before there were just a score of wretched families. If one wealthy, munificent man could effect such a change in the provinces, was there no way of persuading a thousand others in Paris to do the same instead of squandering their money idly (D19492)?

But the path had not been strewn the whole way with roses. To establish the colony on a firm footing Voltaire had needed governmental protection. Choiseul provided powerful support, but his dismissal in December 1770 threatened the whole enterprise with ruin. Fortunately, other patronage was found, foreign trade developed and the community flourished. But Voltaire sought a more permanent economic solution. Ferney was in the pays de Gex, a province in its own right but the smallest and, until Voltaire's coming, probably the poorest in France. It suffered from its peculiar geographical situation. Being cut off from France (but for two roads) by the Jura mountains, it formed an enclave open only to Geneva, Switzerland and Savoy. Therefore, although it was a French province, its business was transacted through foreign states. As such the situation offered limitless possibilities for contraband and the *pays* consequently had to bear a veritable army of excisemen and tax-collectors. Voltaire maintained in a Mémoire on Gex that the prisons were full of smugglers, their families reduced to beggary, trade annihilated and the *pays* deserted.[17] In March 1775 he made his first move in the campaign to free Gex from having to pay indirect taxes, especially the salt-tax (*la gabelle*) to the *fermiers généraux*. Turgot had arrived at the crucial post of *Contrôleur général* (Chancellor of the Exchequer) the previous year. He wanted to carry out radical changes in the system of taxation, reforming the diverse ways of raising public money and instituting a single tax to be levied on all landowners. He also held a strongly liberal belief in the value of free trade and early in his ministerial career issued a decree providing for the unhindered circulation of corn within the country. Such a man was evidently after Voltaire's own heart as the patriarch sought to abolish the arbitrary and ineffective monetary system prevailing in Gex. When the Parlements began to resist Turgot's reforms and riots occurred, Voltaire made clear that he would side with the minister and against the 'abominable superstition of people and Parlement' (D19438, 26 April 1775). By the summer he had completed a memorandum on the situation in the *pays* and submitted it to the government.

With Turgot in charge hopes that had seemed dead find new life. Now, Voltaire tells Frederick, there is a man in France worthy to talk with him. The priests are in despair, the country is at the beginning of a great revolution (D19599). Soon the government has agreed to Voltaire's request to abolish the salt-tax; a price will be agreed with the *fermiers généraux* as an annual indemnity (D19634, 31 August 1775). Voltaire is delighted; it is better than the province had asked for, he writes (D19637). His astute business sense is however not dulled by this stroke of fortune! Perhaps, he tells Fabry, the Mayor of Gex, they can make a profit out of the deal and put the surplus money to road-building (D19634). But when the subsequent negotiations reveal that a hard line is being taken by the government on the amount of the indemnity, Voltaire drops the question of profit-making and indeed disavows it explicitly when writing to Du Pont de Nemours in October (D19701). There still remains room, however, for bargaining on the actual price to pay.

Voltaire offers Turgot 15,000 francs (D19698), but the figure imposed is 30,000 (D19717) and repeated letters to Turgot and others suggesting 20,000 fail completely to get the sum lowered (e.g., D19733, 19742). In the end hard-headed realism wins out. Knowing that he cannot achieve anything further at this stage, he puts on a gracious face and accepts the settlement with gratitude (D19771). But he still wavers a little even now, making one last attempt, though in vain, at reducing it to 25,000 (D19783, 19784, 19817). However, the important fact of enfranchisement has been achieved and that is the essential thing. Reductions were a matter for later, as he told Fabry (D19778).

The reform was due to come into effect on 1 January 1776. On 12 December 1775 '(which, the ever-loyal Wagnière noted, was the twenty-first anniversary of Voltaire's arrival in the *pays*: D19790) the Etats provinciaux (the provincial representative assembly) of Gex met to decide upon the enfranchisement. Hennin reported that Voltaire had expected some opposition (D19803). Perhaps the latter had been too sanguine at first about the details of the settlement, as his letters appear to show, and he now felt he had to carry through a measure he had helped to make unpopular with some. In any case, Voltaire the showman did not neglect the chance to make this an impressive occasion, arriving escorted by twelve dragoons from Ferney, who took up their positions on the square outside the house where the Etats were meeting. When success was won Voltaire opened the window and cried out 'Liberté!' He emerged to cries of 'Vive le Roi, vive M. de Voltaire!' and, his carriage and horses bedecked with laurels and flowers, he made a triumphal tour, accompanied by his dragoons, through several of the villages before returning home (D19800, 19803). It was one of the most moving occasions for the *philosophe* in his whole life, according to Wagnière.[18] Here was one more signal day of brilliant achievement, adding considerably to the legend that had already grown up around his person.

Voltaire's delight at this first ministerial reform by Turgot in the provinces was evident. 'The golden age begins,' he wrote (D19848, 8 January 1776). But 1776, while it would see a new era open in North America, flattered to deceive in France. The Parlements had become increasingly opposed to Turgot's reforms. In May his enemies managed at last to undermine Louis XVI's support of his minister and Turgot was dismissed;[19] it was to be the end of any systematic institutional reform in France before the Revolution.

Voltaire was appalled when he received the news. At his age it seemed to extinguish all hope, and that was, he wrote, 'the worst of all states' (D20213). He foresees the destruction of his colony and the dispersal of its people (D20243). In September he writes that since hearing the news well over three months before he has pursued not a single affair (D20282). Even Voltaire's extraordinary resilience has been sapped at its very centre. The vital energy, still needing an outlet, seems to go into a ferocious attack on Shakespeare in a letter to the Académie Française. Here is not the place to comment upon Voltaire's limitations in judging Shakespeare over a lifetime; though blinkered in his views, he was not wholly devoid of perceptive insights on occasion.[20] But it is sad to see this new crusade expended upon reactionary attitudes, in which it appears that this is the only way left to him to uphold values in France. Voltaire may have won widespread applause (except among the English) when his Letter was read to a public audience at the Academy by d'Alembert in August (D20272), but it was in a negative cause. While declining to share Garrick's venomous tone, one is tempted to agree in substance with the Shakespearean actor's observation to the critic Elizabeth Montagu that Voltaire's remarks were 'the weak and impotent ravings of age' (D20369). At the end of 1776 Voltaire seemed indeed played out: exhausted, disconsolate, powerless.

Even so, there were things to be done. Above all, he turned in every direction seeking help with Ferney, now that there was no one man to help him. Turgot had been replaced by Clugny. The latter had come poorly recommended by Condorcet on both personal and political grounds (D20194); in any case, Clugny died in October and Voltaire found himself appealing to the Genevan-born Necker, who replaced Clugny in part; but would Necker support the interests of Gex against his own birthplace (D20374)? Once again Voltaire was tempted to leave Ferney; he would do so, he told d'Hornoy, if his pays de Gex suffered persecution (D20474, 17 December 1776).

So the end of 1776 lacks any decisive resolution in Voltaire's life. From envisaging the golden era of glorious reform about to begin, he has been relegated in a matter of months to a despairing struggle to save what he can. The grand vision is replaced by tedious but necessary details as he fights to ensure Ferney's survival. During 1776 a complex situation arose over the consequences of replacing the salt-tax. The Etats had decided to buy their salt exclusively from the *fermiers généraux*. But when the arrival of this salt was delayed by over ten months, it became necessary to purchase a short-term supply elsewhere. An entrepreneur, Rose, went off to Berne and committed the Etats of Gex to buying an excessive amount of salt. This was cancelled by the French Government on appeal from the Etats, but an interim provision was still needed and Voltaire requested it on behalf of the Etats in a *mémoire* addressed to the government.[21] The matter is confused and related to personal jealousies. For his part Fabry, supported by Voltaire's old antagonist President de Brosses, felt that the *philosophe* was trying to arrogate himself too much power. This may well have been the case, but the episode remains obscure and would benefit from the closer attentions of modern scholarship.[22]

1776, then, gives way to 1777 in the midst of such limited and harassing concerns. We are at the beginning of the last full year in Voltaire's life, and the events of the past few months serve to remind us of his age. He had long since settled to a steady round of illnesses, most of which served only to safeguard his retreat; to the privacy of his bedroom only the most privileged were admitted and it had served increasingly in the later years as his most assured place of work.[23] Now, however, for a while, there is a sense that even a Voltaire has to grow old. Does one however detect a lightening of the gloom when on 30 December he writes to Fabry that, after all, there is much to be thankful for at Ferney (D20492)? Or is this only a cautious declaration made to a man known to be his enemy? The answers to such questions must lie in the future.

For the moment, let us abandon the narrative and attempt a summing-up of the man as he appeared to those who came to see him. Such a task has been made immeasurably easier through the joint compilation by André-Michel Rousseau and the late Sir Gavin de Beer of observations coming from Voltaire's British visitors.[24] One hundred and fifty reports, varying from the merest allusion to veritable essays on the patriarch and containing a wide range of attitudes as befits the variety of travellers involved, bring Voltaire clearly before us. In the best we recapture something of that most evanescent side to the *philosophe*, yet one without which no proper understanding of him is possible: his phenomenal vitality of presence. It is particularly appropriate in an English-language book on Voltaire to give the stage to these British and American travellers. Nothing comparable exists for the much larger contingent of Frenchmen who came to see Voltaire and it may be feared that a certain distortion will creep in. But remarkable accounts survive of course from his compatriots too and some of these will serve to balance or confirm the opinions of those from beyond the Channel. There is perhaps even an advantage to looking mainly at the British. They were, by and large, free of the endless rumours to which Parisians had been subjected about the *philosophe*'s life for over sixty years. The British were far from unprejudiced about Voltaire; several, even among those who came to see him, felt keen hostility towards him and his views. But there were fewer obstacles to get in the way; the British stood a better chance of a clear view, because (like Voltaire's own Ingénu) they were more ignorant of the distracting details.

By the mid-1760s, a visit to Voltaire was a standard feature of any journey to Geneva. One writer, Antoine Thomas, was sure that his correspondent the chevalier de Taulès would not fail to follow the fashion (Taulès was about to leave for Geneva as secretary to the French ambassador, Beauteville, during the mediation of 1766): 'You do not approach so close to Mecca without making the pilgrimage; and what reprobate has ever been to Rome without seeing the Pope? . . . I am ignorant of the state of devotion amongst *Allah*'s servants; but assuredly Ferney attracts more of the truly devout today than the

Vatican' (D13190, Commentary, 1 March 1766). By the end of Voltaire's life people waited outside the house for him to walk by, 'as though it were a king passing' (D20780). A visit to Ferney necessarily meant gaining a view of Voltaire, otherwise it would have been seeing *Hamlet* without the Prince. This comes through in a wryly amusing poem from an anonymous hand, at the prospect of being asked when the poet returns to England: 'How looks the wonder of the Age?' He dreads the awful confession of failure before his listener:

> Must I be forced to damp his joy
> Each hope of circumstance betray;
> Must I his fondest wish destroy,
> And own I've only seen *Ferney*?[25]

A few deliberately avoided calling, either on principle or because of parental interdiction or from simple indifference.[26] But they formed a very small minority.

Voltaire's fame had so run before him that the very sight of him, the more so in a pre-photographic age, was a novelty avidly coveted. Much though the great man enjoyed flattery, the feeling of being a caged animal must at times have been overpoweringly claustrophobic. When one group of British visitors admitted that they wished only to look at him, he replied: 'Well, gentlemen, you now see me, and did you take me to be a wild beast or a Monster that was fit only to be stared at, as a show?'[27] This incident dated from about 1770; as he grew older, Voltaire became more of a recluse, less good-humoured with the sightseers. One English lady, it was reported in 1776, had at last managed to view the *philosophe*, after many difficulties, but all she got was that he was emerging from his tomb for her, after which he said no more and immediately withdrew (D20383). Very few people therefore come any more to visit him, writes Moultou, the author of this letter; this is confirmed by Lekain on a visit to Voltaire in the same year (D20245).

But for the British generally, and particularly in earlier years, the welcome had been warm. The young Gibbon marvelled at the hospitality afforded one evening in 1763 to his group, when a performance of Voltaire's *L'Orphelin de la Chine* had been followed by an elegant supper and dancing till 4 a.m.: 'Shew me in history or fable, a famous poet of Seventy who has acted in his own plays, and has closed the scene with a supper and ball for a hundred people.'[28] Boswell was impressed by the attentive care he received during his stay the next year,[29] the Duchess of Northumberland was appreciative of Voltaire's politeness in 1772,[30] as the Nevilles were to be a few weeks later[31] and John Morgan had been in 1764.[32] Even as late as 1772, John Moore observed that Voltaire generally had two or three visitors from Paris staying for a month or six weeks and soon replaced by others when they left.[33] Voltaire's isolated life in exile gave him the time and energy he needed for his work. Yet the visits of old friends, as too of strangers if they came well recommended, formed an essential part of his life until the very latest years when the guests were fewer and more choice.

But the welcome might well be bizarre, especially if Voltaire were feeling unwell. A mixed group of British and Russian visitors in 1771 were nonplussed when Voltaire played host while 'placed on his knees in a great chair, over the back of which he leant, and continued opposite to me in this uneasy posture during the whole of supper time'. They took their leave, no less uneasy themselves, and disappointed at their reception.[34] Indeed, Voltaire in a hypochondriac mood could be intimidating. Sickness, as we noted in the first chapter, often served as an excuse and he enjoyed the renown of 'having a colic at command'.[35] Adam Ferguson, visiting Ferney in 1774, discovered that 'His common salutation is, qui veut voir une Ombre.' After that opening, there is no way but 'to let him go on', and in a few minutes 'his tongue becomes as frolicsome as that of a boy of eighteen'.[36]

Being so constantly on show might well have deformed the character of a man far less given to histrionics than Voltaire. In his case it served to fuel a desire to parade, and often to shock, that had always been present. A Scottish visitor, the twenty-year-old James Callandar, displayed the courage or naïveté of youth when reproaching Voltaire for having thrust a forkful of partridge into his own mouth and then continuing to use the same fork for serving everyone else. Voltaire's rejoinder was 'a peculiar laugh of a sardonic kind', accompanying the observation that 'the English were a strange people, and had singular customs'.[37] Quite probably the attribution of English nationality to the noble Callandar was an added insult, as Voltaire was well aware of the separateness of Scotland, being born before the Act of Union when it was a kingdom in its own right.[38] John Conyers rightly noted that there was a despotic quality to such behaviour. Voltaire, head of his house and prince in his domain. could in domestic matters do as he pleased. It was consonant with this position, then, if he chose to appear after everyone else at table or to recall the serving dishes even though everyone had already had enough to eat.[39]

Much of this behaviour must have sprung from petulant boredom, especially in a man of such mercurial moods. But it also relates to

Voltaire's endless capacity for rôle playing, seen in its purest form in the theatre itself. We have had occasion to note the author's fundamental commitment to his plays and deep disappointment if they turned out to be failures. The theatre was for him a place of wonderment, the only pure temple.[40] At Cirey he and Mme du Châtelet had had their own theatre; on his return to Paris after her death there was play-acting at his house, as also later in Berlin, Geneva and Lausanne. The stage was for Voltaire the best *divertissement* which the world could afford. However, opinions of his own acting ability were not high among the British visitors. On Gibbon's first visit to Voltaire in 1757 he was quite taken by the dramatist's declaration, though he recognised it as 'the pomp and cadence of the old stage';[41] but on his return six years later he found that his former enthusiasm had faded and that Voltaire now appeared 'a very ranting unnatural performer'.[42] As for the unadmiring James Callandar, it was hardly to be expected that he would find anything but absurdity in the sight of the dramatist acting in his own plays.[43]

But one must add in fairness that the British have always found the more formal style of the Comédie Française difficult to appreciate. In this respect the comments of French witnesses may give a more balanced impression. Mme de Graffigny, despite finding that Voltaire at Cirey could not play two successive lines without exaggerating, was affected as never before by a tragedy, because his acting was 'divine' (D1876). But it is Lekain's testimony which is particularly impressive, as Lekain was himself one of the greatest actors of the century at the Comédie Française. On his return to Paris from a visit to Ferney early during Voltaire's stay there, Lekain tells of how he had been playing a part in *L'Orphelin de la Chine* and had attracted the playwright's vigorous denunciations for his mishandling of it. Voltaire's sensitivity seems to have frequently been at fever pitch during a dramatic performance; here, as so often, it took some considerable time for him to calm down. But eventually he was mollified, took the text and read from it; and Lekain acknowledges in his letter how much his own view of the rôle had been mistaken, even though he had already played it in Paris with success: 'I would seek in vain to give you an idea of the profound impressions which m. de Voltaire made on my soul, by the sublime, imposing and passionate tone with which he depicted the various shadings in the rôle of Gengiskan. Mute with admiration, he had finished and I listened still.' Back in Paris he plays the part according to his new-found knowledge and the difference is perceptible (D6683, 10 January 1756). Here is a professional tribute to Voltaire's acting skill on grounds of sensitivity, stage presence and intelligence of perception. One could hardly seek for a better testimonial.

These heightened sensibilities at the theatre sometimes led to extraordinary situations. In 1750 Voltaire, present at a performance of his *Oreste* in the Comédie Française, is reported by Mirabeau as waving his arms about and crying out incessantly: 'Ah! que cela est beau! Applaudissez donc!' and so forth. At times he was so carried away by his involvement with the spectacle as to make him, in the eyes of at least one spectator (Mirabeau), a fit candidate for the madhouse (D4095, Commentary). Many years later at Ferney Lekain describes the same state of absorption, though more sympathetically:

he comes to the theatre for relaxation, and this pleasure then occupies his complete attention; there is no soul as sensitive as his; his joy is manifested through burning tears and transports of feeling, which wring the hearts of all the spectators; the scene becomes unique of its kind, for you feel at one and the same time admiration for the work, veneration for its author, and some small sense of illusion in the charm of the presentation.

(D20245, 5 August 1776)

The same suggestion of lunacy which had occurred to Mirabeau in Paris recurs to John Conyers at Ferney in 1765: 'Great wits, says an author, are surely allied to madness; one would imagine this who saw our epic-writer on such a night.' This impression was forced upon him as he watched Voltaire frequently interrupting the action whenever anything displeased him, 'to scold at an empress, or pull the cap of a queen', or to introduce burlesque comments into the part he is himself playing when another character is late on his cue. Conyers feels a painful sense that Voltaire has made a fool of himself.[44]

A similar account of total involvement in the action is given in 1772 by John Moore, who wonders at 'such a degree of sensibility in a man of eighty' and particularly at how the author can still feel such emotions at each renewed performance of plays which, after all, he wrote and which are but 'the fictitious distresses of the drama'. He is curious to know whether such sensibilities would be aroused if the play being performed were by Corneille or Racine.[45] Moore shows here the strengths and weaknesses of plain common sense. Doubtless he was right in his suspicions (which must remain unproven, however, if only because Voltaire by this time apparently attended no other plays but his own). Doubtless a large measure of pure narcissism is involved – one receives the same impression when learning that the château at Ferney is full of busts and pictures of Voltaire.[46] But, as with the *philosophe*'s notorious hypochondria, our purpose here is not to mock or belittle but rather to capture the full sense of this remarkable empathy, so reminiscent in some of these scenes of Diderot's great fictional creation, *le neveu de Rameau*. André Delattre deserves the credit for identifying, perhaps for the first time in such terms, the dionysiac element in Voltaire's make-up.[47] This quality is closely bound up with the immediacy of response which Voltaire's attitudes in the theatre pre-eminently showed and which attracted or repelled, according to the circumstances or the persons present. It relates also to a defect in Voltaire's personality which yet was often a source of strength: his lack of self-awareness. His doctor, Théodore Tronchin, astutely observed this in a letter we have already had occasion to cite: 'Of all men living in the world together, the one he knows the least is himself.'[48] The limitation enabled him to go on being committed to certain situations long after most men, more conscious of their own absurdities, would have withdrawn. It is the other side to his tenacity, which is justly seen as one of his central qualities and for which those such as the Sirven family or Marie Corneille had good cause to be thankful.

This spontaneous, even impetuous, quality underlies the completeness with which Voltaire could impose his personality upon others. To his secretary Wagnière we are once again indebted for giving us a vivid impression of how Voltaire became involved in discussions, initial self-restraint giving way to effortless self-expression:

. . . he would remain silent for a long while, listening to everyone, his head lowered, and appearing to be in a state of stupor or imbecility. When the disputants had more or less exhausted their arguments he seemed to awake, began by discussing in orderly and precise manner their opinions, continued by putting forward his own. You could see him gradually take fire; in the end he was no longer the same man, you felt you saw something supernatural in his whole person, you were carried away by the vehemence of his discourse, of his action, and by the force of his arguments.[49]

Oliver Goldsmith paints a similar picture:

. . . when he was warmed in discourse, and had got over a hesitating manner which sometimes he was subject to, it was rapture to hear him. His meagre visage seemed insensibly to gather beauty; every muscle in it had meaning, and his eyes beamed with unusual brightness.[50]

This charisma was grounded upon a phenomenal vitality which Voltaire had the good fortune to preserve all his life. John Moore found him as 'eager and ardent' on Indian matters in 1773 'as if he was not thirty'; he speculated that Voltaire (then aged seventy-eight) might live another fifteen years yet.[51] Three years later Martin Sherlock found that in discussing literature the *philosophe* 'spoke with the warmth of a man of thirty'.[52] Lekain recounts an extraordinary tale of Voltaire running a foot-race against his nephew, in his eighty-second year, and only just losing (D20245). But such animation was surely obtained at a price and balanced by the days of weakness and dejection. Voltaire's young admirer Amélie Suard, visiting him on several occasions over a fortnight in 1775, captures something of the rapidity with which his state of health went up and down. On her first appearance at Ferney she finds him looking splendidly fit (D19499); two days later he has had a stomach upset and, in his nightcap, looks ten years older (D19501). However, after a further six days he is perfectly restored and looking twenty years younger again (D19505), only to be 'abattu' on her next visit two days later (D19507). One more day passes, and this time 'he has nothing of old age about him except the respect which it inspires' (D19508). When she returns to say goodbye in two days' time he is in bed and claims to be ill, though she finds him full of life and good humour (D19511).

This series of letters offers a fascinating conspectus of Voltaire's physical state; his bodily condition is scarcely the same two days together. The protean quality of his health matches, indeed is an integral part of, the protean quality of his personality. True, a figure as gaunt as Voltaire was, particularly in his later years, would show physical alterations more sharply than most, and the adoption or not of a nightcap or, conversely, a wig made a great difference to his features. But one such feature was particularly important: his eyes. They must have been striking, to impress so many visitors who recalled them later. Mme Suard thought he had 'the most beautiful eyes in the world, so animated still that their brilliance is hardly to be borne' (D19505). Wagnière described them as brilliant and fiery, adding that Voltaire never used spectacles[53] – not even for the smallest print, observes Moultou (D20376). Major Broom noted his 'very piercing eye' and vivacious look in 1765;[54] Thomas Pennant in the same year anticipates Amélie Suard's observation in describing his eyes as 'the most brilliant I ever saw':[55] Samuel Sharpe (1765) remarks on their degree of brilliancy when Voltaire is animated;[56] for Richard Twiss (1768) they were 'particularly expressive';[57] in 1770 Charles Burney notes that they 'are still full of fire; and . . . a more lively expression cannot be imagined';[58] the Duchess of Northumberland (seeing him at the age of seventy-seven) thought they had 'a Fire . . . I never saw in those of a Man of 25;'[59] John Moore (1772) considered them 'the most piercing eyes I ever beheld'.[60] The descriptions abound.

As Peter Beckford expressed it on his visit to Voltaire, 'the activity of his mind was expressed in his countenance'.[61] It was the quality of his intellect which above all gave Voltaire's face so much animation. Roland de la Platière was impressed, when at Ferney in 1769, by the patriarch's retentive memory and powerful thinking, quite as much so, he wrote, as Voltaire's speeches and writings had revealed down the years.[62] Voltaire's thoughts turned naturally to religious and philosophical subjects; John Morgan provides a fascinating example. A small dog crossing the room stopped in front of Voltaire and wagged its tail. The host turned to Morgan's companion Samuel Powel '& as I thought a little abruptly ask'd him, what think you of that little dog; has he any Soul or not, & what do the People in England now think of the Soul'. Mr Powel was, not surprisingly, 'a little startled at this Question put so mal à propos'.[63] The unexpected association of ideas in Voltaire's mind is revealing of how that mind worked. When Boswell visited him they discoursed on many matters. 'At last we came upon religion. Then did he rage.' The rest of the company went in to supper, but the pair remained behind with 'a great Bible before us', disputing with vehemence, so much so that Voltaire became sick and dizzy. Later, having recovered, he expressed to Boswell candidly his intimate religious feelings.[64]

Others did not penetrate so far into Voltaire's soul. Visitors were generally kept on the defensive as he shocked them by blasphemous utterances. Sir James Macdonald confessed that he was tempted to put cotton into his ears against such horrid remarks.[65] John Conyers observed that Voltaire's conversation with men generally turned on blasphemous subjects, the more so if any clerics were present.[66] Priests,[67] saints,[68] Moses,[69] all came in for abuse before various British guests. An inclination to tease was never far removed on these occasions. Voltaire tried to offend Bishop Hervey by asking him whether the greater farce was played in a theatre or in a church, but the bishop refused to be drawn.[70] But a Quaker, Claude Gay, reacted with more earnestness and the atmosphere soured quickly in consequence. When Voltaire began making jokes about sacred matters like the patriarchs and the proofs of Revelation, Gay undertook a coolly rational examination of his audacious utterances: 'Voltaire's vivacity at last turned to downright anger; his eyes flashed fire whenever they met the benign and placid countenance of the quaker . . .' In the end the latter felt he had no alternative but to depart, retiring upon a dignified remark and refusing all entreaty to return; the whole company was left in consternation. As for Voltaire, he withdrew at once to his room.[71] On this occasion at least a guest created confusion by daring to place his concern for truth above the claims of social decorum.

With the ladies Voltaire was more often given to gallantries, or indecencies (the difference between the one and the other often depending upon the hearer's own attitudes). Mme Suard was delighted with his badinage, piquant enough to be flattering without degenerating into tastelessness (D19502). This coincides with Wagnière's memory of his master as possessing a bewitching *politesse* with the fair sex.[72] Even while apparently quite ill, he could still find the strength for a flattering compliment to Princess Dashkof.[73] But John Conyers thought that 'with ladies, he is rather indecent' and 'but too apt to be ludicrous'.[74] It may well be that Conyers failed to appreciate that combination of friendship with overtures of sexual desire which the sophisticated man of society in eighteenth-century France regarded as a civilised ideal in his relations with women.[75]

Whether blasphemous, gallant or dispassionate, Voltaire's talk never failed to be salted with wit. He was not the sort of comic writer who cannot, or will not, reproduce his humour in society; on the contrary, those who met him could have had little doubt that they were in the presence of the man who had written *Candide*. Humour bubbled up out of him, as aphorism, satire, repartee. When the conversation turned to painting in Scotland and Boswell opined that it was not one of his country's strengths, Voltaire at once rejoined: 'No; to paint well it is necessary to have warm feet. It's hard to paint when your feet are cold.'[76] Martin Sherlock asked him, 'How did you find the English fare?' Voltaire, seizing instantly upon the chance of a pun, answered: 'Very fresh and very white.' Sherlock was amazed that a man of eighty-two should have been so quick-witted.[77] What is even more impressive is that these instances (and they could be multiplied) are of witticisms made through the medium of a foreign language, which he probably spoke with 'tolerable fluency'[78] but without possessing anything approaching bilingual mastery. As Samuel Taylor has demonstrated in some detail in a recent paper, humour (rather than the mordant wit which is so often considered to be more characteristic of him) is a fundamental element in Voltaire's personality, with conversation as the supreme outlet for his high spirits.[79] John Moore had summed it up observantly on his visit in 1772: 'The spirit of mirth gains upon him by indulgence. – When surrounded by his friends, and animated by the presence of women, he seems to enjoy life with all the sensibility of youth.'[80]

For Voltaire austerity of outlook was a malady, far worse than the ills of the flesh (D1359).[81] Mme Denis knew whereof she spoke when she pleaded with her uncle not to lose his natural gaiety (D15603). Yet, as Professor Taylor points out, the humour was also a refusal of despair. Mme Suard, a devoted disciple, won Voltaire's confidence sufficiently for him to make the remarkable avowal to her: 'there is no more happiness for me, there has indeed never been any'. When she differed with him, claiming that he had had great satisfactions and, as a lover of glory, had merited and obtained more of it than anyone, he answered: 'Oh, Madame, I did not know what I wanted. It [glory] was my plaything, my doll' (D19507). The sudden void proclaimed here only confirms the observations of Mme de Graffigny and Théodore Tronchin about his constantly frustrated pursuit of fame and approbation.[82] Touching on Voltaire's wit and high spirits, we find ourselves drawn back also to the darker side which underlay it. But Mme Suard was right when she took a constructive line in reply to Voltaire's revelation of the darkness within him; she pointed out that the 'doll' had served not only as self-gratification, as happens with most men, but to delight all who 'are able to think and feel'. Professor Taylor draws attention to the balance in Voltaire's make-up when asserting: 'The activist, ironist and humorist in Voltaire are inseparable . . .'[83]

But one must not forget that, as he himself put it, Voltaire had a monastic vocation in at least one respect: 'I love the cell' (D5821). Only work, he felt, could console the human race for existing (D5767). Wagnière saw that work was essential to his master's life, adding that most of the time they worked eighteen to twenty hours a day. Although, in view of other accounts, these figures are probably exaggerated, only a secretary with total commitment could have stood the strain. Wagnière was accustomed to be called to Voltaire's bedside during the night to take down new thoughts that had come into his master's mind. There were no fixed hours for meals or retiring or getting up.[84] According to Conyers, Voltaire seldom went to bed till daybreak and the next day was not visible till noon.[85] Such a pattern, or lack of it, had been established long ago at Cirey, as Mme de Graffigny witnessed (D1807). Lekain noted that the *philosophe*, as late as 1776, was working regularly ten hours a day (D20245); Charles Burney in 1770 had reported the same detail.[86] By the later years, most of the day was spent in bed, according to Moultou (D20376) and Wagnière, who adds that it was devoted to work.[87] In particular, it appears, the forenoon was set aside for working. Visitors from earlier years, when presumably Voltaire was to be found at his desk rather than in bed at such hours, discovered that

in the forenoon 'he could not bear to have his hours of study inter-
rupted';[88] this observation by Thomas Pennant in 1765 is repeated in
identical terms by John Moore seven years later.[89] Mme de Graffigny
had many years before noticed the same impatience about wasting time
away from his work (D1807), and this was likely only to increase with
age, as Voltaire saw the remaining years being whittled away.

A large part of this time was, inevitably, spent not on composition
but on correction, proof-reading, correspondence with the publishers.
Jeroom Vercruysse has latterly contributed a sympathetic appreciation
of Voltaire's persistence in his repeated attempts to produce a faithful
edition of his works. The 45-volume in-quarto edition, for example,
which began appearing in 1768, took four years of its author's life in
meticulous attention to the state of the text, neglecting nothing: punc-
tuation, lay-out, typography, cancels, distribution. Professor Vercruysse pays deep tribute, well-justified by the manifold instances he
cites, to Voltaire's unremitting efforts and indeed battles with his
diverse publishers, in which insistence, cunning and cajolery, loud
protestation and, all too often, a stoical resignation before the inevitable, play their part. There is, as he says, something admirable in this
stubborn fight, something absurd perhaps but certainly something
exemplary.[90] Let us not altogether overlook this increasingly important
aspect of the writer's life as the years advance, and one which yields as
much as any other the flavour of his personality.

Lekain noted in 1776 that Voltaire's literary studies did not, however, prevent him from attending to the demands of his community at
Ferney and finding ways and means of increasing its trade, prosperity,
happiness. He makes clear how comprehensively the patriarch was
involved, as bailiff, treasurer, house steward, inspector of his animal
livestock (D20245). The *philosophe* was also the *seigneur de Ferney*, and to
the end he kept up both functions assiduously. As *seigneur* he had
installed a gallows on his domain as visible symbol of his overlord-
ship.[91] John Wilkes (1765) reported that his people adored and daily
blessed their benefactor,[92] and John Moore (1772) that he was 'affable,
humane and generous to his tenants and dependants'.[93] For Roland de
la Platière he was a veritable deity, moving and having his being in his
own temple.[94]

We end, then, with the patriarch once more. Dressed as he often was
in outlandish clothes, such as a suit at least thirty years out of date,[95] or
wearing more often than not a nightgown under a flowered waistcoat,[96]
red or black velvet breeches[97] and white stockings,[98] his head covered
by an unpowdered tie-wig beneath a bonnet cap,[99] his costume seemed

absurdly variegated, as though thrown together from a theatrical ward-
robe for a mad King Lear.[100] Yet this was the man who could say, with
justice and pride, that he was 'Lord of a greater extent than the
neighbouring republic of Geneva – I pay no Taxes to the french King
or any other – I enjoy Liberty and Property here & am my own
Master.'[101] The last word may well lie with John Wilkes, who did not
exaggerate in calling him 'the creator of everything useful, beautiful, or
valuable in the whole tract near him, which before was a rude wilder-
ness'.[102]

7 Paris, and Death

As Voltaire entered on the last full year of his life, little suggested the dramatic circumstances in which his final months would be played out. At Ferney his existence continued much as it had done since Turgot's downfall. The period of great crusades is at an end; and even his preoccupation with the colony he has established is more muted. True, Voltaire's indomitable optimism wells up again, as he recovers from the shock of seeing Turgot depart from power. He tells d'Alembert that the small circle of the enlightened will always exist; they will probably never be powerful but, at the same time, they are indestructible (D20501, 4 January [1777]). While this is a far cry from the confident assertions of earlier years that the liberation of men's minds is just around the corner, the remark does not reveal that quality of bleak despair which had pervaded his letters a few months before. If major affairs such as Calas and La Barre are a thing of the past, the reason may be sought rather more in the fatigue of old age (cf. D20684) than in pessimism of outlook. Voltaire is still finding the energy for various enterprises on a minor scale. He adopts a poor young girl, Mlle de Varicourt, the daughter of an impoverished officer who lives nearby, takes her into his house much as he had done with Marie Corneille, and sets about finding her a husband in the marquis de Villette, the marriage being celebrated in Voltaire's own church[1] in November 1777. The marquise, who came to be better known under the sobriquet 'Belle et Bonne', will repay his care by watching over him during his final illness, being present at his death, and continuing thereafter for the rest of her life to worship the *philosophe*'s memory. Lady Morgan, visiting her in 1816, remarked that her apartment (in the house where Voltaire had died) was a sort of temple dedicated to him.[2]

137

Voltaire also threw himself ardently into supporting the Société Economique of Berne when it decided to offer a prize for the best criminal code submitted to it. He himself gave money to augment the prize, wrote his *Prix de la justice et de l'humanité* in response (though he did not submit it for the competition) and characteristically drummed up financial support from important patrons like Frederick (D20743, Commentary) and Catherine (D20745). In smaller compass, these activities display the same flair as ever for promoting a cause and attracting to it the maximum of publicity.

But this is to paint too rosy a picture. Voltaire was also dismayed to hear reports from d'Alembert that the Spanish Inquisition had revived (D20491) and saw that there would yet be many an auto-da-fé and many a chevalier de La Barre to suffer persecution before the day of enlightenment dawned (D20564, 15 February 1777). Judicial oppression was in the air again; Delisle de Sales had been imprisoned for writing a subversive work and was awaiting banishment from France for life. Voltaire was appalled at such continuing fanaticism and frightened on account of the threat it seemed to present once again to himself. The news filled him with renewed despair and was the direct cause, in his view, of a serious stroke which he suffered in March 1777 (D20623); Lekain reports that his life was for a time in great danger and that he was unconscious for over two hours (D20638), and Voltaire speaks of the total amnesia which afflicted him for a couple of days (D20615). In addition, he had considerable financial worries during the early months of 1777. Ready money was short because those like Richelieu who owed him a considerable amount by way of annuities had not paid up. All in all it was a harassing period. One readily understands Frederick's argument when writing to d'Alembert in January 1777 that Voltaire had survived too long; dying a year earlier, he would have escaped his present afflictions (D20539).

Ferney too is continuing cause for concern. Voltaire sees the gradual disappearance from governmental office of those who are capable of offering benevolent patronage (D20730). He complains that the colony is dilapidated (D20683), with workers fleeing in large numbers (D20523). But it seems as if these protests, made not to intimates but to people capable of providing protection for Ferney, are exaggerated in the never-ending cause of winning support and sympathy from powerful patrons. To members of the family like the marquis de Florian the image presented is more hopeful. Voltaire tells the marquis that several houses are going up, even more quickly than expected because of the mild winter (D20505, 6 January 1777). The following autumn he reports with satisfaction that the hamlet is turning into an attractive town (D20810), a view borne out by the marquis de Villette, who speaks of a thriving, orderly community, containing over a hundred houses of pleasing appearance (D20886). On Voltaire's name-day the inhabitants once again show their gratitude by putting on a *fête*, to which the *seigneur* is welcomed in idolatrous fashion and where he revels in the rejoicings (D20826). Clearly Voltaire is anxious about the precarious state of Ferney, feeling that it still needs political support from the French capital in order to flourish. But at the end of 1777 the community remains an outstandingly successful demonstration of Voltaire's liberal paternalism in practice.

With customary resilience, despite the grave stroke which he had suffered, the patriarch once more recovered his health. By June he was in fine form again, according to a neighbour (D20703, Commentary), and receiving the odd visitor (D20719). Despite his frailty his mind was as vigorous as ever, still as well equipped for the rapid aphorism (D20824). A hilarious account survives of a visit made by the unfortunate Barthe to read his play to Voltaire. Such an enterprise betokened a foolish audacity; it received its just reward. After ten lines Voltaire fell to frightening grimaces and contortions. When these had no effect he broke out into loud yawns, complained of being unwell, and eventually withdrew. Barthe had managed to read only the first of his five acts! The rest of the audience had meantime been sitting in horror-struck silence, as Barthe became filled with despair. But the *philosophe* must have suffered some remorse, for on the morrow Barthe was invited back to continue his reading, with promises that there would be no recurrence of the previous day's 'accident'. Alas! Voltaire's temperament was stronger than his desire to be polite. This time he confined himself to yawning, but his patience survived only one more act and during the third he had a fainting fit – which he later described as sent by divine providence to save him from disaster (D20843). The terrifying vitality of the old man had never been more in evidence. In the last two months of 1777 he was engaged on writing three brochures and two tragedies, and still capable of achieving what was denied poor Barthe when he declaimed the whole of *Irène* through from beginning to end before supper, without suffering any after-effects whatsoever (D20972).

Already in 1769 one visitor to Ferney had perceptively summed up the rival attractions for Voltaire of his country retreat and the French capital. Roland de la Platière had declared:

Nothing would be capable of tearing him away from his beloved Ferney, unless perhaps that unfortunate fame as an author which will devour him irresistibly until the grave . . . although he compared very ingeniously the pleasant things of country life with the turbulent agitation of society, he did not persuade me to believe the more in his happiness; he makes it depend too closely on this social world, to which he is still too attached.[3]

We have seen that feelers put out by Voltaire during his years in Geneva finally convinced him that Paris was forever closed to him. Still, hope was never abandoned. With the death of Louis XV and the accession of Louis XVI in 1774 a change seemed to come about at Versailles. It gradually became apparent that no formal order forbidding Voltaire's return had ever existed, as he himself pointed out (e.g., D19588, 3 August [1775]). This knowledge must have been of great comfort. But he had lived so long in exile, had settled in so completely to a way of life as author and patriarch at Ferney that he felt no great compulsion to return, the more so now that he knew it to be possible. As late as the beginning of 1778 it seemed certain that Voltaire would breathe his last amidst his colony in the pays de Gex. The Genevan pastor Moultou, generally an observant neighbour, concluded that the *philosophe* would not go to Paris because he knew that it might well shorten his life (D20972, 4 January [1778]). He had probably divined Voltaire's feelings correctly at the time. But a certain wavering in Voltaire's attitude is soon evident. On 15 January he is talking of visiting Paris in the summer (D20987). The immediate cause is the time and trouble he is devoting to the preparation of his latest tragedy *Irène* for performance by the Comédie Française. By being on the spot he can exercise a closer watch on the casting and rehearsals and ensure that the actors remain faithful to the text. A secondary reason seems to have been the desire, which had never been wholly extinguished, of being received once again at Court. Already in the summer of 1776 he had talked of making the journey on account of Marie-Antoinette and that he had 'a furious passion to have her for my protectress' (D20271; cf. D21027, 21030).

But the visit might, as in 1776, have been postponed indefinitely had not Mme Denis made the first move. She decided to visit Paris, ostensibly to consult medical advice on her own behalf as well as Voltaire's and to carry the play with all its latest revisions to the actors (D21020, 1 February 1778). It is clear from this and a subsequent letter from her on the next day (D21023) that Voltaire had no present expectation of following her when she departed on 3 February with the Villettes. But letters written by Voltaire respectively on the morning and evening of that same day (D21025–6) show him actually changing his mind; by the evening he had decided to leave very soon, and he did so on the 5th, reaching Paris five days later.

The reaction of the French capital to the return of its greatest living son can easily be imagined. People flocked to see him. On the morrow of his arrival he received over three hundred people (D21036, Commentary); his house was never empty during those early days (D21040). The Académie Française sent a special deputation to greet him (D21035, Commentary), and so did the Comédie Française (D21047, Commentary). He met Benjamin Franklin, who asked of Voltaire a benediction for his eight-year-old grandson accompanying him; in the presence of some twenty witnesses, Voltaire blessed the lad in English with the words 'God and liberty' (D21049 and Commentary). The two men were to meet again at the Académie des Sciences, where the audience urged them to embrace à la française and were delighted when they hugged and kissed each other.[4] Indeed Franklin, on a diplomatic mission to France from the nascent United States and due to become before the end of the year the first American ambassador to France, was the only other person in Paris to rival Voltaire in popular acclaim. Mme d'Epinay, linking them together, catches the sense that they are the cynosure of all eyes: 'As soon as they appear at plays, on walks or at academies, cries and hand-clapping never cease. The princes appear; it's not news: Voltaire sneezes, Franklin says: God bless you, and it starts up all over again' (D21170, 3 May 1778).

But the sudden change of pace was not to be borne; many a younger man would have been overwhelmed by it. In addition, Voltaire was working night and day on his play (D21040). Before a week was up, he had fallen victim to fatigue and was suffering much pain, particularly from retention of urine (D21047, 21049). But he pressed on with work, keeping up his rehearsals with the *comédiens* even though at the point of exhaustion (D21077). By the end of February he had become seriously ill and was losing a great deal of blood. Though he continued to spit up blood for another three weeks, once more his remarkable physical vitality pulled him through, and on 21 March he was out and about again. The social round recommenced. Voltaire was to attend the Académie Française on four different occasions, accepted their invitation to preside over the sessions, and inaugurated a project for a new Dictionary (D21173), upon which he, taking the letter A, immediately set to work in a state of considerable fervour.[5]

Public adulation followed him wherever he went, the people calling him *l'homme aux Calas* (D21151, Commentary). Even at home he had only to show himself at the window for a crowd to gather (D21150). The supreme moment came on 30 March, when Voltaire attended the sixth performance of *Irène*, having been too ill to be present at the première a fortnight earlier. As Mme du Deffand had predicted to Horace Walpole in her usual feline manner, the play could not possibly fail, however bad it was, because it would not be judged on its intrinsic merits but as part of the cult of Voltaire (D21096). Her forecast of course proved correct. The play has never been considered one of Voltaire's best and its opening run of seven performances turned out also to be its last. But the actual production of *Irène* was a newsworthy event of the highest importance. Tickets were very hard to come by, and naturally their scarcity value caused their price to soar (D21110, Commentary). The tragedy has ever since been discussed almost invariably in terms of these extrinsic factors. The *Journal encyclopédique*, for instance, concentrated on the fact of its author's age, the enthusiasm of the opening night and the pathos of Voltaire's absence through illness. Hostile critics fell silent, perhaps on orders from influential friends, as Bachaumont intimates in his *Mémoires secrets*.[6]

The delayed appearance of Voltaire at his new tragedy only made the occasion the more dramatic. Watched by large crowds as he made his way in his carriage first to the Académie Française and then to the playhouse, he was received at the theatre with tumultous acclamation. A band including trumpets, tympani, oboes and clarinets added to the air of festivity. An actor brought him a laurel crown, which he gave first to the marquise de Villette sitting next to him, but he was later prevailed upon by d'Alembert to wear it. This appears to have preceded *Irène* (though accounts differ). The play, needless to say, was applauded wildly throughout. At its end the curtain fell, to rise again on a scene in which the bust of Voltaire, set on an altar and covered with laurels, held the centre of the stage; the whole company of actors stood around it, while behind them crowded in a host of spectators who had exceptionally been allowed into the wings for the performance. Once more prolonged applause broke out, after which Mme Vestris, who had played Irène, stepped forward and read a ten-line impromptu poem written in the *philosophe*'s honour by the marquis de Saint-Marc. This itself received two encores, while the *comédiens* continued to heap laurel crowns upon the bust amid scenes of rapturous enthusiasm. Such was the *éclat* surrounding every one of Voltaire's doings at this time that in less than a half-hour an enterprising printer had had two thousand copies of the verses run off. The *Correspondance littéraire* felt that one was transported back to ancient Greece and Rome by this sublime spectacle. A monument had been erected to the glory of genius, as though the stage were a public place; 'for perhaps the first time in France', it added, 'one saw public opinion enjoying the splendour of exercising total sway'.[7] The occasion has justifiably come to be seen as an apotheosis of Voltaire during his lifetime. There is a religious frenzy about the scene which René Pomeau rightly describes as pre-revolutionary in the degree of popular emotion that it evoked.[8]

Happily for him, Voltaire does not appear to have perceived the irony that the man who had all his life fought against religious enthusiasm had become the object of a cult with fanatical overtones and dangerous implications. But the apotheosis should not be seen only in this light. He himself wrote to Frederick expressing satisfaction that the audience had applauded lines in the play saying that Constantine and Theodosius were no more than superstitious tyrants, whereas thirty years before they had been regarded as model princes and even saints. Once more and for the last time in his life he discovers an upsurge of the old optimism about the progress of enlightenment. Perhaps, who knows, within a month he might even be able to pro-nounce a panegyric upon the Emperor Julian the Apostate (D21138)!

In all the adulation, only Versailles stood aloof. Genevan neighbours believed that Voltaire had made the journey to the capital largely because he thought the Queen wished to meet him (D21027, 21030), and Mme du Deffand reported after seeing Voltaire that he probably had hopes of being presented to Louis XVI as well. She guessed right in expressing her doubts that he would win this royal favour (D21077). The only person of note apart from Voltaire who was absent from the opening performance of *Irène* was the King. Everyone else of impor-tance in the Royal Family appeared, and Marie-Antoinette seemed to be paying Voltaire the supreme compliment of writing down those lines which had particularly struck her.[9] But being invited to the Court was another matter. The King, it seems, felt himself obliged to take no official cognisance of Voltaire's presence in Paris, as the latter had arrived without royal permission. Could some compromise be found whereby Voltaire might be received on an informal basis and by the Queen alone? They could, after all, keep off dangerous topics like religion and politics and talk only of Voltaire as writer of epic and tragedy. But if Marie-Antoinette was sympathetically inclined to the idea, she found the King and his counsellors unalterably opposed to it.[10] One can scarcely be surprised at the decision. Louis XVI, given the prudent conservatism of his government ever since Turgot had been dismissed, could hardly have acted otherwise. More interesting is it to note this latest instance of Voltaire's lifelong fascination with monarchs. To the end he felt that they could be a supremely important influence for good. Rare might be the prince who actually helps to advance the cause of enlightenment; nevertheless, in a large state it was only through monarchical government that one could realistically hope for progress.[11]

During the 'crowning' of Voltaire at the Comédie Française the great man had been much moved. Tears pouring down his cheeks, he said: 'They want to kill me. They have overwhelmed me with happiness' (D21139). These remarks sum up cogently the paradox of his situation. The phenomenal welcome he everywhere received was literally destroying him. His doctor, Théodore Tronchin, had predicted as much from the days of Voltaire's first illness soon after the latter's arrival in Paris, adding: 'we shall be witnesses, if not accomplices, of the death of M. de Voltaire' (D21054). But Voltaire's extraordinary stamina managed to delay Tronchin's expectations of an early death. At the beginning of April he was surprising his doctor by calling at his house at 7.30 a.m. when the latter was still in bed. Tronchin concluded that Voltaire was the maddest of the many madmen he had met during his lifetime and reported that the writer expected to live to be at least a hundred (D21143). On 12 April Mme du Deffand found Voltaire as animated as ever he had been; she informed Walpole that he had just bought a new house to which to move from his present abode at the Villettes' (D21151, Commentary). Well into May he was able to keep up a pace that would have laid low most octogenarians. But on 10 May he wrote to the marquis de Florian that he was cruelly ill (D21180); it was the beginning of the end. According to Wagnière he had become so excited over the project to prepare a new dictionary of the Académie Française that he drank a great deal of coffee to keep himself going. Two days later he had a fever, and to counteract that he took an excess of opium.[12]

The delicate physical balance was disturbed. At Ferney over the last fifteen years, according to Wagnière, he had drunk only two or three small cups of coffee daily; indeed, Voltaire was sober and moderate, said his secretary, in everything except work.[13] But the *régime* of Ferney could no longer be maintained when the pressures were so many and various. The Academy Dictionary represented the last irresistible challenge to Voltaire's desires to direct and order a grand campaign; nor can it have aided his health that his fellow-Academicians were less than zealous for the cause and needed to be whipped into action.[14] This time there was to be no reprieve. The illness went on worsening over the next three weeks. An anonymous poem survives, dated 20 May, in which the poet sings Voltaire's praises but is worried about the burden imposed

on him by public fame and gives him some homely advice on how to
look after himself.[15] But the regular meals, regular urination and warm
clothing which the author touchingly counsels Voltaire could no longer
save him. By 24 May he was in desperate straits (D21209–12); late on
the 30th he died. Mme Denis and the marquise de Villette were
amongst those present at the end but not Wagnière who, absent on
business in Ferney and separated from his beloved master for the first
time in twenty-four years, arrived back two days too late to say
farewell.[16]

Wagnière vehemently maintains in his Memoirs that he had been
kept away from Voltaire until too late by Mme Denis, who had at last
achieved her ambition of setting up house again with her uncle in Paris
and meant to keep him there. Wagnière's letters to Voltaire from
Ferney, by contrast, remind his *seigneur* that the colony has been thrown
into consternation by his departure, and the faithful secretary is appalled at the rumours that he may never return; he himself is cut to the
heart and keeps hoping that Voltaire will come back to complete this
fine monument he has built to his own glory and humanity (D21176,
21179, 21191). The Genevan Henri Rieu, in a letter published only
recently, echoes Wagnière's reflections upon Voltaire's unnecessary
journey to the capital and the way in which his secretary was kept at a
distance during his dying days;[17] almost certainly Rieu had shared
Wagnière's confidences and sympathised with them.

All too easily one may convict Mme Denis of utter selfishness in the
way she used Voltaire for her own interests during these last weeks. It is
painful too for any biographer of the *philosophe* to note with what haste
she sold out Ferney to the marquis de Villette, three months after
Voltaire's death, for a sum which Rieu describes as less than half its
value.[18] Under the scapegrace marquis the colony did not fail to
decline. By the end of the year Voltaire's library had been sold to
Catherine and Wagnière travelled to St Petersburg in 1779 to set it up
in the same order as at Ferney. Voltaire scholars in Western Europe
have since had cause to denounce Mme Denis for removing his library
to a place where for long it remained inaccessible, but it would be fairer,
and kinder, to give thanks that this priceless collection has remained
intact, with all that it can tell us (and many a secret lies still to be
revealed within its pages) about what and how Voltaire read.[19]
Nevertheless, Mme Denis's financial greed after her uncle's death was
equalled only by her expeditiousness in despatching these monuments
to his life and learning.

That said, it is not entirely certain that Wagnière was deliberately held at a distance until Voltaire was clearly dying. Quite the contrary. Mme Denis seems to have been keen to obtain his help when she realised Voltaire's grave condition, and she urged Wagnière to return as quickly as possible (D21211), even when on the following day she thought that her uncle was better and began once again to plan for the move to their new house (D21214). Nor is it proven that Voltaire really wanted to return to Ferney and was prevented simply by the evil scheming of his niece.[20] True, Voltaire's last letter to his secretary is deeply moving in its expression of remorse at having left the colony (D21209), and his coachman Pierre Morand reported that these regrets were uttered repeatedly during his final illness (D21210). But this attitude, painfully sincere though it appears, dates only from Voltaire's awareness that he is probably dying. As late as 14 and 15 May, although he is already ill, the tone he takes in letters to Wagnière is quite different. He is still anticipating his move to the new house. As for Ferney, he is not impressed by his secretary's doleful reports, telling Wagnière that d'Hornoy (son of his other niece the marquise de Florian) is protecting the community there more than is realised, while he himself is far more useful to Ferney now that he is in Paris, being more easily able to solicit patronage for it (D21192–3).

The final visit to the capital serves to focus a clear light on Voltaire's attitudes to Paris and the provinces. His feelings are ambivalent, even contradictory on occasion. But despite his full awareness of Parisian frivolity and indifference, he has achieved the dream of decades. Here he is once again at the heart of society, able to see old friends, attend his beloved Comédie Française, the Académie des Sciences, the Académie Française; there is useful work for him to do both in the Academy and in the playhouse; furthermore, he is applauded on all sides. Except for the rebuff from Versailles, he has triumphed over every obstacle. He is not troubled in his conscience about Ferney, believing – quite possibly with justice – that he is an even more valuable *seigneur* now than when he was in the château. Nor has he been completely inactive in Paris on behalf of Gex (cf. D21145).

When Voltaire was first taken ill in February, his reaction was to leave for Ferney as soon as possible (D21047). But once he was well again the thought of fleeing to his sanctum of calm and order gave way to the renewed magnetic attraction of the brilliant capital. Gradually a pattern emerges; he will spend his summers at Ferney and the other eight months of the year in Paris (D21146, Commentary; 21151, Commentary). For the moment, however, it seems he cannot leave, as there is a suspicion that if he does the clergy will prevent his return (D21149).

Wagnière believes that this letter, written by the marquis de Thibouville to Mme Denis, was a lie concocted to keep his master in Paris and that once it had been shown to him it held him tied to the capital and sealed his death.[21] But there is no supporting evidence for this accusation; as late as 20 April Voltaire is talking of an early departure (D21160) and nowhere does he express any sense of being prevented from leaving. Mme Denis may be entirely truthful in saying that her uncle is much more gentle and amiable since he came to Paris (D21178); his letters generally confirm this, revealing few signs of that black depression which would grip him periodically at Ferney. Everything suggests that if he had recovered his health he would have settled easily into an alternating sequence of winter and summer residences in town and country.

   Death ordained otherwise. It did not however catch him unawares. He had long been concerned about what would happen to his body after he died. The custom in Catholic France of burying those who died outside the Church in unconsecrated ground appalled him, since it meant that the corpse was denied a decent burial. Such had occurred in 1730 to the actress Adrienne Lecouvreur, interred in a piece of waste ground because she had died too suddenly to be received back into the Church and therefore remained excommunicated, as were all actors still exercising their profession. The infamy perpetrated on her corpse was all the more horrifying to Voltaire because he was at her bedside when she died;[22] it received lasting commemoration in his *Lettres philosophiques*,[23] as well as becoming the subject of an eloquent poem he wrote in the year of her death.[24] But Voltaire's protest arose not only from affection for the dead *comédienne* or a desire to improve the status of actors; it was instigated too by a peculiarly strong aversion for this repellent act, which filled him with the same horror as ruminations upon the St Bartholomew Day Massacre or Calas being tortured on the wheel.[25] To this was added a terrible dread that he, the scourge of the Church, would suffer similar vengeance. It runs like a leitmotiv through his writing; and this particular fear is probably as much the basis for sudden bouts of panic about possible persecution as the thought of anything that might be done to him in his lifetime. In 1754 he writes to d'Argental that he is ill and expecting to share the fate of Adrienne Lecouvreur (D5691). Fifteen years later he writes to Mme Denis explaining why he took Communion at Ferney; it was necessary in order to avoid scandal for himself and his family. By contrast, what did his fellow-writer Boindin achieve by refusing to submit to the law of the land? Nothing but pain for his family, 'and he was thrown on the refuse dump' (D15596). To Martin Sherlock in 1776 he reflected on how much better off were the English: 'Ah! Sir, you are happy, you may do any thing; we are born in slavery, and we die in slavery; we cannot even die as we will, we must have a priest.'[26] Throughout his life from at least the 1730s he knew that he would have to make an 'art of dying'.[27]

So the first illness in Paris in February 1778 caught him somewhat by surprise. At Ferney he had prepared a situation which would lead to burial in his church (or more precisely, in a tomb which was half-in half-out of it: cf. D20719). But by coming to Paris he had upset this delicately contrived state of affairs. He realised that the clergy were probably hostile and that death would overtake him before he had made his peace with them. D'Alembert found him terrified by the perilous state in which he had placed himself (D21052). Thereafter Voltaire quickly set about removing himself from such dangers. Three days after d'Alembert's visit he warmly welcomed one abbé Gaultier, who had declared that he wished to see him in order to save his soul from damnation (D21066, 21070). Gaultier made several visits to Voltaire's bedside, obtaining the following declaration on 2 March:

I the undersigned declare that, suffering for the last four days from a vomiting of blood at eighty-four years of age, and having been unable to drag myself to church, M. the curé of Saint-Sulpice having kindly added to his good works that of sending me M. the abbé Gaultier, priest, I confessed to him, and that if God disposes of me I die in the holy Catholic religion in which I was born, hoping from the divine mercy that it will deign to pardon all my faults, and that if I have ever caused scandal to the Church I ask pardon for that from God and the Church . . .

(D. app. 499)

The declaration was duly witnessed by Voltaire's great-nephew the abbé Mignot and his friend the marquis de Villevieille. Nothing was lacking to ensure that the document would be thoroughly respectable. As for the contents, they too are orthodox – as far as they go. But there is no reference to the divinity of Christ, that cornerstone of the faith upon which Voltaire had expended so many attacks during his lifetime, just as there is no explicit disavowal of his own writings. In the confrontation between priest and penitent it was the latter who had the better achieved his aims. Voltaire had found the cleric he needed: decent, unfanatical and naïve, 'un bon imbécile', as he summed him up to Wagnière. However, the abbé, it appears, recognised at once the equivocal nature of the declaration, declaring to Wagnière that it did not signify a great deal. He probably saw it as a promising base upon which to build in future visits. As it was, Voltaire seems to have eluded an attempt by the priest to give him Communion, alleging that he was still spitting blood.

The abbé was engaged with one who had had long practice in wily tactics. Unknown to him, he had in fact seen Voltaire for almost the last time. His usefulness to the *philosophe* now at an end, he was simply denied admittance when next he called. Voltaire made a show of apology, explaining that the only priest he could now see was the curé de Saint-Sulpice (the abbé de Tersac), who had since claimed prior right of access to Voltaire's soul and been graciously granted it (D21091). Gaultier was fobbed off with a general remark that Voltaire would be glad to see him when he was a little better (D21102). Despite plaintive letters from the abbé later on (including the day of Voltaire's death) that no one would allow him to see the great man (D21128, 21221) he had, quite simply, been dismissed from the latter's spiritual service. His sole consolation was to be admitted (after his final letter to Voltaire) to the dying man's bedside a few hours before the end, but accompanied by the curé de Saint-Sulpice. By then, however, Voltaire was in no fit state to make any further retractions. The final words of the *philosophe* to the two representatives of the Catholic Church were piteous but unyielding: 'Let me die in peace!' The great prize had eluded the zealous abbé.[28]

So too had it eluded everyone else. Voltaire died as he lived, a deist. His true declaration of faith had been made in writing on 28 February in Wagnière's presence: 'I die worshipping God, loving my friends, not hating my enemies, detesting superstition' (D app. 497). Although the curé de Saint-Sulpice took over from Gaultier the prerogative of visiting Voltaire, he made no further progress with his parishioner's conversion; the visits seem to have been of a purely courteous nature and never in private, according to the marquis de Villette.[29] Besides, Voltaire was now convalescing, and doubtless the curé saw little profit in attempting to extract any new confessions until the fear of death became more immediate once again. When in May the end was near, the curé lent his assistance to a macabre arrangement that would secure Voltaire the respectful disposal of his body that he sought, though not in Paris. In consequence, the Chief of Police was able to direct the government minister responsible that it should be transported out of Paris for burial at Ferney (D21208); the minister transmitted the necessary authorisation to d'Hornoy. Once clear of the capital, the mourners could arrange to have the body embalmed (D21218–19). But strict secrecy was enjoined in order to secure the success of the plan, the news of Voltaire's death was to be concealed for some hours afterwards, and action was taken to ensure that the journals also maintained silence (D21220; cf. D21032, Commentary).

This plan was executed once Voltaire had died. After a hasty embalming the body was clad in a nightgown and nightcap, placed in a coach and smuggled out of the capital. In the event, the decision to go to Ferney was cancelled; it was feared that resistance from the bishop of Annecy might prove insuperable. The abbé Mignot took the corpse to the abbey of Scellières, in Champagne, of which he was the commendatory Abbot; and there he prevailed upon the prior to bury it with due ceremony in the church, pending an eventual transfer to Ferney. As it was, the interment took place only just in time. The Archbishop of Paris, getting wind of the family arrangements, wrote with all speed to the Bishop of Troyes urging him to prevent such a burial within the latter's diocese. When this proved to be too late, the abbey prior was made the scapegoat and removed from office. Only the prompt action of Mignot had ensured that Voltaire would not, at his end, become some awful kind of Flying Dutchman, with no safe haven to receive his body. Nor was it ever to reach Ferney; there too the clergy had definitively barred the way.[30]

For some, there could scarcely exist a more odious symbol of the authoritarianism of the Catholic Church under the Ancien Régime than this episode. One might die only within the Church, or else be an outcast. The account of Voltaire's ingenious manoeuvres to find a middle way commands respect and compassion. Yet in the end they would have proved insufficient but for the devotion, ingenuity and – it should not be forgotten – privileged position of members of his family. Even so, the spectacle of Voltaire's body, ill-embalmed and increasingly offensive, being removed from Paris as though it were contraband goods, testifies eloquently to the barbarous nature of a society which could so abuse its most famous member and vilify human dignity.

The final triumph must however lie with Voltaire. His dead body was defenceless against insult, but while he lived his genius could still bestride the world even as he lay on his deathbed. There is no way more fitting to close his life than with his very last letter. It is addressed to the chevalier de Lally-Tolendal, whose father had been executed in 1766 for alleged treason after his defeat by the English in India; it was the fate of Admiral Byng in reverse and upon grounds as slender. Voltaire had led the fight to clear Lally's name, and at last came the news that here too he had won. The letter is poignantly simple: 'The dying man recovers life at learning this great news; he embraces M. de Lally most tenderly; he sees that the King is the defender of justice; he will die content' (D21213, 26 May [1778]). The 'calm of mind, all passion spent' is moving as it takes on the Voltaire rhythms for one last time with the same assured art and economy as ever. From the paradoxical expression of joy in the opening remark, he moves through affectionate greetings to a simple political statement, and lastly to the philosophical leave-taking of his correspondent in particular and of the world at large. When one reflects on the circumstances in which this letter must have been composed by a debilitated figure near to death, and sees that it is yet a model of ordered elegance, one grasps something of the extraordinary capacities of Voltaire's mind. It might well be termed his testament: in politics, the campaign for justice with the king as lynch-pin of the system; in art, the classical qualities of balance, concision, clarity.

Such was the man. What influence did he have on his own world and on posterity? As Lanson put it in his classic biography, the question is almost impossible to answer with any degree of precision.[31] This was the situation when Lanson wrote seventy years ago and it has not changed significantly since then, even though the amount of scholar-ship undertaken on Voltaire in the interim is immeasurable. Yet, as Lanson adds, the reality of Voltaire's influence cannot be doubted.[32] His literary production extended over more than sixty years; according to Besterman's count[33] what is extant runs to fifteen million words. From the production of his first tragedy *Oedipe* in 1718, he dominated the Comédie Française during his lifetime (D70, Commentary). His epic poem *La Henriade* was considered, even by a coolly detached observer like Mathieu Marais, to be a masterpiece and the glory of the French nation when it first appeared (under its original title *La Ligue*) in 1723 (D135, Commentary). Already by the 1730s, according to Jean-Jacques Rousseau, his fellow-writers hung upon his every word.[34] The Voltaire Catalogue at the Bibliothèque Nationale recently published contains 5,618 entries of works by him; the nearest author to that is Cicero, with fewer than three thousand. One can easily lose oneself in endless statistical detail where Voltaire is concerned. Better, perhaps, to convey some sense of his moral standing among his contemporaries. The very banality of John Moore's comment in 1772 makes it the more representative: 'This extraordinary person has continued to excite more curiosity, and to retain the attention of Europe for a longer space of time, than any other man this age has produced, monarchs and heroes included. – Even the most trivial anecdote relating to him seems,

in some degree, to interest the Public'.[35] Such is his fame that in 1770 a
group of friends and admirers, including Diderot, Grimm, Marmontel,
d'Alembert and Helvétius, united under Mme Necker's guidance to
commission a statue of him by one of the most distinguished of French
sculptors, Pigalle.[36] By then it was common in France to refer to the
century as 'le siècle de Voltaire' (cf. e.g., D16813). What was fame in
some eyes was notoriety for others. Diderot is echoing orthodox popular opinion when he has a character in his *Jacques le fataliste* (*c.* 1773)
equate Voltaire with the Antichrist.[37] Be that as it may, by the last
weeks of Voltaire's life John Adams was summing up public opinion
generally when reporting the conversation at a dinner party he
attended in Paris. The great man was extolled to the skies as the 'grand
Monarch of Science and Literature'. The table concluded that after his
death 'the Republic of Letters would be restored. But it was now a
Monarchy . . .' (D21156, Commentary).

For a major writer like Diderot, who ranks alongside Voltaire in
twentieth-century critical esteem, the shadow cast by the latter was
enormous, even inhibiting. Jacques Chouillet sums it up concisely in
saying that Diderot might well have phrased it: 'Etre Voltaire ou
rien'.[38] When Voltaire died Diderot wrote of the immense void that had
been created in all branches of literature, asserting that 'your name . . .
will go down to the most distant posterity and will perish only amidst
the ruins of the world.' There follows an enumeration of Voltaire's skill
in epic, tragedy, light poetry, mock-epic, history and narrative, as well
as his achievement in introducing Locke, Newton, Shakespeare and
Congreve to France. He then passes on to praise Voltaire's 'striking
actions', his courageous defence of oppressed innocence, his creation of
a new town at his own expense; 'which amongst us would not give his
life for one day like yours?'[39] It is the tribute of a modest man, the more
striking because that man was himself a great writer possessed of
outstanding sensitivity and judgment. His view, encompassing so
much of Voltaire's work in this broad sweep, is therefore of particular
value as testimony in the year of Voltaire's death.

Soon would come the great collective edition of Voltaire's works,
organised by Beaumarchais as a worthy monument to the memory of its
author. It was published at Kehl, just across the Rhine from Strasbourg,
because Voltaire's Complete Works could still not be printed in France.
The Archbishop of Vienne, for instance, informed his parishioners in a
pastoral circular that it would be a mortal sin to subscribe to or in any
way aid the sale of this edition. Even the Prospectus, when it appeared
in 1781, aroused great hostility from the clergy, necessitating a total

ban on all reference to the work in French journals. The publication of the first volumes was condemned by the Archbishop of Paris in 1785 and the Government ordered the edition to be suppressed. But the volumes went on appearing until the whole work was complete by 1789. Unfortunately, Beaumarchais's gesture led him into financial ruin; while poor administration on his part was a prime factor, the continued political opposition from the Church to the man it saw as its greatest enemy doubtless also played a significant part.[40]

Despite these difficulties, however, Voltaire was much read in the years before the Revolution; and the *cahiers de doléance* in which the three Estates of the realm presented their grievances to the Etats-généraux on the eve of that great event contain a remarkably close similarity to Voltaire's programme of reform, in the view of one recent commentator, who argues that if, as is widely believed, the *cahiers* reflect a true image of the France of 1789, Voltaire continued to represent French aspirations at the very close of the Ancien Régime. The Declaration of the Rights of Man stresses the same ideals as Voltaire: liberty of speech, press, assembly, religion; equality before the law rather than social equality; right to property and security; the law of the secular State as the highest authority; reform in criminal procedures abolishing torture, unnecessary punishment, and arrest without due legal process; equitable taxation.[41]

It is with the early period of the Revolution that Voltaire's influence can be most closely associated, and one may suitably date the highwater mark as 11 July 1791, the day on which his remains were brought back to Paris to be placed in the Panthéon, the newly created national secular shrine, at the close of a magnificently solemn procession through the streets of the capital. It was a second apotheosis of the 'saint' who had prepared the way for the Revolution, representing the victory of reason, philosophy, justice and tolerance, as Roland de la Platière's wife, Mme Roland, now a prominent figure in events, saw it.[42] Just as his first 'crowning' at the Comédie Française had unleashed unique demonstrations of fervour, so now 'le roi Voltaire', returning in triumph over arbitrary Church-dominated power, showed the way to a new patriotic cult which would reach its height in the desperate years just ahead.

In 1791, with the split between the Revolution and the Ancien Régime now definitive, Voltaire was of particular relevance to the movement of public opinion. But from 1792 the battle against the Church and for religious tolerance and social equality was won. Political life became more democratic as the lower social classes began to play a larger part. The focus of interest amongst the *philosophes* gradually passed to Rousseau, who had come to equal Voltaire in popular appeal and by 1793 to overtake him. This general impression is borne out by a recent statistical analysis of references to Voltaire and his fellow-*philosophes* during the years 1791–3.[43]

But the history of Voltaire's influence during the Revolutionary period still needs to be written, as too that of the *philosophe*'s presence and standing during the following century. The only important work undertaken in this area so far is by André Billaz,[44] who has charted the reaction of Romantic writers to Voltaire. As he shows, Voltaire was the supreme negative reference for the Romantics, representing all that they wished to destroy in terms of outmoded attitudes and literary style. But it was not easy to reject a figure who had shown so much diversity. If Voltaire had made overtures to enlightened despotism he had also fought for liberty and prepared the Revolution. If for Chateaubriand his anti-Christian attitudes were odious, he still represented the best of French classical tradition, not to be rejected or lost. So too, broadly felt other writers of the generation of 1800 like Mme de Staël and Constant. But after 1815 the break became more complete in literary matters, as Voltaire was deemed to lack the imaginative breadth of a Shakespeare or a Schiller and his ironic wit was considered offensive to devotees of the new melancholy. However, many of the younger Romantics were attracted to the political Voltaire who had fought for the Rights of Man. Under the Restoration he became a symbol, for such as Stendhal, of the liberal values that had once more been crushed by a reactionary régime in which the Church had regained the ascendant. From 1817 to 1829 almost every year saw a new edition, and sometimes several, of Voltaire's complete works: 'Balzac's France buys Voltaire in massive quantities'. As political author he was the darling of the freethinking bourgeois; as literary custodian of classical values he appealed by virtue of *La Henriade* and his tragedies to the more traditional elements of society.[45]

Such contradictions testify to the almost suffocating comprehensiveness of the *philosophe*. It was impossible for the next fifty years to escape his universal presence, whether thundered at from the pulpit or extolled on the tribune or taught in the classroom. He was used at every turn in the political debates of the century, against religious superstition but for religion, for monarchy but against privilege. With the fading of time this impression gradually became diluted and merged into more simplistic positions: Flaubert's Homais, the apothecary in *Madame Bovary* (1857), contemptible in his complacent support for half-baked scientific ideas of the day, is a 'Voltairean', but a monstrous deformation of the *philosophe*. In 1878, on the centenary of Voltaire's birth, celebrants of his memory were necessarily drawn into a rigid anticlericalism, even if they did not begin by taking that position.[46]

Gradually that view too has died away. Two hundred years on from Voltaire's death an attempt is being made to see him rounded and whole. It is a major academic industry, involving a dozen major conferences on Voltaire and Rousseau throughout the world in 1978, a hundred contributors working under the general editorship of W. H. Barber and his Editorial Board on the *Oeuvres complètes* and a Voltaire Foundation at Oxford which is itself a sizeable and growing concern. Studies large and small on the master cease not to flow in amidst much else to the *Studies on Voltaire and the eighteenth century*. Paul Valéry's cogent remark on Voltaire (in his 1944 oration at the Sorbonne on the 250th anniversary of Voltaire's birth) would be even truer today: 'Voltaire lives, Voltaire endures: he is unendingly topical.'[47]

How much he matters, though, outside the ranks of academic specialists, is harder to say. Lanson saw that his rôle as a populariser, with the supreme ability to set public opinion in certain directions, makes it harder to dissociate his influence from the collective movement of the Enlightenment than is the case with a more clear-cut, less protean intellect like Montesquieu or, one may add, the marquis de Sade. It is above all the Voltairean spirit, preaching tolerance and intellectual freedom, hating oppression, which one can discern as his enduring legacy. In some respects it is not well suited to an age like ours, where a sceptical approach to absolute dogmas is conspicuous mainly by its absence, and even when it is present is rarely combined with the energy Voltaire put into everything he did. Goldsmith spoke true in asserting that 'no man can more truly be said to have lived'.[48] Action, and commitment: the question is often raised as to whether Voltaire was sincere. Good faith is difficult to determine in any writer, especially one of such sophistication as Voltaire. Since he lived in a society where he often feared for his safety the question becomes even more complex. Countless times he did not hesitate to disavow works and attitudes which were in danger of compromising him or to publish under pseudonyms (the Bibliothèque Nationale catalogue lists 175 in all). But in a larger sense his sincerity can hardly be doubted, as he ceaselessly fought the *infâme* with increasing awareness of his own position and the nature of his enemy. Flaubert sums it up in a letter:

For me he is a *saint*! . . . Do you obtain such results when you are not sincere?

. . . In short, that man seems to me ardent, relentless, convinced, superb. His 'Ecrasons l'infâme' has on me the effect of a crusading call. His whole intelligence was a war machine. And what makes me cherish him is the disgust which Voltaireans inspire in me, people who laugh at the important things: Did *he* laugh? He gnashed his teeth![49]

Voltaire declared that in his view history required the same art as tragedy, with an exposition, a crux, a dénouement (D7792). Whatever the validity of that theory, one is tempted to apply it to his own life. For all his exiles, alarums and disappointments, he was a happy man: partly because of his marvellously buoyant temperament, but also because in the end circumstances were good to him. A life is not a work of art. Yet in Voltaire's existence one can trace as in a well-constructed play the growing self-knowledge and the gradual discovery of how and where he could make a permanent impression in the world. He was rich and he lived long; in both these respects he was fortunate. Eventually he knew that his true rôle was as a *philosophe*, his true home a remote château just inside France but where he was lord of his own demesne. At the end, a glorious dénouement was granted him in Paris, with honours few have ever experienced. Death will always come, as Sartre once put it, too soon or too late. In Voltaire's case the timing was almost right; only a few last days of doubt and remorse and pain cloud the picture, and even there his intelligence shines forth to the very end. He was a great man; and the gods who had blessed him with such bounteous talents smiled upon him and made his life one of rare meaning.

Chronology

	Voltaire	Other
1694	21 November: born.	
1701	13 July: Voltaire's mother dies.	
1702		Queen Anne succeeds William III to English throne.
1703	October – enters Jesuit collège Louis-le-Grand.	
1704		Newton, *Optics*.
1706	Introduced to Société du Temple by abbé de Châteauneuf.	Mme du Châtelet born.
1710		Leibniz, *Theodicy*.
1711	Leaves Louis-le-Grand.	
1712		Rousseau born.
1713	September: goes to Holland as secretary to the French ambassador: affair with Pimpette. 18 December: leaves Holland.	Diderot born. Treaty of Utrecht.
1714	January: starts law studies with Maître Alain; meets Thieriot.	George I succeeds Queen Anne to English throne.
1715		1 September: Louis XIV dies. Louis XV comes to throne. Regency of duc d'Orléans until 1723.

Voltaire	*Other*
1716 May: exiled to Sully-sur-Loire (chez le duc de Sully). October: returns from Sully.	Leibniz dies.
1717 17 May: Bastille.	D'Alembert born.
1718 11 April: leaves Bastille: sent to Châtenay. June: begins using name of Voltaire. 12 July: returns to Paris. 18 November: 1st performance of *Oedipe*.	Fréron born.
1719 Awarded gold medal and watch by George I of England. (1719–23): worldly life; frequent visits to and stays at country châteaux.	
1720	Collapse of John Law's System.
1721	Montesquieu, *Lettres persanes*.
1722 1 January: Arouet *père* dies. January: receives pension from Regent. July–October: visits Low Countries.	
1723 *La Ligue* appears (later title: *La Henriade*). November: attack of smallpox.	Louis XV's personal reign begins.
1724	
1725 September: three of Voltaire's plays being performed during celebrations of Louis XV's wedding. November: receives pension from Queen.	
1726 January–February: Chevalier de Rohan quarrel. April: Bastille. 10 May: leaves Calais for England.	Swift, *Gulliver's Travels*. Cardinal Fleury becomes effectively Prime Minister of France (until 1743).

Voltaire   *Other*

c. July: secret return visit to
France briefly.
September: Voltaire's sister,
Mme Mignot, dies.

1727   January: presented at English   April: Newton dies.
       Court.   10 June: George I dies: George
                                               II succeeds to English throne.
1728   January: *Essay on Epick Poetry*,
       January: *Essay upon Civil Wars in*
       France.
       March: publishes *La Henriade* in
       London.
       c. May: *Essai sur la poésie épique*
       (French translation).
       November: leaves England.
       Spends winter in Dieppe.

1729   March: returns to Paris, at first
       secretly.
       (1729–30) with La Condamine,
       makes fortune in Paris lottery.

1730   March: Adrienne Lecouvreur
                                               dies; buried in unconsecrated
                                               ground.

1731   *Histoire de Charles XII* printed at
       Rouen: police seize part of the
       edition.

1732   13 August: 1st performance of
       Zaïre.
       Begins work on *Siècle de Louis*
       XIV.

1733   *Le Temple du Goût* appears.   Pope, *Essay on Man*.
       Becomes linked with Mme du
       Châtelet.
       August: *Letters Concerning the*
       English Nation (English version
       of *Lettres philosophiques*) published
       in London.

1734   April: *Lettres philosophiques*
       published in France.
       May: *Lettre de cachet* for arrest of
       Voltaire; he goes into hiding.

Voltaire	*Other*
June: *Lettres philosophiques* publicly burned in Paris. July: settles at Cirey. October: Mme du Châtelet joins Voltaire at Cirey.	

1735   March: allowed to return to Paris.

1736   April–July: in Paris for the Jore affair.
August: begins correspondence with Frederick.
November: *Le Mondain* appears.
December: flees to Holland.

1737   January: *Défense du Mondain* appears.
March: returns from Holland to Cirey.

1738   1st edition of *Eléments de la philosophie de Newton* appears.
December: Mme de Graffigny arrives at Cirey to stay until February 1739.

February: M. Denis marries Voltaire's niece.
December: Desfontaines, *Voltairomanie* appears.

1739   May: visits Brussels with Mme du Châtelet.
August: leaves Brussels for Paris.
December: returns to Low Countries, after Cirey.
Essai sur le Siècle de Louis XIV appears.

1740   Publishes Frederick's *Anti-Machiavel*.
August: goes from Low Countries to meet Frederick at Cleves.
November–December: visits Frederick in Berlin; returns to Low Countries.

31 May: Frederick becomes King of Prussia.
16 December: Frederick invades Silesia: War of Austrian Succession begins.

1741   1 April: *Mahomet* first performed (at Lille).

Voltaire   *Other*

November: returns with Mme
du Châtelet to Paris.
December: returns with Mme
du Châtelet to Cirey.

1742   *c.* February: returns with Mme
du Châtelet to Paris.
August: *Mahomet* first performed
in Paris.
August–October: visits in
French provinces and to
Brussels.
November: back in Paris.

1743   April: fails to obtain Cardinal   Condorcet born.
Fleury's chair in Académie
Française.
June: leaves for diplomatic
mission in Berlin.
August: Berlin and various
places in Germany.
October: leaves Berlin for
Brussels and Paris.

1744   April: returns to Cirey.   Pope dies.
April–July: composes *La Princesse*   M. Denis dies.
de Navarre.   Louis XV declares war on
October: returns to Paris for   England and Austria.
rehearsals of *La Princesse de*
Navarre.
(1744–45): beginning of love
affair with Mme Denis.

1745   18 February: Voltaire's brother   11 May: French victory at
Armand dies.   Fontenoy.
23 February: *La Princesse de*   Mme de Pompadour becomes
Navarre first performed at   titular mistress of Louis XV.
Versailles.   Swift dies.
1 April: appointed Royal
Historiographer.
May: *Poème sur Fontenoy* appears.

1746   25 April: elected to Académie
Française.
November: appointed gentleman

Voltaire	*Other*
of King's bedchamber. Beginning of friendship with d'Alembert.	
1747 July: *Zadig* appears in Holland (under title *Memnon*). October: flees Versailles for Sceaux with Mme du Châtelet.	Diderot and d'Alembert begin work on *Encyclopédie*.
1748 February–August: in Lorraine with Mme du Châtelet. August: returns to Paris. September: back in Lorraine. December: returns to Cirey.	Treaty of Aix-la-Chapelle ends War of Austrian Succession. Montesquieu, *De l'esprit des lois*. La Mettrie, *L'Homme machine*.
1749 February–June: Paris. June: brief visit to Cirey with Mme du Châtelet. July: returns to Lorraine with Mme du Châtelet. 10 September: Mme du Châtelet dies. October: back in Paris.	Buffon, *Histoire universelle* begins to appear. Diderot, *Lettre sur les aveugles*. July–November: Diderot imprisoned at Vincennes.
1750 June: leaves Paris for Berlin. Beginning of Hirsch scandal.	Rousseau, *Discours sur les sciences et les arts*. *Prospectus* of the *Encyclopédie*.
1751 September: La Mettrie reports to Voltaire 'orange and peel' remark by Frederick. December: *Le Siècle de Louis XIV* appears.	Vol. I of *Encyclopédie* appears. La Mettrie dies.
1752 Quarrel with Maupertuis. December: *Diatribe du docteur Akakia* appears. December: *Diatribe du docteur Akakia* publicly burned in Berlin. *Micromégas* appears.	First official condemnation of *Encyclopédie*.
1753 26 March: leaves Berlin. 4 June: detained at Frankfurt. 7 July: leaves Frankfurt. October: settles in Colmar. *Annales de l'Empire*.	Grimm begins editing *Correspondance littéraire*.

Voltaire	Other
1754 Takes Easter Communion at Colmar. June: abbey of Senones. June–November: Colmar. December: Visits Geneva for first time.	Rousseau, *Discours sur l'inégalité*. Fréron's *Année littéraire* begins to appear.
1755 February–March: settles at Les Délices. *La Pucelle* appears in a pirated edition. 31 July: forbidden to put on plays at Les Délices. December: *Poème sur le désastre de Lisbonne* completed.	Montesquieu dies. 1 November: Lisbon earthquake.
1756 *Essai sur les moeurs* appears. August: d'Alembert visits Les Délices. Tries to save Admiral Byng.	29 August: Seven Years War begins with Frederick II's invasion of Saxony.
1757 Gibbon visits Ferney for first time.	4 January: Damiens attempts assassination of Louis XV. 14 March: Admiral Byng shot. 5 November: Frederick II victorious over French at Rossbach. November: Vol. VII of *Encyclopédie* (including article 'Genève') appears.
1758 July–August: at Schwetzingen. October: purchases Tournay. Definitive break with Rousseau.	D'Alembert abandons *Encyclopédie*. Rousseau, *Lettre à d'Alembert sur les spectacles*. Helvétius, *De l'esprit*. Choiseul becomes Foreign Secretary (and effectively Prime Minister) until 1770.
1759 January–February: *Candide* appears. February: purchases Ferney.	Suppression of privilege for printing of *Encyclopédie*. French military and naval defeats at Quebec, Minden, etc.

Voltaire	*Other*
1760 December: receives Marie Corneille at Ferney and adopts her. *Anecdotes sur Fréron.*	2 May: 1st performance of Palissot, *Les Philosophes.* George II dies; George III succeeds to English throne.
1761 Ferney church rebuilding completed (1761–5) Organises edition of Corneille's works, with Voltaire's *Commentaires*, by subscription.	Rousseau, *La Nouvelle Héloïse.* 13 October: Marc-Antoine Calas found hanged.
1762 15 April: opens Calas campaign.	January: Elisabeth Sirven found dead. 9 March: Jean Calas executed at Toulouse. Jesuit Order suppressed in France. Catherine proclaimed Empress of Russia. Rousseau, *Emile.* Rousseau, *Du contrat social.*
1763 December: *Traité sur la tolérance* appears. Marie Corneille married, with dowry from Voltaire. Gibbon visits Ferney for second time.	Seven Years War ends: Treaty of Paris.
1764 First edition of *Dictionnaire philosophique* appears. *Commentaires sur Corneille* appear. December: gives up Les Délices. Boswell visits Ferney.	Disbandment of Jesuit Order in France. Mme de Pompadour dies. Beccaria, *Of Crimes and Punishments.* Condemnation of Sirvens.
1765 Involved in Genevan political problems	*Encyclopédie* resumes publication. 9 March: rehabilitation of Calas.
1766 *Commentaire sur le livre des délits et des peines.* Supports Genevan Natifs. Tries to persuade Diderot and others to emigrate with him to Cleves.	1 July: La Barre executed.

Voltaire	*Other*
1767	January: Collonge affair. March: 1st performance of *Les Scythes*. July: *L'Ingénu* appears. Defends Marmontel's *Bélisaire*.	February: Marmontel, *Bélisaire* appears.
1768	1 March: Mme Denis leaves Ferney for Paris. Takes Easter Communion.	
1769	Takes Communion. 27 October: Mme Denis returns to Ferney.	
1770	*Questions sur l'Encyclopédie* begins to appear.	D'Holbach, *Système de la nature*. Genevan Natifs flee to Ferney. December: Choiseul falls from power.
1771		Helvétius dies. Acquittal of Sirvens.
1772		Final volumes of *Encyclopédie* appear. Thieriot dies.
1773		Diderot goes to Russia.
1774		10 May: Louis XV dies; Louis XVI comes to throne. Turgot becomes *contrôleur général des finances*. Goethe, *Werther*.
1775	May, October: fêtes at Ferney in honour of Voltaire and Mme Denis. June: Amélie Suard visits Ferney. Frees pays de Gex from indirect taxes.	Beaumarchais, *Le Barbier de Séville*.
1776	August: *Lettre à l'Académie Française* on Shakespeare read to the Académie by d'Alembert.	Turgot dismissed by Louis XVI. American War of Independence begins. Fréron dies.

Voltaire	*Other*
1777 October: fête at Ferney in honour of Voltaire. November: marriage at Ferney of marquis de Villette to 'Belle et Bonne'. *Prix de la justice et de l'humanité*.	Necker in charge of finances (until 1781).
1778 5 February: leaves Ferney for Paris. 16 March: *Irène* first performed. 30 March: Crowning of Voltaire at Comédie Française. 30 May: Dies.	2 July: Rousseau dies.

Notes

Preface

1. *Mémoires sur Voltaire* (1826).
2. *Voltaire et la société au XVIIIe siècle* (1867–76).
3. A. Delattre, *Voltaire l'impétueux* (1957), p. 13.
4. *ibid.*, p. 14.
5. *The Complete Works of Voltaire*, ed. T. Besterman. Vols. 85–135 (1968–77). All references to Voltaire's letters are to this edition, cited as indicated in the footnote on page 1.
6. G. Lanson, *Voltaire* (1910), p. 161.
7. T. Besterman, *Voltaire* (1976), p. 583. All references will be to the 3rd edition.
8. Some characteristically perceptive comments have been made along these lines by L. Gossman in a brilliant article, 'Voltaire's Heavenly City'. It must be added, however, that his general position is somewhat different from the one taken in this study.
9. H. Mason, *Voltaire* (1975).

Chapter 1: Youth, and England

1. Some doubts remain about both place and date. Voltaire often claimed that he was born on 20 February 1694 (cf. e.g., letters to Collini and Damilaville, 20 February 1765, D12410–11) but elsewhere contradicts this. It seems likely that he was himself uncertain (cf. letter to d'Argental, D20493) and preferred to believe in the February date because it gave him almost an extra year – a cause for pride especially as he grew old (cf. e.g., letter to marquis d'Argence, 30 October 1777, D20869). A baptismal record in the parish of Saint-André-des-Arts dated 22 November 1694 (Mol. I, p. 294; cf. Archives Nationales, Minutier Central, Etude CVIII, 471) seems to give conclusive confirmation to the later date, which is now generally accepted by biographers (cf. also *infra*, n. 2). The time and place of baptism would also appear to rule out the legend that he was born in Châtenay on the outskirts of Paris, notwithstanding the proclamation of the Café Le Voltaire, in the Place Voltaire of that town. Voltaire himself claims to have been born in Paris (*Epître à Boileau*, Mol. X, p. 397).

167

2. Pierre Bailly: 'Mme Arouet . . . has been very ill, having given birth to a son three days before,' 24 November 1694, Desnoiresterres, I, p. 4.

3. 'il n'en a parlé qu'une seule fois, dans ses oeuvres de jeunesse, et ce fut pour faire une plaisanterie déplacée' (R. Pomeau, *La Religion de Voltaire*, p. 35). However, on his visit to Voltaire at Ferney in 1770, Charles Burney noted the picture of Voltaire's mother on the walls of the château (G. de Beer and A.-M. Rousseau edd., *Voltaire's British Visitors*, p. 140). It is presumably the same portrait which is mentioned in the posthumous inventory of Voltaire's belongings (D. app. 503, p. 369). This detail, though slight, may suggest a somewhat greater degree of emotional attachment than is generally assumed.

4. Desnoiresterres, I, pp. 180–2. Cf. also R. E. A. Waller, 'Voltaire and the regent', *SVEC* 127 (1974), pp. 7–12, on the relatively severe sentence Voltaire received when imprisoned in 1717, and the possible reasons for it.

5. For a succinct bibliography on the question, cf. D62, Commentary.

6. Theodore Besterman sets out the evidence for believing that Voltaire was a bastard (*Voltaire*, pp. 20–3). But the grounds are insubstantial (and Voltaire's nieces themselves firmly refuted the thesis: D6968). It is at least equally reasonable to argue with Pomeau (*La Religion*, p. 35) that Voltaire wished to confer an ideal father on himself as an expression of hostility to his true father. This squares with Voltaire's own promotion of his assumed father, Rochebrune, an obscure poet and librettist, into an attractively intelligent author and officer (D6968).

7. cf. e.g., letters to her in 1756, D6681, 6697, 6792.

8. *La Religion*, p. 28.

9. cf. D277, and Pomeau's incisive discussion of this episode (*La Religion*, pp. 82–4).

10. Mol. X, p. 231.

11. cf. D70, Commentary, which cites C. Alasseur, *La Comédie française au 18ᵉ siècle* (Paris 1967), pp. 138–41.

12. cf. O. R. Taylor ed., *La Henriade*, p. 21.

13. *ibid.*, p. 33.

14. *ibid.*, pp. 51–3.

15. *ibid.*, pp. 55–60.

16. Peter Gay finds a 'new awareness' of this sort in the *Lettres philosophiques* (1734) (*Voltaire's Politics*, p. 48); but one may antedate this essential outlook by well over a decade.

17. G. Lanson ed., *Lettres philosophiques*, revu et complété par A.-M. Rousseau (Paris 1964), 2 vols, I, p. 61.

18. *ibid.*, I, p. 24.

19. *ibid.*, II, p. 29.

20. cf. A.-M. Rousseau, *L'Angleterre et Voltaire*, pp. 58–64; D. J. Fletcher, 'The Fortunes of Bolingbroke in France in the eighteenth century', *SVEC* 47 (1966), pp. 211–14.

21. There is even a reference to personal ill-health dating from 1719 in an *Epître à M. de Genonville* (Mol. X, p. 246).

22. Desnoiresterres, IV, p. 172.

23. De Beer and Rousseau edd., p. 176.

24. D344: the passage indicates that Voltaire is assuming he was not the son of Arouet but of Rochebrune.

25. cf. e.g., letter to Mme du Deffand, 19 May 1754, D5822. A number of instances of

Voltaire's attitude to ill-health are cited in a useful article by R. Waldinger, 'Voltaire and medicine', *SVEC* 58 (1967), pp. 1777–806.

26. (J. Dubois): *Relation de la maladie, de la confession, de la fin de M. de Voltaire* (Geneva 1761), p. 5.

27. *La Vie de Voltaire* (Geneva 1787), p. 45.

28. cf. L. Foulet ed., *Correspondance de Voltaire (1726–1729)* (Paris 1913), pp. 220–32.

29. A.-M. Rousseau, *op. cit.*, pp. 76–7.

30. O. R. Taylor ed., *La Henriade*, pp. 60–2.

31. L. Foulet ed., *Correspondance*, p. 38, n. 1.

32. For a recent careful account of the Regent's British policy, cf. J. H. Shennan, *Philippe, Duke of Orléans: Regent of France 1715–1723* (London 1979), pp. 51–75.

33. It is interesting to note that even the 1723 edition attracted 30 subscriptions from England: cf. O. R. Taylor ed., *La Henriade*, p. 44.

34. cf. *ibid.*, pp. 28–31; R. Pomeau, 'Voltaire en Angleterre: Les enseignements d'une liste de souscription', *Annales publiées par la Faculté des Lettres de Toulouse* IV (1955), pp. 67–76.

35. cf. N. Perry, *Sir Everard Fawkener, SVEC* 133 (1975), p. 147.

36. *op. cit.*, p. 79.

37. From the Court at Fontainebleau he had written to the marquise de Bernières: 'I found myself almost always up in the air, cursing my life as courtier, running uselessly after a little good fortune which seemed to present itself to me, and which fled with great speed as soon as I thought to grasp it' ([17 October 1725], D252). But a month later he has changed his mind when writing to the same marquise, now that he has received his pension from the Queen: 'I no longer complain of the life at Court' (13 November [1725], D255).

38. A.-M. Rousseau, *op. cit.*, p. 79.

39. L. Foulet ed., *Correspondance*, pp. 58–9, n.

40. In any event, Louis XV signs an order in late June 1727 permitting Voltaire to spend three months in Paris, D320.

41. A.-M. Rousseau, *op. cit.*, p. 63.

42. *ibid.*, p. 117.

43. Lanson ed., *Lettres philosophiques*, gives a full list of what Voltaire might have seen at the London theatres, including Lincoln's Inn Fields and the Haymarket as well as Drury Lane (II, pp. 92–5).

44. A.-M. Rousseau, *op. cit.*, pp. 120–1. Rousseau considers the story authentic and cites this version as dating back to 1728, hence not open to scepticism as part of a legend that might have grown up around the later Voltaire.

45. *La Religion*, p. 76.

46. Foulet argues that Voltaire might have learned of Pemberton's book from announcements in the journals (ed., *Correspondance*, p. 96, n. 2); while this is possible, Voltaire's remark to Thieriot seems to suggest an acquaintance with the book rather than just a summary of it.

47. Lanson ed., II, p. 320, n. 50.

48. A.-M. Rousseau, *op. cit.*, pp. 127–31.

49. 'Voltaire and Samuel Clarke', *SVEC* 179 (1979), pp. 47–61. If Voltaire was dazzled by Clarke's intelligence, he also found the English cleric's metaphysical speculations insecure and over-abstract: 'une vraie machine à raisonnements', as he puts it in the seventh *Lettre philosophique* (Lanson ed., I, p. 79): cf. A.-M.

Rousseau, *op. cit.*, pp. 134–5. At Ferney in 1764 he will describe Clarke to Boswell as a 'metaphysical clock' (A.-M. Rousseau, *op. cit.*, p. 135); one wonders whether 'Clock' is not intended as a punning witticism on the Englishman's name.

50.   A.-M. Rousseau, *op. cit.*, p. 99.

51.   'Voltaire en Angleterre', pp. 72–3. It is however necessary to add that Voltaire also sought the patronage of the Queen of France, referring to his epic poem as 'a solid though poetic work, which has as its basis the Catholic religion and loyalty to sovereigns', 25 April 1728, *SVEC* 179 (1979), pp. 166–7. The political orientation, though it exists, must not be seen in unduly simplistic terms.

52.   A.-M. Rousseau, *op cit.*, p. 104.

53.   *ibid.*, pp. 109–11.

54.   O. R. Taylor ed., *La Henriade*, p. 67.

55.   *The Present State of the Republic of Letters*, January 1728; cf. *ibid.*, p. 68.

56.   O. R. Taylor ed., p. 75.

57.   A.-M. Rousseau, however, points out that the profits on *La Henriade* may be more apparent than real and that Voltaire probably made his money in England from secret business speculations (*op. cit.*, p. 154 n.).

58.   *ibid.*, p. 88.

59.   *ibid.*, p. 84.

60.   *ibid.*, pp. 97–8.

61.   Rousseau suggests a possible reason for any quarrel that may have occurred as attributable to money matters connected with publishing (*ibid.*, pp. 152–3).

62.   ed., *Correspondance*, p. 277.

63.   J.-C. Guédon, 'Le Retour d'Angleterre de Voltaire et son séjour chez Jacques Tranquillain Féret de Dieppe', *SVEC* 124 (1974), pp. 137–42.

64.   *op. cit.*, pp. 140–6.

65.   *ibid.*, p. 113.

66.   *ibid.*, pp. 153–4.

67.   *ibid.*, pp. 149–51, citing W. Calhoun, 'Voltaire and Sir Robert Walpole: A new document', *Philological Quarterly* 46 (1967), pp. 421–4.

68.   I have discussed the *Lettres philosophiques* as a literary work in my *Voltaire* (London 1975), pp. 107–24.

Chapter 2: Luxury, and Cirey

1.   The episode is recounted in detail by J. Donvez, *De quoi vivait Voltaire?* (Paris 1949), pp. 39–55; this book, though begging many questions of detail, still remains the best guide. The whole subject of Voltaire's financial affairs, however, stands in need of a full new treatment in the light of abundant new evidence that has come to light in recent years, particularly in the Besterman edition of the Correspondence. Cf. also, T. Besterman ed., *Voltaire's Household Accounts* (Geneva 1968).

2.   Later in life, he gave lapidary expression to his perspicacity: 'Pour faire sa fortune dans ce pays-ci, il n'y a qu'à lire les arrêts du conseil [In order to make one's fortune in this country, one needs only to read the edicts of the Council]', Mol. I, p. 75.

     This quotation is taken from the *Commentaire historique*, which I have treated throughout this study as an autobiographical work, for the reasons given by Besterman (*Voltaire*, p. 621).

3. Donvez, p. 145.
4. Besterman, *Voltaire*, p. 167; Besterman ed., *Voltaire's Household Accounts*, p. iii.
5. Delattre, *Voltaire l'impétueux*, p. 61.
6. Mol. I., p. 45.
7. cf. P. M. Conlon, *Voltaire's literary career from 1728 to 1750, SVEC* 14 (1961), p. 31.
8. A.-M. Rousseau points out that this is the only case in French literature of a first-rate writer producing a major work in a foreign language: 'Letters concerning the English Nation', *SVEC* 179 (1979), p. 25.
9. Voltaire denounced Thieriot to cardinal Fleury for publishing against his wishes; this, he said, only paved the way for a French edition while he was absent from Paris (D722 [24 April 1734]); a similar protestation of innocence is made to the minister Maurepas (D723). The newly wed duchesse de Richelieu adds her voice on his behalf (D729, 29 April 1734). The next month Voltaire disavows the edition to Maurepas as full of errors and additions (D749) and in June again appeals to Fleury for protection (D761). Although the *procureur général* Joly de Fleury remained unimpressed by Voltaire's disavowal (D791, 8 October 1734), Voltaire's case gradually won favour. Joly de Fleury eventually produced a letter of disavowal from Voltaire (but perhaps written by the former?) which he thought might be considered satisfactory (D825, 9 January [1735]), and this smoothed the way with Chauvelin (D828). Even then, however, the affair dragged on another couple of months before permission to return to Paris was granted. It must have helped Voltaire that Josse was seen to be the villain, and the author's own loud protestations played their part as well, as too the influential support he could call upon; but doubtless the authorities felt that it was time to remind Voltaire he could no longer placate them with ease after his numerous skirmishes with them.
10. cf. the lively new biography by René Vaillot, *Madame du Châtelet* (Paris 1978).
11. 'I love luxury, and even soft ease.' References to the poem will be based on the text established by André Morize in his *L'Apologie du luxe au XVIIIᵉ siècle et 'Le Mondain' de Voltaire* (Paris 1909).
12. 'Voltaire at Cirey: Art and Thought', *Studies in Eighteenth-Century French Literature presented to Robert Niklaus,* edd. J. H. Fox *et al.* (University of Exeter 1975), p. 1. The particular works referred to are set out in the Notes (p. 12).
13. Voltaire had sent out a number of manuscript texts to friends, one of them Bussy de Rabutin, who died shortly afterwards. The poem, discovered amongst his papers, was deemed amusing enough to be copied and distributed across Paris (Mme du Châtelet speaks of three hundred copies, D1273).
14. The statements should not perhaps be taken entirely at face value, as Besterman's Commentary to the letter makes clear; Mme du Châtelet may have wished to correct an impression perhaps given in an earlier letter that her love for Richelieu had revived. This might well be so, without invalidating the sincerity of her expressed feelings for Voltaire.
15. Morize ed., p. 139. It is interesting to discover the same line in an early edition unknown to Morize, also based on a manuscript copy of 1736 and conceivably the original version of the poem; cf. C. Dédéyan, 'Une version inconnue du "Mondain"', *RHLF* 49 (1949), pp. 67–74. It comes from a collection entitled *Le Docteur Gelaon ou Les Ridiculités anciennes et modernes* (1737).
16. G. Ascoli, *Voltaire: Poèmes philosophiques* (Paris, n.d.), p. 41.
17. Morize had attributed its composition to September 1736 or earlier (p. 8), which

is now made more precise by the discovery of Mme du Châtelet's letter. Ira Wade thinks it was written at Cirey late in 1735 (*Studies on Voltaire*, pp. 37–8), largely on the basis of Voltaire's letter to Thieriot of 3 November in that year; but as he admits, the similarities are not particularly compelling or profound and no other evidence appears to support this thesis. One may however allow the possibility that this marks the seminal moment of the poem; but there remains the basic question: if as Morize rightly says, *Le Mondain* is 'la profession de foi, spirituelle et épicurienne, d'un Parisien libertin' (p. 34), why write it at all at Cirey? René Pomeau (*La Religion de Voltaire*, p. 238), takes a different line, considering the poem to be written in Paris during the euphoria after the success of *Alzire* and celebrating the poet's joy at rediscovering the city; to which one must rejoin that the correspondence from that visit contains scarcely a single expression of contentment, let alone joy, being a doleful tale throughout of Voltaire's failures and humiliations.

18. cf. my 'Voltaire's Poems on Luxury' in *Studies in the French Eighteenth Century presented to John Lough*, edd. D. J. Mossop *et al.* (University of Durham 1978), pp. 108–22, from which some of this material has been drawn.

19. cf. J. Ehrard, *L'Idée de nature en France dans la première moitié du XVIIIe siècle* (Paris 1963), p. 383.

20. Thieriot received, for instance, the profits from the London 1733 edition of the *Lettres philosophiques*.

21. Dubuisson speaks of Voltaire as having already in 1735 made large and generous loans to a score of young men (D884).

22. cf. D. Williams ed., *Commentaires sur Corneille*, Vol. I.

23. Bibliothèque Nationale, MSS Fonds Fr. 13694, f. 199; cited by Conlon, p. 47.

24. It originally appeared under the chevalier de Mouhy's name, but the chevalier very probably did no more than publish the work: cf. Mol. XXII, p. 371, n. For a full account of the Desfontaines–Voltaire quarrel, cf. T. Morris, *L'Abbé Desfontaines et son rôle dans la littérature de son temps*, SVEC 19 (1961), esp. pp. 49–68.

25. No place, no date; bound with *Le Préservatif*, Bibliothèque Nationale, Shelf No. Zz.3529.

26. The quarrel was however to remain active for a while yet, Voltaire publishing a further Mémoire in February 1739, Mol. XXIII, pp. 27–45; but Desfontaines was eventually obliged to apologise and disavow the *Voltairomanie* during 1739 (cf. letters from the marquis d'Argenson to Voltaire, D2032, 2041, 2057).

27. Vaillot, p. 177; Frederick does, however, deliver Thieriot a stern reprimand and urge him to seek reconciliation with Voltaire (D1823, 1973), while defending Thieriot to Mme du Châtelet as being weak but not malicious (D1826, 1933).

28. cf. E. Showalter, 'Sensibility at Cirey: Mme du Châtelet, Mme de Graffigny, and the *Voltairomanie*', SVEC 135 (1975), pp. 181–92, which links most perceptively the troubles of Mme de Graffigny with the larger matter of the *Voltairomanie* and sets both in the context of a deteriorating relationship between Voltaire and Mme du Châtelet at Cirey. He also refutes in conclusive manner the old accusation that Mme de Graffigny had sent a copy of *La Pucelle* to Lunéville.

29. D2961; cf. also D2956, 2963, 2979, 2990.

30. *Voltaire and Mme du Châtelet* (1941); *Studies on Voltaire* (1947); *The Intellectual Development of Voltaire* (1969).

31. cf. R. A. Leigh, 'An anonymous eighteenth-century sketch of Voltaire', SVEC 2

(1956), pp. 241–72. As Professor Leigh makes clear, this 'minor masterpiece', which Voltaire received in 1735, summed up incisively the major criticisms made of him: inconsistency, superficiality, shabby moral character, anti-Christianity, love of limelight, greed for gain, lack of patriotism, unoriginality.

32. Lanson ed., II, p. 29.

33. art. *cit.*, p. 4.

34. Mol. I, p. 88.

35. D3171, 3172, 3179, 3181, 3186, 3200, 3213: the episode is a delightfully instructive example of Voltaire getting his way with initially recalcitrant authorities.

36. Mol. I, p. 89: 'My Henry IV [i.e. *La Henriade*], and my *Zaïre*,/and my American *Alzire*,/have never won me a single glance from the King;/I had a thousand enemies with very little fame. Whereas honours and goods at last are showered upon me/for a fairground farce.'

37. Longchamp and Wagnière: *Mémoires sur Voltaire*, II, pp. 137–49.

38. Mol. I, p. 87.

39. Of the 156 letters compiled by Theodore Besterman for his edition of *Lettres d'amour de Voltaire à sa nièce* (Paris 1957), 82 are wholly or substantially in Italian.

40. Voisenon, *Oeuvres complètes* (Paris 1781), IV, p. 181; cited by Vaillot, p. 291.

41. Besterman argues realistically that Voltaire was only discussing stage business with the actress (*Voltaire*, p. 270). Vaillot seems to endow the Gaussin episode with an importance not justified by the evidence he adduces (*op. cit.*, p. 231).

42. Longchamp and Wagnière, II, pp. 200–205.

43. *ibid.*, II, pp. 250–62.

44. I have discussed the importance of *Zadig* to Voltaire's philosophical evolution in my *Voltaire*, pp. 52–7.

Chapter 3: Frederick, and Berlin

1. Voltaire's use of imagery here to express his viewpoint is a clear prefiguration of the final chapter in *Candide*. To Frederick, he writes: 'Les souris qui habitent quelques petits trous d'un bâtiment immense ne savent ni [si] ce bâtiment est éternel, ni quel en est l'architecte, ni pourquoi cet architect a bâti. Elles tâchent de conserver leur vie, de peupler leurs trous, et de fuir les animaux destructeurs qui les poursuivent. Nous sommes les souris. . . . [The mice who live in some few little holes of a huge building do not know whether that building is eternal, nor who is its architect, nor why that architect has built it. They try to preserve their lives, to populate their holes, and to flee the predatory animals which pursue them. We are the mice . . .]' Cf. the Dervish's reply when Candide poses the question of evil's existence: 'Quand Sa Hautesse envoie un vaisseau en Egypte, s'embarrasse-t-elle si les souris qui sont dans le vaisseau sont à leur aise ou non? [When His Highness sends a ship to Egypt, is he concerned whether the mice in the ship are comfortable or not?]' (ed. J. H. Brumfitt, Oxford University Press, 1968, p. 148). Candide's decision to cultivate his garden is in line with the mice in the letter to Frederick who concentrate on survival. The parallel serves to remind us of the essential continuity of Voltaire's thought between 1736 and 1758; the only important difference is that in *Candide* the hero's actions are more specifically a response to the problem of evil.

2. The bibliographical complexities surrounding *La Pucelle* are such that the canto

numbers Frederick cites do not necessarily relate to the later printed versions. Cf.
J. Vercruysse ed., *La Pucelle* (1970).
3. The genesis and publication of the *Anti-Machiavel* make a complicated story. A
reliable account is to be found in C. Fleischauer's critical edition, *SVEC* 5 (1958).
4. *Voltaire*, p. 264.
5. Mol. I, p. 16.
6. cf. *infra*, Ch. VI.
7. Bibliothèque Nationale, MSS Fonds Fr. 15204, f. 11. (I have modernised the
French.) D2375, Commentary reproduces the poem, but with some minor errors
of transcription.
   'No, despite your virtues; no, despite your charms,/My soul is not content./No,
you are but a coquette,/Conquering hearts and never giving yourself.'
   'My soul perceives the worth of your divine charms;/But do not imagine that it
is content./Traitor, you leave me, to follow a coquette;/I for my part would not
leave you.'
8. 'I leave you, 'tis true; but my torn heart/Will fly back unceasingly towards
you;/Four years you have been my mistress,/A love of ten years must be preferred;/I fulfil a sacred duty./Hero of friendship, you yourself approve my
action./Farewell, I depart in despair./Yes, I go to the knees of an adored one,/But
I give up that which I love.' (D2378).
9. *Voltaire*, p. 251.
10. *Voltaire and the Century of Light*, pp. 66–7.
11. cf. e.g., Voltaire's tender reproaches to Thieriot (D1748, 7 [January 1739]).
12. cf. *supra*, p. 20.
13. Mol. X, p. 474 (1716).
14. *Oeuvres de Frédéric le Grand* (Berlin 1846–57), Vol. XVIII, p. 25. (D. app. 60 gives
the wrong page reference.) It is scarcely surprising that Mme du Châtelet should
have seen Frederick as a rival (cf. e.g., D2778). Did she, one wonders, intend it
specifically sexual sense?
15. Mol. I, p. 27.
16. These remarks strikingly prefigure the famous observation of Clausewitz that
'war is simply a continuation of political intercourse, with the addition of other
means' (*On War* (1832), edd. and trans. M. Howard and P. Paret (Princeton
1976), p. 605). Frederick's campaigns play an important part in Clausewitz's
work.
17. Indeed, one such letter (D2623, [30 June 1742]) got Voltaire into considerable
trouble, since it was opened by the censors, who informed the world that Voltaire
had praised Frederick for stealing a march on the French *premier ministre*, Cardinal
Fleury, by the peace treaty he had made. The resulting indignation at Voltaire's
'unpatriotic' attitudes briefly threatened to involve him in yet one more flight
from Paris (D2625, Commentary). This fortunately did not occur, probably
because Voltaire made due apology (e.g., D2626), including to Fleury himself
(D2644, 2655).
18. Mol. I, p. 92.
19. *ibid.*, p. 36.
20. *La Religion de Voltaire*, p. 277.
21. To add, however, a balancing factor, Voltaire came to realise that if he went to
Paris he might not be permitted to return to Prussia (cf. e.g., D4525, 20 July

[1751]). But this serves only to strengthen the argument that he had thrown in his lot with Frederick.

22. Catalogue of exhibition 'Voltaire, voyageur de l'Europe', at Sceaux, 1978, p. 7.
23. *Commentaire historique* (1776), Mol. I, p. 92.
24. Mol. X, p. 442 (1772).
25. Duvernet claims that this information, reaching Voltaire via Thieriot while he was still making up his mind whether to go to Berlin, enraged him so much that it was the determining factor (pp. 113–14). As much of Duvernet's information seems to have come from Thieriot, the story is probably well-founded; but one suspects that Voltaire's decision, however irrationally motivated, was not based on a simple fit of temper.
26. For interesting new light on this episode, cf. C. Mervaud, 'Voltaire, Baculard d'Arnaud et le prince Ferdinand', *SVEC* 183 (1980), pp. 7–33. Cf. also the full account in R. L. Dawson, *Baculard d'Arnaud: life and prose fiction, SVEC* 141–2 (1976), esp. pp. 142–93.
27. Desnoiresterres makes some perceptive comments on this letter, pointing out that, whateverer the miseries of life in Paris, there were both 'la cour et la ville'; if you tired of the former, Parisian society still offered its compensations. But in Prussia, 'la ville' in this sense was non-existent (IV, pp. 178–9).
28. He uses the phrase in a letter to Countess Bentinck (D4524, 18 July [1751]).
29. *op cit.*, pp. 10–11.
30. As he put it in his *Mémoires:* 'Je résolus dès lors de mettre en sûreté les pelures de l'orange [I resolved from that moment to safeguard the orange peelings]', Mol. I, p. 38.
31. The authenticity of this letter is still uncertain, as the original has never been found. Cf. L. Velluz, *Maupertuis* (Paris 1969), p. 124 n.
32. For a fuller account, cf. C. Fleischauer, 'L'*Akakia* de Voltaire', *SVEC* 30 (1964), pp. 7–145; J. Tuffet ed., *Histoire du docteur Akakia et du natif de St-Malo* (Paris 1967), pp. lxviii–xcii.
33. *Mémoires*, Mol. I, p. 38.
34. *Journal et mémoires*, ed. Rathery (Paris 1859–67), VII, p. 419; cited in A. D. Hytier, 'Frédéric II et les philosophes récalcitrants', *Romanic Review* 57 (1966), p. 174.
35. *op. cit.*, p. 170.
36. *Mon séjour auprès de Voltaire* (Paris 1807), p. 56.
37. *op. cit.*, p. 171.
38. *Mémoires*, Mol. I, p. 42. Cf. also D5308–5464, *passim*, and Collini, pp. 81–94.
39. cf. Besterman's development of this point, *Voltaire*, p. 342.
40. 'L'Auteur arrivant dans sa terre, près du lac de Genève', Mol. X, pp. 365–6.
    'Liberty! liberty! your throne is in these parts:/ . . . /Come down to my hearths on your fine festive days./Come and create for me there a new destiny.'
41. cf. my *Voltaire*, pp. 163–4.
42. cf. C. Mervaud, 'Julien l'Apostat dans la correspondance de Voltaire et Frédéric II', *RHLF* 76 (1976), pp. 724–43.
43. *Voltaire's Politics*, p. 170.
44. 'Portraits de Frédéric II dans la correspondance prussienne de Voltaire', paper given at Mannheim Conference on 'Voltaire and Germany', May 1978, and to be published in the *Transactions*. I am indebted to Mme Mervaud for kindly allowing me to see the text.

45. ed. F. J. Crowley (University of California 1938), p. 199.
46. cf. M. Fontius, *Voltaire in Berlin* (Berlin 1966).
47. H. Duranton paper, Mannheim Conference, May 1978; to appear in the *Transactions*.
48. Collini, p. 32.
49. e.g. Luiscius's tragi-comic acceleration of experiences (Mol. I, p. 10), the awful punishment inflicted by Frederick's father on the deserting soldier, and the gratuitously ridiculous act of mercy awarded the latter at Voltaire's request (pp. 30–1).
50. cf. *ibid.*, p. 10.
51. *ibid.*, p. 29: 'trente-six' is often used familiarly in French to denote an indeterminate large number, e.g. 'avoir trente-six raisons de faire quelque chose': 'to have umpteen reasons for doing something'.
52. *Mes Entretiens avec Frédéric le Grand: Mémoires et Journal de Henri de Catt*, Vol. XXII (1885), p. 137; cited by C. Mervaud, 'Voltaire, Baculard d'Arnaud et le prince Ferdinand', p. 33.
53. *Voltaire's British Visitors*, p. 77.
54. *ibid.*, pp. 135–6.
55. Mol. I, p. 96.

Chapter 4: Geneva, and Candide

1. cf. Mme Denis's letter to J.-R. Tronchin, D6352.
2. R. Naves, *Voltaire et l'Encyclopédie* (Paris 1938), p. 42.
3. Mol. XIV, pp. 133–5. Cf. G. Gargett, 'Voltaire et l'affaire Saurin', *Dix-huitième Siècle* 10 (1978), pp. 417–33.
4. *Voltaire et l'Encyclopédie*, p. 43.
5. cf. R. Pomeau, *La Religion de Voltaire*, pp. 304–5. The matter is gone into at greater length in G. Gargett, 'Voltaire and Protestantism', Ph.D. dissertation, University of East Anglia, 1974, pp. 127–306. A revised version of the latter has just appeared in *SVEC* 188 (1980).
6. R. N. Schwab and W. E. Rex, *Inventory of Diderot's Encyclopédie*, Vol. VI, *SVEC* 93 (1972), p. 236.
7. *Oeuvres complètes*, edd. B. Gagnebin and M. Raymond, Paris, Vol. I (1964), p. 496.
8. cf. *ibid.*, pp. 494–5; letter from Rousseau to Vernes, 22 October 1758, *Correspondance complète de Jean-Jacques Rousseau*, ed. R. A. Leigh, Geneva, Banbury and Oxford, 1965– , Vol. V, no. 715.
9. cf. M. Launay, *Jean-Jacques Rousseau: écrivain politique 1712–1762* (Cannes/Grenoble 1971), p. 49; H. Lüthy, *La Banque protestante en France de la Révocation de l'Edit de Nantes à la Révolution* (Paris 1959–61), 2 vols, II, pp. 54–5.
10. cf. Leigh ed., Rousseau, *Correspondance*, Vol. V, app. 197.
11. For a full discussion of the controversy surrounding Rousseau's *Lettre à d'Alembert*, cf. the edition by M. Fuchs (Lille/Geneva 1948).
12. cf. E. Showalter, *Madame de Graffigny and Rousseau*, *SVEC* 175 (1978), pp. 32–3.
13. As Leigh points out, however, there is very little reference to Rousseau's second *Discours* in Voltaire's letter; at best he would have had time only to cast a glance over it; ed. *cit.*, Vol. III, no. 317, Commentary.
14. Of course, Voltaire inveighed throughout his life against man's ridiculous pro-

pensity for seeking out metaphysical truths that must forever elude him; but the idea that striving after knowledge of the natural world might also be overweening pride, as seen here in Rousseau's letter, does not seem to occur to him. Cf. e.g., letter to Mme du Deffand, D13207, 12 March 1766.

The Moland and Besterman Indexes yield a single reference to Faustus, of no great significance, at Mol. XXVI, p. 492.

15. Epistle I, vv. 289–94; ed. M. Mack (London/New Haven 1950), pp. 50–1.
16. Mol. IX, p. 474.
   'Elements, animals, human beings, all is at war./Admit it we must, *evil* exists on earth.'
17. cf. R. A. Leigh, 'From the *Inégalité* to *Candide*', in W. H. Barber *et al.* edd., *The Age of the Enlightenment: Studies presented to Theodore Besterman*, pp. 66–92.
18. *ibid.*, p. 89.
19. Mol. XXIV, pp. 166–79.
20. *Utopia and Reform in the Enlightenment* (Cambridge University Press 1971), p. 77.
21. I have discussed the literary aspects of *Candide* in my *Voltaire*, pp. 57–73. For the benefit of those unfamiliar with the *conte*, the following synopsis may help to illuminate the details in the text:

The naïve Candide, brought up in the castle of the Baron of Thunder-ten-tronckh in Westphalia, is expelled when he falls in love with the Baron's daughter Cunégonde. Henceforth he wanders the world, undergoing, witnessing or hearing of a dreadful succession of misfortunes, catastrophes, and atrocities. Forcibly enrolled in the army of the Bulgares, he becomes involved in a battle with the Abares which ends in terrible carnage. He flees to Holland and rediscovers his childhood tutor Pangloss, who had taught him to believe in the doctrine of Optimism. They are taken by a charitable Anabaptist, Jacques, to Lisbon, only to arrive in the middle of an earthquake and storm, in which they are shipwrecked and Jacques is drowned. A subsequent auto-da-fé is held by the Portuguese Inquisition in order to prevent a recurrence of such disasters. Pangloss is hanged, Candide beaten and later rescued by Cunégonde, who has providentially arrived on the scene. They flee to America. Candide is forced to abandon Cunégonde and takes refuge in a Jesuit colony in Paraguay which turns out to be run by her brother; but a quarrel leads to a further flight, this time to the Utopian kingdom of Eldorado. Though all is happy and prosperous there Candide (accompanied by his faithful servant Cacambo) decides to leave, provided with sufficient wealth to ensure that henceforth they will, at least financially, be masters of their destiny. They meet Martin, a Manichean who sees only evil on earth, and travel with him to Europe, where they are swindled in Paris, witness Admiral Byng's execution and, by way of Venice, reach Constantinople in pursuit of Cunégonde. They come upon Pangloss (who had survived the hanging) and Cunégonde's brother, who have both ended up in the galleys, and purchase their freedom. Cunégonde is found, and a small band of friends is formed, who settle on a plot of land near Constantinople. Pangloss is still as much an Optimist as ever, despite all he has suffered. He consults a dervish-philosopher on metaphysics and is curtly told that all such discussions are futile. A similar lesson on a more practical level is taught by an old man who has achieved a contented and fruitful existence in cultivating his own piece of land. Candide learns that the only right attitude to life is to 'cultivate our garden'.

NOTES

22. ed. H. T. Mason, *Zadig and Other Stories* (Oxford University Press 1971), p. 101.
23. The doctrine of Philosophical Optimism arose from the concern, felt with particu-
    lar intensity from the late seventeenth century, to reconcile a belief in divine
    justice with the existence of evil. Leibniz had presented his own solution in his
    Essais de Théodicée (1710), seeing God as subject to the laws of reason and therefore
    able to create only an imperfect world; by His goodness He has created, therefore,
    'the best of all possible worlds'. Pope's optimistic views (which seem to relate to a
    different tradition, tracing back through English thinkers) are expressed above all
    in his *Essay on Man* (1733–4). For a lucid account of the ideas involved, cf. W. H.
    Barber, *Voltaire: Candide* (London 1960), pp. 41–9.
24. cf. also *Voltaire's British Visitors*, p. 37.
25. *ibid.*
26. *L'Angleterre et Voltaire*, pp. 219–31.
27. ed. J. H. Brumfitt (Oxford University Press 1968), p. 55. All references will be to
    this edition.
28. '. . . mice in a ship about the intentions of those steering it.'
29. cf. *supra*, p. 173, n. 1.
30. Brumfitt ed., p. 148. 'When His Highness sends a ship to Egypt, is he concerned
    whether the mice in the ship are comfortable or not?'
31. *ibid.*, p. 60.
32. *ibid.*, pp. 60–1.
33. *ibid.*, p. 148. ' "What then is to be done?" said Pangloss. "Keep silent," said the
    dervish.'
34. *ibid.*, p. 111.
35. R. Pomeau ed., *Essai sur les moeurs* (Paris 1963), 2 vols., II, p. 383.
36. Brumfitt ed., p. 104.
37. *ibid.*, p. 110.
38. *ibid.*
39. *ibid.*, p. 124.
40. *ibid.*, p. 113.
41. Desnoiresterres, V, p. 292, citing Formey, *Souvenirs d'un citoyen* (Berlin 1789), II,
    p. 230.
42. René Pomeau rightly lays emphasis on this latter motive; ed., *Candide* (Paris
    1959), pp. 35–6.
43. R. Pomeau, 'Une esquisse inédite de "l'Ingénu"', *RHLF* 61 (1961), pp. 58–60.
44. N. L. Torrey, 'The Date of composition of *Candide*', *Modern Language Notes* 44
    (1929), pp. 445–6.
45. L. Perey and G. Maugras, *La Vie intime de Voltaire aux Délices et à Ferney (1754–1778)*
    (Paris 1885), pp. 241–2.
46. Brumfitt ed., p. 72.
47. cf. e.g., letter to Frederick, D1331, 27 May 1737; letter to President Hénault from
    Berlin, D4958, 25 July [1752].
48. cf. I. O. Wade, *Voltaire and 'Candide'* (Princeton 1959), pp. 176–7.
49. ed., *Candide*, pp. 40–1.
50. *ibid.*, pp. 263–4.
51. Brumfitt ed., p. 106.
52. ' – Qu'est-ce qu'optimisme? disait Cacambo. – Hélas! dit Candide, c'est la rage de
    soutenir que tout est bien quand on est mal. [What is optimism? said Cacambo. –

Alas! said Candide, it is the mania for asserting that all is well when one is not.]'
(Brumfitt ed., p. 107).

53. The word *infâme* used substantively appears first in Voltaire's letters in June 1759 (D8338, to Frederick, [*c.* 5 June 1759]), in response to Frederick's own use of it a few weeks before when writing to Voltaire (D8304); cf. A. Raymond, 'L'Infâme: superstition ou calomnie?', *SVEC* 57 (1967), pp. 1291–306. By *l'infâme* Voltaire essentially is referring not so much to the Catholic Church as such as to the excesses of all organised religions in the direction of fanaticism, superstition and intolerance. Pomeau gives an excellent summation (*La Religion de Voltaire*, pp. 314–16) but seems to conclude too readily on the evidence that Voltaire was attacking Christianity as such.

54. No reference has been made thus far to two useful studies linking *Candide* to the Correspondence: G. Murray, *Voltaire's 'Candide': the Protean Gardener, 1755–1762*, *SVEC* 69 (1970); P. Ilie, 'The Voices in Candide's Garden, 1755–1759', *SVEC* 148 (1976), pp. 37–113. Murray has the great merit of undertaking basic spadework and indicating the rich possibilities; his reading of *Candide* is fertile and stimulating, though in my view given to exaggerating Voltaire's capacity for intellectual rôle-playing. Ilie is more measured in this respect and reaches persuasive conclusions; but his view perhaps overstates the ambivalence in Voltaire's attitudes during the Geneva period. While the opinions expressed in this chapter differ considerably from those in both works, it would be ungenerous not to state a debt of gratitude to them for their ability to put old questions in a new and challenging way and thereby to encourage further thinking on the subject.

Chapter 5: Ferney, and L'Ingénu

1. 'Voltaire à la Bibliothèque Nationale', *Catalogue général des livres imprimés à la Bibliothèque Nationale*, Vol. CCXIV (Paris 1978), p. xii.
2. Vol. I, pp. 71–3.
3. J. Balcou: *Fréron contre les philosophes* (Geneva 1975); this excellent account has now become the standard work on Fréron.
4. *ibid.*, p. 285.
5. *ibid.*, p. 61.
6. 'A un premier commis', 20 June 1733, Mol. XXXIII, p. 353.
7. Gita May, 'Voltaire a-t-il fait une offre d'hospitalité à Rousseau?' *SVEC* 47 (1966), p. 102.
8. 'Epître à la marquise du Châtelet, sur la calomnie', Mol. X, pp. 282–8.
9. For a comprehensive account of the matter, cf. H. H. Freud, *Palissot and 'Les Philosophes'*, *Diderot Studies* 9 (1967), esp. pp. 176–92 for Voltaire's reactions; and R. Naves, *Voltaire et l'Encyclopédie*, pp. 70–86.
10. For details on this, as on the whole background to the Calas case, cf. D. D. Bien, *The Calas Affair* (Princeton 1960).
11. It has been generally believed that Voltaire treated this request for help with callous detachment; Gargett, *op. cit.*, pp. 375–85, demonstrates that this is a false reading of the evidence and that Voltaire's attitude here is not inconsistent with that to be shown a few months later on behalf of Calas.
12. René Pomeau summarises various discussions of the case over the last hundred years (*La Religion de Voltaire*, p. 326, n. 66).

13. *ibid.*, p. 334.
14. The problem of Voltaire's attitude to the people has received much attention. Particularly useful statements on the subject are R. Mortier, 'Voltaire et le peuple', *The Age of the Enlightenment: Studies Presented to Theodore Besterman*, pp. 137–51; and P. Gay, *Voltaire's Politics*, esp. pp. 335–9, which takes a more liberal view.
15. cf. B. Gagnebin, 'Le Médiateur d'une petite querelle genevoise', *SVEC* 1 (1955), pp. 115–23.
16. An excellent study of the historical background to *L'Ingénu* has been provided by F. Pruner, 'Recherches sur la création romanesque dans *L'Ingénu* de Voltaire', *Archives des lettres modernes* XXX (1960).
17. ed. W. R. Jones (Geneva/Paris 1957), p. 178. All references to *L'Ingénu* will be to this edition.
18. My italics. There seems no very persuasive reason for choosing this date (the Moland edition gives 8/9 October, though without explaining why); indeed, the attitudes expressed are reminiscent of the letters to Richelieu of 15 September and 8 October.
19. 'lively but innocently good-natured'.
20. Jones ed., p. 93.
21. 'infinite wit, wide reading, a fiery imagination and extraordinary memory, exuberance and heedlessness in much greater profusion. But it is only a matter of cultivating and correcting. Leave it to me.'
22. Jones ed., p. 123.
23. *ibid.*, p. 93.
24. *ibid.*, p. 91.
25. *ibid.*, p. 82.
26. *ibid.*, p. 138.
27. *ibid.*, p. 141.
28. *Voltaire l'impétueux*, p. 24.
29. 'Voltaire's *L'Ingénu*, the Huguenots and Choiseul', *The Age of the Enlightenment*, pp. 107–36. On Voltaire's connections with the government over the French Protestants at this time, cf. also G. Gargett, 'Voltaire, Gilbert de Voisins's *Mémoires* and the problem of Huguenot civil rights (1767–1768)', *SVEC* 174 (1978), pp. 7–57.
30. Jones ed., p. 116.
31. *ibid.*, p. 133.
32. *Voltaire dans ses contes* (Paris 1967), pp. 295–317.
33. art. *cit.*, p. 118.
34. For details, cf. my 'The Unity of Voltaire's *L'Ingénu*', *The Age of the Enlightenment*, p. 105.
35. For a comprehensive account of the affair, cf. J. Renwick, *Marmontel, Voltaire and the 'Bélisaire' affair*, *SVEC* 121 (1974).

Chapter 6: Ferney, and the Patriarch

1. cf. R. Naves, *Voltaire* (Paris 1966), p. 70.
2. D14789, 1 March 1768. Besterman devotes a useful chapter to this single day in Voltaire's life, *Voltaire*, pp. 525–34.
3. The 'affaire des manuscrits' still remains obscure. Most commentators consider La Harpe guilty of theft, but a recent article by A. Jovicevich places the main

blame on Mme Denis and considers La Harpe's guilt in the affair to be of only secondary importance ('Voltaire and La Harpe – l'affaire des manuscrits: a reappraisal', *SVEC* 176 (1979), pp. 77–95).

4. cf. the account of the correspondence between Voltaire and Mme Denis 1768–9 by H. Micha, *Voltaire d'après sa correspondance avec Madame Denis* (Paris n.d.), pp. 115–46.

5. *La Religion de Voltaire*, pp. 442–3.

6. *Correspondance littéraire*, ed. M. Tourneux (Paris 1877–82) 16 vols, VIII, p. 63.

7. cf. Pomeau, *La Religion*, pp. 354–7, for an inventory of these years.

8. cf. *ibid.*, pp. 395–6.

9. C. Duckworth: 'Voltaire at Ferney: an unpublished description', *SVEC* 174 (1978), p. 65.

10. D19508, [?12 June 1775]. It is particularly ironic, therefore, that when Condorcet, condemned to death under the Terror, called on Mme Suard and her husband for help, he was turned away from their door and died shortly afterwards (1794), either by his own hand or from exposure.

11. A reliable account of the affair has been provided by H. Hancock, 'Voltaire et l'Affaire des Mainmortables: un ultime combat', *SVEC* 114 (1973), pp. 79–98.

12. *Voltaire*, p. 552.

13. Gita May, 'Voltaire a-t-il fait une offre d'hospitalité à Rousseau?', p. 102.

14. *Voltaire's British Visitors*, p. 103.

15. Moultou reports that some houses were sold against annuities settled upon the lives of Voltaire and Mme Denis on generous terms (D19639), and Wagnière confirms this, *Mémoires sur Voltaire*, I, p. 65.

16. *op. cit.*, I, p. 385.

17. Best. app. 374, *Voltaire's Correspondence*, ed. T. Besterman (Geneva, 1953–65), 107 vols, XCV, p. 301. (This appendix has not been reprinted in the definitive edition of the Correspondence and will appear elsewhere in the *Oeuvres complètes* now being prepared: cf. *SVEC* 165 (1977), p. 150.)

18. *op. cit.*, I, p. 91.

19. Turgot's fall is analysed in detail by Condorcet to Voltaire, D20194, [June/July 1776].

20. cf. R. Naves, *Le Goût de Voltaire* (Paris 1938); D. Williams, *Voltaire: literary critic*, *SVEC* 48 (1966); Besterman, *Voltaire*, pp. 131–58; my *Voltaire*, pp. 11–16.

21. cf. *supra.*, n. 17.

22. The best account known to me remains Desnoiresterres, Vol. VIII, pp. 81–9.

23. Longchamp and Wagnière, I, p. 93.

24. *SVEC* 49 (1967).

25. A.-M. Rousseau, *L'Angleterre et Voltaire*, Vol. II, p. 292, n. 16a.

26. *ibid.*, p. 292; cf. de Beer and Rousseau edd., p. 197.

27. De Beer and Rousseau edd., p. 138.

28. *ibid.*, p. 61.

29. *ibid.*, p. 89.

30. *ibid.*, p. 153.

31. *ibid.*, p. 158.

32. *ibid.*, p. 71.

33. *ibid.*, p. 160.

34. *ibid.*, p. 147.

35. *ibid.*, p. 154.
36. *ibid.*, p. 176; cf. *supra*, p. 8.
37. *ibid.*, p. 99.
38. *ibid.*, p. 15.
39. *ibid.*, p. 118.
40. cf., in *Le Monde comme il va*, the praises heaped on the 'temple' which turns out to be a theatre, as compared with the repellent spectacles at the other, ecclesiastical, 'temple'. *Romans et contes*, ed. H. Bénac (Paris 1960), pp. 68–9, 72.
41. De Beer and Rousseau edd., p. 34.
42. *ibid.*, p. 60.
43. *ibid.*, p. 100.
44. *ibid.*, p. 115.
45. *ibid.*, p. 166.
46. *ibid.*, p. 188.
47. *op. cit.*, p. 33.
48. D6985, 17 September 1756; for an earlier reference to this letter, cf. *supra*, p. 96.
49. *op. cit.*, I, p. 54.
50. De Beer and Rousseau edd., p. 27. Unfortunately, some small measure of doubt still exists as to whether Goldsmith actually met Voltaire; if not, his portrait is so clear that he most probably received it from an eye-witness at Ferney; cf. *ibid.*, p. 14.
51. *ibid.*, p. 172.
52. *ibid.*, p. 181.
53. *op. cit.*, I, p. 94.
54. De Beer and Rousseau edd., p. 93.
55. *ibid.*, p. 95.
56. *ibid.*, p. 105.
57. *ibid.*, p. 129.
58. *ibid.*, p. 141.
59. *ibid.*, p. 153.
60. *ibid.*, p. 159.
61. *ibid.*, p. 66.
62. Gita May art., p. 100.
63. De Beer and Rousseau edd., pp. 72–3.
64. *ibid.*, pp. 89–90.
65. *ibid.*, p. 108.
66. *ibid.*, p. 117.
67. *ibid.*, p. 162.
68. *ibid.*, p. 129.
69. *ibid.*, p. 181.
70. *ibid.*, p. 97.
71. *ibid.*, pp. 64–5.
72. *op. cit.*, I, p. 93.
73. De Beer and Rousseau edd., p. 146.
74. *ibid.*, p. 117.
75. L. Spitzer has some interesting comments to make on this phenomenon in 'Pages from Voltaire', *A Method of Interpreting Literature* (Smith College 1949), pp. 94–7.
76. De Beer and Rousseau edd., p. 85.

77. *ibid.*, p. 184.
78. cf. *ibid.*, p. 130.
79. 'Voltaire's humour', *SVEC* 179 (1979), pp. 101–16.
80. De Beer and Rousseau edd., p. 161.
81. cf. *supra*, p. 10.
82. cf. *supra*, p. 96.
83. art. *cit.*, p. 107.
84. *op. cit.*, I, p. 93.
85. De Beer and Rousseau edd., p. 116.
86. *ibid.*, p. 140.
87. *op. cit.*, I, p. 93.
88. De Beer and Rousseau edd., p. 94.
89. *ibid.*, p. 161. The similarity is however so close that one wonders whether the statement has not been copied by one from the other. Moore's observations appeared in 1783, Pennant's in 1793.
90. 'Voltaire, Sisyphe en Jermanie: vers la meilleure des éditions possibles', *SVEC* 179 (1979), pp. 143–57.
91. cf. de Beer and Rousseau edd., p. 139.
92. *ibid.*, p. 103.
93. *ibid.*, p. 163.
94. Gita May art., pp. 100–101.
95. De Beer and Rousseau edd., p. 175.
96. *ibid.*, pp. 129, 187.
97. *ibid.*, pp. 129, 153, 187; Besterman D20780.
98. *ibid.*, pp. 129, 153, 187; Gita May art., p. 99; Besterman D20780.
99. *ibid.*, pp. 116, 129, 153, 175–6, 187.
100. *ibid.*, pp. 116–17.
101. *ibid.*, p. 75.
102. *ibid.*, p. 103.

Chapter 7: Paris, and Death

1. The church had been rebuilt by Voltaire in 1761. He added the famous inscription 'Deo erexit Voltaire' (which survives on the church to this day), adding that it was the only church dedicated to God rather than to one of His intermediaries.
2. Desnoiresterres, VIII, p. 510.
3. Gita May art., pp. 101–2; cf. *supra*, p. 96.
4. Aldridge, *op. cit.*, p. 401; cf. also A. O. Aldridge, *Franklin and his French Contemporaries* (New York University Press 1957), pp. 9–11.
5. D21174; cf. also Longchamp and Wagnière, I, p. 153.
6. For these and other details, cf. L. Willens, 'Voltaire's *Irène* (1778) and his illusion of theatrical success', *SVEC* 185 (1980), pp. 87–101.
7. ed. *cit.*, XII, p. 71; cf. also D21134; 21137, Commentary; 21139.
8. *La Religion de Voltaire*, p. 451.
9. Desnoiresterres, VIII, pp. 267–8.
10. *ibid.*, pp. 256–8.
11. cf. P. Gay, *Voltaire's Politics*, pp. 309–10 and *passim*; R. Pomeau ed., *Politique de Voltaire* (Paris 1963), pp. 38–43.

12. Longchamp and Wagnière, I, pp. 153–5; cf. also Desnoiresterres, VIII, pp. 342–8.
13. *op. cit.*, I, pp. 92–3.
14. *Correspondance littéraire*, XII, p. 94; cf. also Desnoiresterres, VIII, pp. 364–6, citing a letter from Théodore Tronchin.
15. 'Lettre de Polichinelle à monsieur de Voltaire: du 20 mai 1778' (Paris 1778), BN Shelf No. Ye 26447.
16. Longchamp and Wagnière I, p. 160.
17. J. Vercruysse ed., 'Lettre de Henri Rieu sur les derniers jours de Voltaire', *SVEC* 135 (1975), pp. 193–8.
18. *ibid.*, p. 197.
19. An invaluable catalogue has now been produced (M. P. Alekseev and T. N. Kopreeva edd., *Biblioteka Vol'tera: Katalog Knig* (Moscow/Leningrad 1961), and a multi-volume edition of Voltaire's marginal jottings in the books he read has begun appearing: *Corpus des notes marginales de Voltaire*, Vol I: A-B (Berlin 1979). Cf. also S. S. B. Taylor, 'Voltaire's marginalia', *SVEC* 135 (1975), pp. 167–80.
20. Mme Denis has traditionally played the rôle of villain in Voltaire biographies. There are evident defects in her character; but her loyalty to her uncle in remaining with him for two decades in the social desert of Ferney cannot be simply dismissed as pure self-seeking, and it is evident that she was popular in the colony, as witness the *fête* to celebrate her recovery from illness in 1775. She deserves the attention of a biographer in her own right.
21. *op. cit.*, I, p. 148.
22. Desnoiresterres, I, p. 430.
23. Lanson ed., II, p. 159.
24. Mol. IX, pp. 369–70.
25. Here again we touch upon the fascinating question of Voltaire's intense and sometimes macabre relationship with his own body, already clear from his chronic hypochondria (cf. *supra*, pp. 7–10). A study of this topic still remains to be written. Some very helpful hints are provided by L. Gossman, 'Voltaire's Heavenly City', p. 82, n. 12.
26. De Beer and Rousseau edd., p. 185.
27. The term is taken from J. McManners' inaugural lecture at Oxford, *Reflections at the Death Bed of Voltaire: The Art of Dying in Eighteenth-Century France* (Oxford 1975). Professor McManners outlines the problem and Voltaire's personal response to it in a masterly synopsis.
28. The classic account of Voltaire's dealings with the Catholic clergy in 1778 remains Desnoiresterres, VIII, pp. 219–44, 357–62; Pomeau has added some further documents, *La Religion de Voltaire*, pp. 451–5, as has the Besterman edition of the *Correspondence*: cf. also the penetrating analysis of these events by McManners, *op. cit.*, pp. 19–23.
29. *Courrier de l'Europe*, 17 April 1778; cited in Desnoiresterres, VIII, p. 241, n.
30. cf. Desnoiresterres, VIII, pp. 389–400.
31. *Voltaire*, p. 202.
32. *ibid.*, pp. 203–4.
33. *Voltaire*, p. 598.
34. *Confessions*, Bk V, *Oeuvres complètes*, ed. *cit.*, Vol. I (1964), p. 214.
35. De Beer and Rousseau edd., pp. 158–9.

36. *Correspondance littéraire*, ed. *cit.*, IX, pp. 14–15. The statue is now in the Louvre.

37. *Oeuvres romanesques*, ed. H. Bénac (Paris [1959]), p. 619.

38. *SVEC* 185 (1980), pp. 225–36. The phrase is borrowed by the author from a remark made by the young Hugo about Chateaubriand.

39. *Essai sur les règnes de Claude et de Néron* (1778), *Oeuvres complètes*, edd. J. Assézat and M. Tourneux, Paris, Vol. III (1875), pp. 253, 342.

40. Desnoiresterres, VIII, pp. 455–8; G. Barber, 'The Financial History of the Kehl Voltaire', *The Age of the Enlightenment*, pp. 152–70.

41. R. Waldinger, *Voltaire and Reform in the Light of the French Revolution* (Geneva/Paris 1959), pp. 97 ff.

42. cf. R. O. Rockwood, 'The Legend of Voltaire and the Cult of the Revolution, 1791', *Ideas in History: Essays Presented to Louis Gottschalk*, edd. R. Herr and H. T. Parker (Duke University Press 1965), pp. 110–34.

43. R. Galliani, 'Voltaire et les autres philosophes dans la Révolution: les brochures de 1791, 1792, 1793', *SVEC* 174 (1978), pp. 69–112.

44. *Les Ecrivains romantiques et Voltaire* (Université de Lille – III 1974).

45. R. Pomeau, 'Voltaire à la Bibliothèque Nationale', Catalogue Voltaire, Bibliothèque Nationale', pp. xiii–xiv.

46. R. Galliani, 'Voltaire en 1878', *SVEC* 183 (1980), pp. 91–115.

47. *Voltaire* (Paris 1957): cited in A. Sareil ed., *Voltaire et la critique* (Englewood Cliffs, New Jersey 1966), p. 176.

48. 'Memoirs of M. de Voltaire', *Collected Works* (Oxford 1966), Vol. III, p. 227.

49. Letter to Mme Roger des Genettes [1859–60?], *Oeuvres complètes*, ed. R. Descharmes, Paris, Vol. II (1923), p. 410.

Selected Bibliography

SVEC = *Studies on Voltaire and the Eighteenth Century*, ed. T. Besterman (1955–76), H. Mason (1977–   ), Geneva and later Banbury 1955–

Mol. = L. Moland ed., *Voltaire: Oeuvres complètes*, Paris 1877–85, 52 vols

A. O. Aldridge, *Voltaire and the Century of Light*, Princeton 1975
W. H. Barber *et al.*, edd., *The Age of the Enlightenment: Studies presented to Theodore Besterman*, Edinburgh and London 1967
T. Besterman, *Voltaire*, London, 1969: 3rd ed., Oxford 1976
T. Besterman ed., *The Complete Works of Voltaire*, Geneva, Banbury and Oxford, 1968–
   Vol. 2: *La Henriade*, ed. O. R. Taylor, 1970
   Vol. 7: *La Pucelle*, ed. J. Vercruysse, 1970
   Vols 53–55: *Commentaires sur Corneille*, ed. D. Williams, 1974–5
   Vols 85–135: *Correspondence*, ed. T. Besterman, 1968–77
J. H. Brumfitt ed., *Candide*, Oxford 1968
P. M. Conlon, *Voltaire's Literary Career from 1728 to 1750, SVEC* 14 (1961)
G. de Beer and A.-M. Rousseau, *Voltaire's British Visitors, SVEC* 49 (1967)
A. Delattre, *Voltaire l'impétueux*, Paris 1957
G. Desnoiresterres, *Voltaire et la société au XVIIIᵉ siècle*, Paris 1867–76, 8 vols
P. Gay, *Voltaire's Politics*, New York 1965
L. Gossman, 'Voltaire's Heavenly City', *Eighteenth-Century Studies* 3 (1969–70), pp. 67–82
G. Lanson, *Voltaire*, Paris 1910

G. Lanson ed., *Lettres philosophiques*, revised by A.-M. Rousseau, Paris 1964, 2 vols

Longchamp and Wagnière, *Mémoires sur Voltaire*, Paris 1826, 2 vols

H. Mason, *Voltaire*, London 1975

Gita May, 'Voltaire a-t-il fait une offre d'hospitalité à Rousseau?', *SVEC* 47 (1966), pp. 93–113

A. Morize, *L'Apologie du luxe au XVIIIe siècle et 'Le Mondain' de Voltaire*, Paris 1909

R. Naves, *Voltaire et l'Encyclopédie*, Paris 1938

R. Pomeau, *La Religion de Voltaire*, 2nd ed., Paris 1969

A.-M. Rousseau, *L'Angleterre et Voltaire*, *SVEC* 145–7 (1976), 3 vols

M. Tourneux ed., *Correspondance littéraire*, Paris 1877–82, 16 vols

I. O. Wade, *Voltaire and Madame du Châtelet*, Princeton 1941

Studies on Voltaire, Princeton 1947

Voltaire and 'Candide', Princeton 1959

The Intellectual Development of Voltaire, Princeton 1969

Index